NEW ENGLAND AT 400

NEW ENGLAND AT 400

From Plymouth Rock to the Present Day

Eric D. Lehman

Globe
Pequot

Guilford, Connecticut

Globe
Pequot

An imprint of The Rowman & Littlefield Publishing Group, Inc.
4501 Forbes Blvd., Ste. 200
Lanham, MD 20706
www.rowman.com

Distributed by NATIONAL BOOK NETWORK

British Library Cataloguing in Publication Information available

Library of Congress Control Number Available
ISBN 978-1-4930-4348-4 (cloth : alk. paper)
ISBN 978-1-4930-4349-1 (electronic)

♾™ The paper used in this publication meets the minimum requirements of American National Standard for Information Sciences—Permanence of Paper for Printed Library Materials, ANSI/ NISO Z39.48-1992.

ACKNOWLEDGMENTS

Thanks to my editor, Amy Lyons, and Jarrad Peter Rosa, Emilia Rivera, Michael Lockshier, Ethan Perkus, Stephen Healey, Jim Lampos, Christopher Collier, Eddie Podbielski, John Burgeson, David and Trena Lehman, and David K. Leff. Thanks also to New Englanders like Anne Bradstreet, Miantonomi, Emily Dickinson, Henry David Thoreau, Mark Twain, Charlotte Perkins Gilman, John Winthrop, Abigail Adams, Phillis Wheatley, Edna St. Vincent Millay, Amy Lowell, and Henry Wadsworth Longfellow, who provided phrases for some of the chapter titles. The libraries and work of the New Haven Historical Society, Connecticut Historical Society, Vermont Historical Society, Maine Historical Society, the Connecticut Humanities Council, the New England Historical Society, and the University of Bridgeport were valuable, as was the Massachusetts Historical Collections and the incredible interlibrary loan system here in Connecticut. And thanks as always to my wife, Amy Nawrocki.

CONTENTS

INTRODUCTION

On the 400th anniversary of the landing at Plymouth, it's time to look back, commemorate, and reflect on what New England has meant to its people, and to the world. Yankee wordsmith Noah Webster once said, "Every child in America should be acquainted with his own country. He should read books that furnish him with ideas that will be useful to him in life and practice. As soon as he opens his lips, he should rehearse the history of his own country." Answering "Who are we?" is an important part of answering "Who am I?" Or maybe it's the other way around.

So, what is New England? There have been many answers over the past four centuries. After all, every generation of immigrants and natives, puritans and patriots, has defined this land anew. Is John F. Kennedy a product of the same culture as John Winthrop? How does the poetry of Anne Bradstreet relate to the Route 128 tech corridor of the 1970s? Do the whalers of the 19th century lead directly to Dunkin' Donuts?

The answers are not immediately obvious; even in the inaugural date we find contradictions and uncertainties. After all, when the pilgrims arrived at Plymouth, French, Dutch, and English fisherman had been trading with Algonquin-speaking Native American tribes for a century. The Algonquins were the latest in a series of peoples that had migrated to, conquered, and settled this corner of North America for at least ten thousand years. They worked with birch bark and clay, rawhide and stone. They traveled on canoes and lived in wigwams. The various tribes called themselves the Abenakis, the Wampanoags, the Pequots, the Narragansetts. But they did not call their home New England, or even think of this territory as a cohesive whole. When does this shift occur?

It could have happened during John Cabot's voyage in 1497, the first to claim this land for England and find the rich fishing waters off the coast. Maybe when the Dutch built trading posts along the Connecticut River or when the French built a station on Mount Desert Island. Or maybe it happened in 1606 when John Robinson, William Bradford, and

William Brewster met in Brewster's home in Scrooby, Nottinghamshire, to discuss a possible plan for emigration. The strongest contender comes in 1614 when Captain John Smith mapped the coastline and named the territory. One of the harbors he named Plymouth, and two years later published what was essentially an advertisement called "A Description of New England."

Nevertheless, the first permanent European settlement in 1620 seems as good a place as any to mark when "New England" becomes a full, lived reality. The forty decades that followed have been some of the most consequential in the history of the world, especially for such a tiny seventy-thousand-square-mile piece of land, with a population that never rose above half a percent of the earth's total. As we dig down into that history, it becomes clear that New England and New Englanders have lasted for a long time. What's more, they seem ready to continue, at least as long as one person stands up to speak his or her mind at a town meeting, one meal of fried whole-belly clams is served in a seaside shack, or one copy of *Walden* rests on a bookshelf.

Some people might say that this kind of continuity is an illusion, that history doesn't matter, that identity is as insubstantial as a farmhouse ghost. Perhaps. But though change is constant and transformation inevitable, we are still influenced by those who came before us, by the events that shaped the culture that shaped us. The decision of a judge three hundred years ago may not seem to affect us, but the culture it created does. We live the way we do now because of a battle, a design, an invention. A city, a house, a single human being. And as we explore more and more, we find that it is never just one thing; it is many things. There is no summing up, no heart of identity. Rather, it is diffused throughout, in all the years at once, and in the spaces between, like the blood running throughout your body.

That is why history helps us—by giving us not facts but stories. A story allows for a more complex identity, a lived philosophy, a greater truth. It can more accurately tell us who we were, who we are, and who we might become, alone and together. In that way, and in others, a book like this does not mark an ending, but a beginning. Turn the page.

CHAPTER I

From *Mayflower* to Muskeetoes

1620s

THE *MAYFLOWER* TREMBLED IN THE WIND. WATER SEEPED IN AS WAVES sprayed over the bow, and the assembly on their knees in the hold prayed loudly and long. One man was flung overboard but held onto the topsail halyard while the others pulled him back in hand by hand. The sails were taken down and waves and wind beat upon the tiny craft over and over. A midship beam cracked and with great effort they screwed it back into place and fixed it with a post.

After nine stomach-churning weeks at sea, the miserable passengers sighted a long strip of sandy beach. On November 11, 1620, men with iron waistcoats and salt-corroded muskets stepped onto the gray autumnal shore. As the silent, empty days passed, they carried juniper wood for fires back to the ship, desecrated Indian graves to get tools, found bowls and pots in abandoned teepees, and even unearthed tobacco and herring in baskets. A beached whale provided oily sustenance for a time, as they scouted the land. Three weeks after the first landing, a shore party was attacked with arrows as they rummaged through graves, and fled back to the *Mayflower*. Later that day the tiny ship sailed across the wide, shallow bay to a place they called Plimouth.

As Christmas Day dawned, sick and tired, terrified of the wilderness and the "savages" who lurked in it, the colonists began to build against the growing cold. Some dug cave shelters in the sides of hills where they could survive until spring. A few of the more industrious copied the bark wigwams of Indians, with hemlock boughs for bedding. Unfortunately, none were professional carpenters or expert botanists. Like most people in the 17th century, they could hunt and fish, but were certainly not the most skilled of their countrymen.

Former postmaster William Brewster and enigmatic soldier Myles Standish tried to keep the 101 passengers calm. "The Saints," as the core group called themselves, were primarily nonconformists from the Scrooby church in Yorkshire, England, who disagreed with the Archbishop of Canterbury on the authority of scripture. Although they could not legally leave England, ten years earlier some had snuck over to Holland anyway. A merchant named Thomas Weston convinced these vagabonds to move to "New England," where no established church could exert its will upon them.

After their long exile, Brewster and other Saints formed a joint-stock company, with a charter from James I. They hired Standish as a sort of escort, after finding the price of Captain John Smith of Virginia too high. Forty-one men and women had left Delftshaven on July 22, stopping in Southampton to pick up sixty poor unbelievers, whom they called "Strangers." They chartered the *Mayflower*, a 180-ton square rig that had formerly been used to transport wine.

They knew the terrible story of the Virginia colony of Roanoke, which had been settled by 117 people four decades earlier and had disappeared like a whisper in the wind. They shuddered at the fate of the settlers of Jamestown in 1607, where two-thirds died in the first nine months. Now, thirteen years later and hundreds of miles to the northeast, the Plymouth group desperately harvested the last remnants of wild strawberries and watercress, and fished for crabs and lobsters. Foxes and wolves stole their meat and birds and deer fled from their guns. By March 1621, half were dead from scurvy and starvation. The young William Bradford writhed in his cot with terrifying pains in his hip, tended to by Myles Standish. He tried to remember his Bible or maybe his Seneca. "What could they see," Bradford wrote of his fellow colonists later, "but a hideous and desolate wilderness, full of wild beasts and wild men?"

A few weeks later, one of those "wild men" appeared, asking for "beer" in English, and calling himself Samoset. A second man named Tisquantum, or "Squanto," soon arrived with even better English language skills. He had lived in the area now called Plymouth until 1614 when he was kidnapped, converted, taught English in London, taken to Newfoundland, then back to England, and finally back home to New England. Upon his return, he found most of his tribe dead from the epidemic that had raged across the area in 1616. Just two years earlier, Captain John Smith had scouted the area, and found "goodly, strong, and well-proportioned people" as well as corn and mulberry farms aplenty near Quincy and Weymouth. Now, in 1621, along the Taunton River, explorers found empty cornfields and villages, where thousands must have lived in earlier times. The first European who settled near Mount Wollaston wrote that "the bones and skulls" piled around empty villages seemed to him "a new-found Golgotha."

When the *Mayflower* anchored in Cape Cod Bay, Squanto was essentially a prisoner of the surviving Pokanoket Wampanoag Tribes, and they used him as their interpreter and spy. He did not bend so easily to their needs, though. He had seen the power and extent of London, the weapons and ships, and his own people were gone. The English were now in some ways his people, and he seemed determined to help. He brought the settlers to the coves with the fattest eels, and shepherded them to trading sessions for beaver pelts.

The most powerful sachem in the area, Massasoit, visited the tiny village and sat down to a meal of roasted venison. A treaty followed, one that both sides would keep, at least for the next few decades. On a return expedition, Myles Standish and Squanto explored Boston Bay together, meeting with different Wampanoag Tribes, making deals for furs. Near the Blue Hills they found many abandoned gardens and cornfields, recently grown wild. As the summer wore on, Squanto and other friendly Wampanoags continued to teach these sickly European refugees how to grow corn and catch herring.

The Algonquin-speaking civilization of New England might have been devastated by European epidemics, but they had plenty of wealth and wisdom to give. Living in seasonal villages that included two hundred or three hundred people, they met at large meetings throughout the year to trade stone hatchets and reed baskets. The tribes cleared the underbrush with fire, maintained paths, and cultivated berry bushes and fields of corn. Winters were spent inland at hunting camps in snug birch-bark wigwams, and summers were spent by the shore piling up oyster and clam shells into huge hills that could be seen for miles. And Squanto was not an anomaly; many were already wearing European clothes and carrying European artifacts. A few could speak French or Dutch better than the English colonists could.

By autumn 1621 nearly all the remaining settlers had chopped down trees with their broadaxes and built log homes. After the harvest, the young governor William Bradford invited their Wampanoag friends to a gathering, and ninety showed up. The settlers didn't have enough food, so the Indian hunters headed into the woods, bringing back five deer in short order. A three-day party ensued, including wine made from the wild grapes. Standish paraded his "training band" back and forth and held target practice. When, on November 9, 1621, the *Fortune* arrived with thirty more settlers, the little Plymouth Colony seemed permanently part of the fabric of the land they called New England.

Not everyone was happy about that. In January 1622 the Narragansetts sent a messenger with a bundle of arrows tied together by a snake skin. When Squanto saw it, he interpreted it as a threat, and Standish sent the skin back with bullets inside. Another Wampanoag, Hobamock, was close to the sachem Massasoit, and not at all close to Squanto. They soon envied and hated each other, and their intrigues led to a near-death escape by Squanto, after he offended Massasoit. Standish stood up for his friend, and the incident passed. But then in 1622, while helping a ship to round Cape Cod, Squanto caught a fever and died.

Life at the little colony went on without him. One thing the settlers did not lack was wood for the fireplace, and after the first winter, few died of cold even on the most bitter winter days of that little Ice Age. Women and children planted corn, tapped maple trees, and molded clay into bricks and pots. Huge turkeys and partridges roamed the woods, "fat, sweet, and fleshy." While lice, fleas, and "muskeetoes" presented daily problems, as Bradford put it: "They are too delicate and unfitted to begin new plantations and colonies, that cannot endure the biting of a muskeeto."

Larger problems arose from the communal lifestyle; both men and women complained when they had to labor for other families, while the aged complained they had to work as hard as the young. All this was "a kind of slaverie" and mutual respect diminished. But, as Bradford said, "though some do it not willingly, and others not honestly, yet all do it." After all, a much greater fear drove them, lurking just beyond the dark forest edge. Great branches of pines and oaks reached toward them as if to pull civilization apart.

Myles Standish trained militia, and provisions were stocked in a small fortified house. New settlers began to arrive and build new houses and villages. As the Plymouth Colony began to look more and more like an actual colony, Massasoit knew that the English, weak as they were now, could be a valuable ally against the powerful Narragansett. In 1621 he had already used Standish to help him consolidate power, and two years later the new colony of Wessagusset precipitated a new crisis. The starving settlers there had stolen corn several times from nearby Massachusetts tribes, the small robberies of corn echoing the larger robbery of the land. Now, through his messenger Hobamock, the sachem whispered news of a widespread conspiracy to take revenge and wipe out the colonists.

One-third of the settlers at Jamestown, Virginia, had just been massacred, and fears were running high. The Plymouth colonists quickly built a fort. But rather than waiting, Standish decided to take forward action and trekked forty miles north to Wessagusset. On April 6, 1623, he lured a parley from an unfriendly tribe into a blockhouse and slammed the door. Then he, Hobamock, and a few other armored Englishmen jumped and killed seven of the strongest men. With his own hands, the short but tough Standish killed their tallest, strongest warrior.

The most generous interpretation might be that Standish had only killed a few men, and in doing so, stopped the violent death of many on both sides. Or there may have been no conspiracy at all, and this may have been a smaller group that Massasoit wanted to neutralize. Whatever the case, everyone in the region feared Standish as a ruthless murderer now. Many formerly friendly Indians stopped trading, and others fled the area. And despite this ostensible victory, the Wessagusset settlers retreated, leaving behind a failed plantation.

New colonists moved in a few months later, including Thomas Morton, who had left life as a London lawyer to fly falcons in the wilderness of North America. Over the next two years, Morton became a very successful trader, learning to admire the Algonquin culture, which he called more "civilized and humanitarian" than the English. Then he learned that the leaders of the small settlement had been selling indentured servants to Virginia plantations. Furious, he organized a "free community" amongst the rest, and the slave traders fled. Morton changed the name of the village to Ma-re Mount, and on May 11, 1627, he and the bachelor men of this small colony erected a maypole, invited Wampanoag men and women, and began their revels. After all, this was a new land, not subject to the laws or mores of England, and people were free to do as they wished.

Morton was not interested in a religious crusade, but he was definitely interested in creating a utopia. Just not the utopia the Plymouth elders had envisioned. Bradford called Morton the "lord of misrule," saying that he and his small group "set up a Maypole, drinking and dancing about it many days together, inviting the Indian women for their consorts, dancing and frisking together (like so many fairies, or furies rather) and worse practices." Still, they had to find an excuse that would hold up in court, or at least the court of public opinion, and Morton gave them one. He sold "pieces, powder, and shot" to the Indians. The other settlers saw the danger in this, whatever they thought of Morton's more frolicsome behavior.

Bradford ordered that he stop both activities. Morton first ignored him, then successfully argued his case, putting those London lawyer skills to good use. Back in Ma-re Mount, he remained defiant, calling Myles Standish "Captain Shrimp," tapping hogsheads of claret, and roasting clams and birds on the fire. He and his followers had "prosperity and hope" and charged the Plymouth group with a "thirst after Beaver." One of his favorite books, *Don Quixote*, gave him insight into the absurdity of the situation, and he was able to maintain a good humor.

When, the following year, Morton held another celebration, complete with an eighty-foot maypole topped with deer antlers, Myles Standish gathered eight soldiers and marched to Ma-re Mount to cut down this idol. This done, he pursued Morton, who slyly escaped and made his house ready for defense. Unfortunately, while Standish waited outside, Morton and two companions got drunk, and Standish captured him again, dragging him back to Plymouth in chains. After a trial he was left to starve on an island off the coast, but after some of his Wampanoag friends provided him with food, he slipped back to England, where he continued to plague the efforts of the Plymouth colonists until his dying day.

Morton was not the only one exiled from Plymouth. Others not living a godly enough life were banished, and found sanctuary to the west in what would become Rhode Island, or in New Amsterdam amongst the Dutch. And yet, more and more settlers arrived. Nantasket and Thomson's Island were settled, and a fur-trading station appeared on the Kennebec River in 1627. By 1629 Salem, Marblehead, Hull, Braintree, Lynn, Weymouth, Quincy, Oyster River, Dover, and Strawberry Bank had been founded by independent settlers. Dozens of European fishing vessels could be seen off the coast.

In a red waistcoat and purple cloak, Governor William Bradford walked confidently along the gray shores of Cape Cod Bay. Alongside him were his friends, the lanky Reverend William Brewster, holding a small cane in his hand, and stocky Myles Standish, with his armor and musket. Plymouth had increased corn production, becoming self-sufficient, if not wealthy. The "Saints" found more time to argue metaphysics, wrangling over questions of grace, corruption, and predestination.

As far as they were concerned, they had built their utopia, defeating wilderness, "wild men," and sinners alike. But they could not know that their little utopia on the shore was only the thin wedge of the axe.

CHAPTER 2

Strawberries and Severed Heads

1630s

The *Arbella* arrived off Salem at four in the morning on June 12, 1630. Sailors shot off two small cannons, and passengers jumped eagerly onto the shore to gather strawberries. The desultory villagers shared what beer and venison they had with the new arrivals, who looked around at the poverty-stricken settlement with unease. Is this wasteland what they had struggled for? On board the *Arbella* eighteen-year-old Anne Bradstreet watched the shore dejectedly, anxious and fearful of both the wisdom of this venture and her own suitability for it. "I came into this country, where I found a New World and New manners at which my heart rose." Misinterpreted by many over the centuries, Bradstreet was actually confessing that she felt like throwing up.

Her fellow passenger John Winthrop was not optimistic either. His son had already failed to find haven or wealth in Barbados, and he himself had traveled as far as Constantinople and Venice looking for a new home for his group of nonconformists. He and the other Puritans knew they had to do something, though, to escape the "wickedness" of England. Or was that escape the wrong course? "It will be a great wrong to our own Church and Country to take away the good people," he wrote. Maybe they should stay and try to make things better.

Some did. But others, like Winthrop and Bradstreet, decided to create a refuge of purity in the wilderness of North America, a shining example for believers worldwide. It was not a hiding place, they told themselves; it was a beacon, the kingdom of God on earth. They would, quoting

Matthew 5:14, create a "city upon a hill," in this new colony around Massachusetts Bay.

After leaving Salem, Winthrop and the families that followed him traveled southwest to the mouth of a deep harbor, and set up a second home in Charlestown. It was not much better than Salem, covered with rotting food and trash. Winthrop had already started building a house frame, and on September 7, 1630, he brought it across the Charles River to a treeless peninsula, occupied by one man, William Blackstone, who lived in a hut on what is today Beacon Hill. Most followed him, and "this place was called Boston."

Despite increasing numbers of settlers, survival was nearly as difficult as it had been ten years earlier. Wolves attacked herds of cattle and pigs, and scavenged the bodies of the dead. Winthrop's son Henry drowned the first summer. On another occasion, lost only a few miles from home, Winthrop shivered all night in front of a campfire, singing Psalms, pacing back and forth, clutching his compass and his matchbook. Throughout his troubles, Winthrop tried his best to keep his mind on God, but after he was elected governor, duties kept getting in the way. Indeed, government was itself a sacred task. The world to him was theological, not material, and to curb human depravity was the primary role of the government.

Although the Bay Colony maintained a greater separation of church and state than any country in Europe, when a few dissenters in a Watertown church spoke in a generous manner about Catholic churches, Winthrop debated them. However, other members of the church, superficially agreeing with Winthrop, formally condemned and refused to take communion with those who held the radical opinion that Catholics were Christians. Winthrop hustled back to Watertown to argue against this strict reprisal, as well. Excessive purity could be just as big a problem as excessive tolerance, at least as far as he was concerned. Both of these errors were errors of righteousness, and led to separatism, something to be avoided at all costs.

As more and more ships arrived, the Bay Colony soon outnumbered and outproduced Plymouth. The settlers came from all over England in families with nearly equal numbers of women and men. After two months huddled together on the small ships, they clustered together on the rocky shores of Massachusetts before setting out to found villages and home-steads of their own. Two-thirds of the settlers relocated at least once, with many making several moves.

All these different congregations and communities from Eng-land could not possibly hold together. There, the Puritans were loosely organized around protests to the existing order. In New England, little disputes between them began to appear. And according to theological doctrine, those differences were dangers to both the souls of the "mis-guided" and to the sociopolitical health of the community. The paradox was that everyone thought he or she knew God's will. This naturally led to schisms, but also to excessive credulity. Someone as intelligent as preacher John Cotton began to believe superstitious tales of malevolent births.

Another brilliant and charismatic man, Roger Williams, fell into a different sort of trap. Born in London in 1600, Williams attended Cam-bridge University, married a lady's maid named Mary Brainard, and became a private chaplain. He befriended fellow dissidents Winthrop, Cotton, and Thomas Hooker, following them to the Massachusetts Bay Colony. As minister in Salem, Williams tried to convert members of the local tribes, but also learned their languages and customs. He was less progressive when it came to women, suggesting they should wear veils. Luckily for them, his friend John Cotton argued that doing so showed too much submission to their husbands.

Williams had a fiery conviction that God spoke through him. "Abstract yourself with a holy violence from the Dung heap of this Earth," he wrote. In 1633 he went south to preach to the Plymouth Colony but "begane to fall into some strange opinions," according to William Brad-ford. Some theological differences had to be accepted, but Williams's separatist views and fanatical zeal combined like gunpowder. He wrote a tract that condemned both the English king and the authority of the Bay Colony. Brought before the General Court in Boston, he gave satisfactory answers; the offending tract was destroyed and he was allowed to serve as the pastor at Salem.

Two years later he stood a second time before the elders of the col-ony for his "newe and dangerous opinions," and on October 9, 1635, was convicted of sedition and heresy. Temporarily out of the governor seat, Winthrop privately warned his old friend to flee to Narragansett Bay while at the same time publicly condemning him. Williams fled into the wilderness just as officers of the court came to arrest him, wading through snow drifts and crossing ice-choked rivers until he reached the Plymouth sachem, Massasoit's, village. The friendly chief welcomed him, gave him food and shelter for the rest of the winter.

Like Roger Williams, Thomas Hooker chafed under Bay Colony rule, but stayed quieter about it. Born in Leicester, England, Hooker had gone to school with John Cotton, and married Susanna Pym, sister of the parliamentary leader who later opposed Charles I. He preached at Chelmsford, began to criticize the Anglican Church, and in 1630 was forced to appear before the High Commission Court and threatened with torture. Out on bond, he fled to the Netherlands just ahead of the law, and then to Boston, arriving in 1633. He settled in Cambridge and acquired a reputation for his ability to console the sick, the dying, and the spiritually distressed.

He had watched the trial of Roger Williams, and waited. Then, on May 31, 1636, Hooker and his followers, the "Visible Saints of New Town," left the Bay Colony with their horses, livestock, and a herd of cattle. His sick wife was dragged on a litter by a horse, as the group struggled along the Great Indian Trail all the way to the banks of the Connecticut River. There, amongst giant elm trees and blackberry bushes, the tiny community of Windsor had been founded two years earlier by Roger Ludlow. He admired Hooker and they rejoiced to be in the same new colony.

Hooker set up a village he called Hartford, to the south of Windsor and to the north of another hamlet of ten houses, Wethersfield, both of which also welcomed more settlers that summer. The local sachem, Sequassen, accepted these intruders as protection against the Pequot Tribe. Hooker opened town meetings to set rules, including inaugurating chimney inspections and forbidding children to swing on gates.

Hartford occupied the land formerly used by Dutch traders, who could only watch in frustration as the property they had "bought" was seized by others. Down at the mouth of the large Connecticut River,

Colonel George Fenwick and Captain Lion Gardiner had built on the site of another Dutch fort, preparing their new Saybrook Colony for the rumored arrival of Puritan leader Oliver Cromwell. Farther up the Connecticut River, William Pynchon settled a spot where the Westfield and Chicopee Rivers meet the main flow, calling it Springfield.

Meanwhile, Roger Williams had recovered from his winter ordeals, and bought land from the Native Americans at the head of Narragansett Bay, which he named New Providence. Others had already moved into the area, including Boston's original settler, William Blackstone. Things had grown too crowded up there, and he had fled to the woods, one of the first of the irascible New Englanders who preferred solitude.

These new colonies and settlements trespassed on the territory of the Pequots and Mohegans, catching the attention of another brilliant man on a mission. Son of the Mohegan sachem, Uncas married the daughter of the Pequot sachem and paid tribute to that larger and more powerful tribe. As early as 1634, Uncas had rebelled but was defeated and forced to make obeisance to Sassacus, the Pequot chief. That same year an epidemic of smallpox wiped out huge numbers of Native Americans, just before the English settlers moved into their territory. Uncas bided his time, improving his English skills and making friends.

Back in the village of Boston, another controversy was brewing. Anne Hutchinson had arrived a few years earlier, already a mother of a grown son and wife to a dim-witted husband. She set about improving her new home, inviting local women for discussions of the preachers' latest sermons. She soon became more than just an interpreter, giving her own sermons to eager listeners, preaching that her fellow Puritans had given themselves to work rather than to grace.

In that crisis year of 1636, her brother-in-law by marriage, John Wheelwright, arrived into this religious foment after being forced out of an English vicarage for supposedly selling church offices. Now, in a sermon at Boston, he called those who "walked in a covenant of works," "antichrists." Naturally, the elders of the other churches who did "walk in such a way" did not appreciate this sort of accusation. As a woman, Hutchinson was even more terrifying to the ministers. More than once she actually led her followers out of the meetinghouse during a sermon, supporting John Cotton and Wheelwright's ideas of "antinomianism" and "familism." A minority of colonists supported these ideas, too, but a year after Hooker and Williams had left, the sitting governor and all the magistrates who might have sympathized with Hutchinson and Wheelwright were voted out.

By then Winthrop and the other English colonists had a new problem. The death of an English sailor and his crew in a fight with Native Americans led to a retributive raid that swept up the entire Pequot nation into a fury of righteous anger. The Connecticut settlers were outnumbered, but they had allies. Roger Williams had befriended the Narragansetts, and Windsor's Captain John Mason had befriended the Mohegans. In fact, Uncas warned Mason that the Pequots were going to attack the fort at Saybrook, and they did, besieging it throughout the winter of 1636/1637. In April, Pequots attacked Wethersfield, killing nine people and kidnapping two young girls.

In May, Captain Mason led seventy-seven English, sixty Mohegans, and four hundred Narragansetts and Niantics against the Pequots. The Narragansetts and Niantics mostly abandoned the march, leaving the Mohegans and English outnumbered by a strong Pequot force. Instead of engaging it, Mason turned to one of the nearby Pequot forts, where hundreds of women, children, and elderly men lay sleeping after a feast. Mason and the English and Mohegan soldiers crept up to the twelve-foot-high walls of the fort and forced their way inside past a few arrows. Grabbing branches from the fires, they tossed them onto bark, straw, and timber. Soon the fort was an inferno, with hundreds screaming in agony. Some soldiers, seeing what they had done, were "moved by pity" and saved a few lives amidst the chaos. The rest of the Pequots inside were burned or shot when they tried to flee.

The Pequot warriors returned to their fort to find the charred and twisted bodies of their families. In a blinding rage they pursued the soldiers to the harbor, where the colonists embarked with a few prisoners, and according to Mason himself, a large collection of severed human heads. William Bradford wrote later that he thought it God's justice, but also said, "It was a fearful sight to see them thus frying in the fire and the streams of blood quenching the same, and horrible was the stink and scent thereof." Roger Williams protested, saying, "Nature knows no difference between Europeans and Indians." But this was a minority view. Reflecting the opinion of the majority, John Mason wrote, "Thus the lord was pleased to smite our Enemies in the hinder Parts, and to give us their Land for an Inheritance."

Sassacus and the rest of the Pequots fought on, but Mason and the Mohegans confronted them again in a brutal hand-to-hand brawl in the swamps of western Connecticut. Sassacus escaped and attempted to find refuge amongst the Mohawks. Instead, they killed him and sent his body parts to Boston. More heads and hands arrived as tribute from other tribes, including three pairs of severed Pequot hands that Roger Williams sent on to John Winthrop, believing this to be common courtesy toward the donors.

At the end of summer 1637, with the Pequot threat on the wane, Winthrop and the Bay Colony called an assembly, ostensibly trying to make harmony between the religious factions. But friends of Wheelwright and Hutchinson were subtly removed from the court, and the leaders of the opposition were deprived of their weapons. Wheelwright was asked to retract his opinions. He did not, but the court deferred its sentence at the request of Winthrop, who was still trying to make peace amidst "the heat of contention." Finally, on a Monday morning in November, Wheelwright was tried again, and again refused to admit guilt. On Tuesday he was convicted of sedition and banished.

Hutchinson's trial followed a few days later. Winthrop, Anne Bradstreet's husband, and other leaders of the colony accused her of slandering the ministers and disturbing the peace. However, unlike Wheelwright and other men, she had never written down her opinions or spoken them from an actual pulpit, and so the very thing that made her actions so dangerous protected her. She did well on the first day, and on the second, John Cotton defended her. Hutchinson defeated the judges during questioning. But she could not defeat her own overconfidence, and confessed, or rather rejoiced in "immediate revelation," saying, "You have no power over my body, neither can you do me any harm—for I am in the hands of the eternal Jehovah, my Saviour, I am at his appointment." She continued in this vein, telling them to "take heed how you proceed against me—for

I know that, for this you go about to do to me, God will ruin you and your posterity and this whole state."

Whether theology or politics, this statement could not stand. Her banishment was deferred until spring, and she was put into a private house with plenty of provisions. There were protests by many churchgoers, and she unrepentantly continued to speak to people with the same "errors" as before. In March she was formally excommunicated, after which observers found that "she gloried in her sufferings."

During the winter, Wheelwright had sheltered in New Hampshire, where he bought a piece of land from the Indians and founded Exeter with twenty families of followers. Hutchinson nearly followed him but changed her mind and headed to Rhode Island. Other dissenters, women and men, were whipped and banished. Farmers and trappers unwilling to live under the sort of religious oligarchy they had fled in England moved quietly to the frontier in New Hampshire and Maine. A few even fled to New Amsterdam to join the Dutch.

Meanwhile, the survivors of the Pequot Tribe were absorbed into the surrounding tribes, particularly the Mohegans. In September 1638 Uncas made himself a vassal of the Connecticut Colony, but at the same time achieved dominion over the other Native Americans between the river and the Narragansetts. The Mohegans were now a regional power.

In the words of one Bay Colony minister, the prosecutions of the heretics and the defeat of the Pequots "arose and fell together." A day of celebration followed for success against both threats. As governor, John Winthrop joined the celebrations, remaining committed to keeping the colony's unity for the rest of his life. Nevertheless, he somewhat contradictorily remained good friends with Hooker and Williams, and even reconciled with Wheelwright a few years later. "For this end, we must be knit together in this work as one man," he wrote. "We must entertain each other in brotherly affection, we must be willing to abridge ourselves of our superfluities for the supply of others' necessities. We must uphold a familiar commerce together in all meekness, gentleness, patience and liberality. We must delight in each other, make others' conditions our own, rejoice together, mourn together, labor, and suffer together, always having before our eyes our commission and community in the work, our community as members of the same body."

These were good ideas. And yet somehow, the fragmentation of that community had also led to good ideas. After all, Roger Williams's opinions on Native Americans and slavery were centuries ahead of his time, and his banishment for theological disagreements led him not to establish his own "spiritual unity," but instead to promote religious freedom, so that no one would be "molested for his conscience." The first "heretical" Baptist Church in America was founded in Providence shortly afterwards. The heretic Anne Hutchinson was reviled by most contemporaries, but her "minority opinion" would provide inspiration to women and men of the future.

For the rest of Uncas's life, he would fight a losing battle trying to meld the interests of his tribe and the settlers. But he and other allied native peoples would continue to give the colonists more and more radical ideas about diversity and personal freedom. Before the end of the decade, Thomas Hooker signed the Fundamental Orders of Connecticut, which safeguarded the powers of all officials and "vested" those powers in the people in a way that no document ever had. It also significantly failed to mention anything about the English king, or Parliament, or anything to do with a separate authority.

It was the beginning of a series of new experiments, ones that would create a new people, a greater New England, and the founding principles of the United States.

CHAPTER 3

So Must We Be One

1640s

ON APRIL 14, 1638, THREE SHIPS SAILED DOWN THE CLEAR, OYSTER-filtered waters of Long Island Sound, turned north between two arms of land, and after disembarking on a small island in the salt marshes, the passengers knelt and listened to a sermon called "Temptations of the Wilderness." From the heights, Chief Momauquin of the Quinnipiac Indians watched them. The few hundred settlers on the ships already outnumbered his smallpox-ridden tribe, and Momauquin quickly signed a treaty of protection against the Mohawk with Governor Theophilus Eaton, for what they called "long water land." Eaton suggested the tribe move onto what would become the nation's first Indian reservation.

Surveyor John Brockett laid out the first planned city in the colonies, with nine squares that included a central green just large enough to hold 144,000 bodies, the number of people these Puritans thought would make it into heaven. Eaton and the Reverend John Davenport named this town New Haven, imagining as so many others had, an ideal theocratic state that controlled timber and property sales. They based their constitution on the law of Moses, allowing for no separation between church and state.

Soon more literate, middle-class English settlers arrived, with New Haven and the neighboring Connecticut colonies booming from eight hundred to fifty-five hundred settlers in six years. A New Haven brewer named Stephen Goodyear purchased all of Long Island not yet claimed for a bargain of 110 pounds. Settlers from New Haven moved there, the first of many emigrations from New England into the rest of America.

Meanwhile, a group of settlers headed to Virginia encountered storms and settled Martha's Vineyard instead. Fishermen planted houses on the Isles of Shoals. The Bay Colony doubled in size during those years, flush with beaver furs and board pine, and both Boston and New Haven began trading with the Caribbean, the Azores, and the Canaries. They were joined by Newport, founded in 1639 by a group of settlers that included the exiled Anne Hutchinson and soon to be the largest settlement in Rhode Island. To the north, along the coast of Maine and New Hampshire, the rocky shore hid small bays where hamlets of fisherfolk settled throughout the 1620s and 1630s. Protected by salt marshes and thickets of tough brush, they turned their backs on the wilderness and kept their eyes to the sea, drying fish on the rocks and packing hogsheads for export to Boston and beyond.

On Richmond Island, Maine, English merchant Robert Trelawney secured fishing rights for Casco Bay in 1631, bypassing Massachusetts and sending products directly to England. By the 1640s the operation had failed, and the territory north of the Piscataqua River began to look promising to the acquisitive Puritans of the Bay Colony, who seized it in 1641. Other colonies also suffered. Puritan leader Oliver Cromwell had never come to Saybrook as rumored, and the settlement declined before merging with Hartford. And Plymouth was troubled by a crime wave—from minor blasphemies to witchcraft, from adultery to bestiality, punished as Leviticus demanded. They had also become a very small part of a much larger New England.

Meanwhile, the English Parliament was about to go to war with the English king, a bitter conflict that would last the entire decade. Migration to New England slowed to a trickle, and many in the colonies questioned the whole idea of leaving England in the first place, since they were clearly needed there. George Fenwick of Saybrook returned to the home country to fight, Hugh Peter of Massachusetts left to serve as chaplain to Oliver Cromwell, and Samuel Desborough of Guilford became keeper of the Great Seal of Scotland.

For the colonists who stayed, another war loomed. The sachem of the Narragansett, Miantonomi, had watched the Pequot War, at first with satisfaction and later with horror. He questioned John Mason's tactics and the subsequent bondage of the Pequot, and knew that his tribe could be next. As the most powerful chief in southern New England, he had a voice, and he began to use it, paddling up and down rivers in hollowed log canoes, using paths his people had used for centuries. But instead of searching for turtles or trout, he was searching for allies. The Native Americans still outnumbered the English colonists, if only they could unite.

Sitting around fires on Long Island and eastern Connecticut with men in breechcloths and skirts, Miantonomi talked of war. "For so are we all Indians as the English are, and say brother to one another; so must we be one as they are, otherwise shall all be gone shortly," he said in summer 1642 to the Montauk Indians. "We shall all be starved." Like Uncas, perhaps he realized that like it or not he was a "New Englander" too. He just had a different solution.

Uncas had added the Hammonasset Tribe to his Mohegan dominions, and was now as strong as the Pequots had been ten years earlier, particularly since he stayed allied to his friend John Mason's Connecticut Colony. He and Miantonomi had an argument over the old Pequot lands, and in 1642 the Narragansetts invaded with a force of a thousand men. Uncas met him near what is today Norwich and offered single combat. Miantonomi refused, saying, "My men have come to fight, and they shall fight." Uncas gave a signal and rushed the Narragansetts, driving them back and taking Miantonomi prisoner. The Mohegans took him to trial in Hartford, and after the colonists sent him back, Uncas's brother struck Miantonomi fatally in the head with a hatchet.

A few months later, Virginia colonists were massacred by the surrounding tribes and this execution of the Narragansett sachem seemed like a wise precaution. Both this threat and the raging English Civil War led to a meeting of the Plymouth, New Haven, Connecticut, and Massachusetts Bay Colonies. John Winthrop, Theophilus Easton, and the others reached an agreement in September 1643: "a firme and perpetual league of friendship and amytie" called the Articles of Confederation for New England. Primarily a military alliance, the United Colonies of New England would support each other for defense against native tribes, the French, or the Dutch in New Netherland.

Two years later, in 1645, a thousand Narragansett warriors again attacked the Mohegans to avenge the death of Miantonomi. Early success led to other tribes joining the fight, and Uncas found himself under siege at his home village of Fort Shantok. The colonial federation put together a force of three hundred men that included the feared warriors Myles Standish and John Mason. The Narragansetts sent a parley, insisting their argument was with Uncas, not the English. However, the combined force of the colonial confederacy convinced the tribe to sign a treaty of "firm and perpetual peace" not only with the English but with Uncas and his allies. The strength of the New England Confederacy had been demonstrated convincingly; it was now the single most powerful group along the Atlantic coast of North America.

Rhode Island had not been invited to join the other colonies, because Roger Williams and his people were still considered too radical, not to mention the Quakers, Catholics, and other supposed heathens who lived there. Worried that this new alliance would lead to the other colonies dividing up Rhode Island, Williams slyly stole to England to meet with Parliament, which somehow took time off from its war with the king to grant him a charter. Having secured Rhode Island as a full colony, he returned in triumph and served as governor, banning indentured servitude and continuing to shelter refugees from other colonies.

One of those refugees was Samuel Gorton, who had emigrated from Lancashire in 1637 and, after being pushed out of Plymouth, moved to Portsmouth, Rhode Island. His backtalk annoyed the magistrates there, too, and he was whipped out of town. In Providence, he bought land from the Narragansett, preached to a splinter sect, spent countless hours meditating, and tried to expunge formal ceremony during worship services. But after more antiauthoritarian acts, he was grabbed by militia, dragged to Massachusetts, and sentenced to hard labor. He seemed even too radical for the radical Roger Williams, who wrote to John Winthrop, "Master Gorton having abused high and low at Aquidneck, is now bewitching and bemadding poor Providence."

After a trip to England to gain an order of protection, Gorton named his settlement after his patron, the Earl of Warwick. He wrote that he "left my native country to enjoy liberty of conscience in respect to faith toward God and for no other end." Eschewing his former antiauthoritarian views, in 1651 he became president of the Colony of Rhode Island and Providence Plantations. He helped ban slavery and, like Williams before him, moved from radical youth to "professor of the mysteries of Christ" to civil leader. And yet he retained his own strange opinions about spiritual matters, refusing to compromise his most cherished beliefs. Rhode Island had become an experiment on how far religious tolerance could go.

Others were mellowing a bit, too, trying to get along. In 1643 John Winthrop had written a conciliatory letter to the exiled John Wheelwright in New Hampshire. Wheelwright wrote back, saying he would not change his beliefs, but that he wanted "to bring about reconciliation and peace." A year later, the Bay Colony retracted its order of banishment, though in doing so pretended Wheelwright had admitted wrongdoing. In 1647 he finally returned to Massachusetts, taking a job in Hampton, and was given more than that: land, money, and eventually a vindication from the court.

Even the old scallywag Thomas Morton showed up in possession of protective papers from Parliament, in good spirits after successfully shredding the Plymouth Colony's charter. He went to the wilds of Maine where he was left alone for the most part, until he died. Other early settlers were disappearing too. Anne Hutchinson had moved to New Netherland, but had found herself in the middle of another war with Native Americans after the Dutch massacred Lenape camps. She and her family were murdered during the reprisals. Thomas Hooker's Hartford now boasted a town crier, treasurer, school, and biennial fair, all paid by taxes. In 1647 it was hit by a strange epidemic that swept through New England, but though many contracted it, most survived. One of the hundred exceptions was Hooker himself.

And then, the impossible happened. On January 30, 1649, Oliver Cromwell and the victorious Parliament executed King Charles of England. Two months later, just after learning this shocking fact, John Winthrop passed away. As he lay in his sick bed with fever and cold, he at least could look on a world that seemed finally, after long labors, to be turning to the values he had championed. The seeds of self-government and union had been planted, and would rise up perennially for the next century, until their full and majestic flowering.

CHAPTER 4

A Country beyond Sight

1650s

By 1650 Anne Bradstreet had come a long way in the two decades since she felt like vomiting at the first sight of America. Despite chronic poor health, she had borne eight children and written about such varied subjects as medicine, motherhood, and theology. Her book of poetry, *The Tenth Muse Lately Sprung Up in America*, was published in England and became an instant best seller. Everyone there always enjoyed the latest gossip from America, but this was something different, a thoughtful treatise on finding love, faith, and the rewards of hard work. "Was ever stable joy yet found below? Or perfect bliss without mixture of woe?" she wrote, reflecting the optimism felt by many. Their moral crusade seemed to have been justified—New England was thriving and Oliver Cromwell and the Puritan Parliament had conquered the Old.

Many settlers had left England for economic as well as spiritual reasons, and rejoiced in small liberties of agricultural and local governance. And what they took the greatest joy in were the sovereignties and duties of owning land, a house, a home. There was slate and marble for building, but most houses were wood, and with questionable chimneys, fire became a top concern. Each home kept a ladder and selection of fire buckets; Joseph Jericks of Lynn built the nation's first fire engine in 1650. Ten to fifteen family members and servants jammed into one narrow-windowed house and thought themselves lucky.

Women like Anne Bradstreet spent a good deal of their day inside these houses, spinning, weaving, and bleaching: creating bed sheets and wardrobes of stockings, doublets, shirts, and woolen suits. They filled candle molds with fish oil, tallow, or bayberry wax. They used flint and steel to light a tinder bundle, keeping the fire all day, turning a roasting spit by the light of a Betty lamp, filling warming pans with hot coals. Outside they kept small kitchen gardens for herbs, and whitened the sides of their small houses with a wash of powdered clamshells.

Kitchens gathered toasting forks and gridirons, pewter platters and salt cellars. At tables hewn from oak, families feasted on rye 'n' injun bread and soused pork, while iron bean pots bubbled over the kitchen fire. The settlers cooked pumpkins when they had to, but preferred squash. Apple trees had grown from European seeds, and the fruit was used in every way imaginable. To drink, the family might have milk, cider, grape juice, or other fermented beverages—anything to avoid plain, unsanitary water. Other than soup spoons, most ate with their hands; only rich families like the Winthrops used forks. They could also afford to scrape sugar from cones into imported tea. The wealthier might also have green cotton waistcoats, silk gowns, or scarlet cloaks, perhaps a bracelet or locket, or a brass door knocker. But the difference between rich and poor in New England of the 1650s was not great enough to spark much envy.

In the fields and forests, men could be seen shearing sheep, reaping hay, setting traps for beaver and fox. Tar and pitch and salted fish were packed into barrels, while thick planks of oak and tall masts of white pine were cut and exported. Huge oysters and lobsters were harvested using native methods, while cod were netted by the thousands off the coast. Heath hens made easy targets for muskets, as did the annual flocks of passenger pigeons. Hundred-strong herds of cattle roamed the muddy mire of Boston Common and the swampy flats north of New Haven. Thousands of sheep grazed in Massachusetts and laws were soon passed to protect them; the owner of a dog who killed a sheep had to hang the dog and pay double the price. Bounties were set on wolves, and their shaggy heads were nailed to the outer walls of meetinghouses.

In many towns singing was banned, though few missed it. Sometimes bowling was permitted, but betting on it was not. Smaller offenses like cursing or dancing would only rate a fine. Laws against fancy dress and tobacco use were passed, but rarely enforced. Drink was not a problem until it became a problem, though drunkards and those who served them were sometimes prosecuted. However, a pub was deemed necessary, and Massachusetts actually fined towns for not providing one. These were often built at ferries or crossroads, and served townspeople as well as travelers, all gathering for a mug of cider or beer, a slice of cake, and a roast chicken. Often both women and men hurried directly from a cold church to a warm tavern for a hot toddy.

Burglars and highwaymen were branded on the forehead with the letter "B" and second offenders were hanged, though capital crimes did need two or three witnesses to merit appearance in court. Arsonists were whipped and made to pay double damages, and Massachusetts added the cutting off of an ear if the crime was on the Sabbath. Indians were prosecuted for murder of other Indians, and in the early years, Europeans were sometimes executed for murdering Indians, too. Suicides were buried along the side of the highway under a cairn.

Small conflicts between settlers were often caused by the tangled web of vague and conflicting land grants, charters, patents, and boundary lines. Disputations over theology continued to split churches and send parishioners into the wilderness to start a newer, purer community, like the nine families who left Lynn to found Sandwich or the settlers who quarreled with Anne Hutchinson and moved to Newport. Sometimes, though, families just found it too far to walk or ride to church every Sunday and built another church, and thus another town, down the road from the old one. Such a community might need a blacksmith, and one would make his way there. His son would begin a trade, his wife would farm the land, and others would join them.

A few threats of war surfaced during those years. The New England Confederation had signed a separate treaty with the Dutch in New Amsterdam in 1650, but in 1652 war broke out between England and Holland. Since they bordered Dutch territory, the Connecticut and New Haven Colonies asked for assistance. Massachusetts and Plymouth refused, and the alliance began to waver. However, in 1654, when official war was declared in Europe, Connecticut grabbed the small Dutch outposts along the river and made ready their forts. Rumors flew that the Dutch had allied with the Mohawk and Niantics and were going to crush New Haven. A combined force of Cromwell's and Connecticut's soldiers made ready to attack New Amsterdam. However, no attack came, peace was declared, and the English attacked the French at Port Royal instead.

As dictator of England, Oliver Cromwell did not become the generous benefactor that New Englanders hoped for. On October 1, 1651, Parliament passed the first Navigation Acts, instructing the colonies to use English ships and to sell certain goods like tobacco or salt fish directly to England. These acts set an alarming precedent for more laws and more restrictions, which would trouble the colonies over the next century. However, the region did receive one bonus from Cromwell—captured Scots to use as indentured servants. The practice of indentured servitude was common, and the first slaves had arrived in 1638. Like the Scots and other servants, these slaves sat in church with the rest of the community and were allowed trial by jury. They could marry and could take their owners to court, and could usually buy their freedom. Nevertheless, they were slaves.

During those years, the ambitious New Haveners boasted their own iron foundry, and had taken back Greenwich from the Dutch. They even tried to settle Delaware, but were expelled by the Swedes. The Connecticut Colony had been joined by John Winthrop Jr., who had gone to the Temple Bar in London, and dabbled in alchemy and other sciences but, with his father, had given up the crumbling ramparts and bell towers of medieval England for the promise of America. He had earlier helped found the Saybrook Colony, built a farm on Fisher's Island, and opened up the "Pequot Country" to settlement. He threw his considerable energies into New London before being named governor of his adopted colony in 1657.

The border between the New London settlers and Rhode Island remained just as undefined as the one between the Mohegans and Narragansetts. For much of the decade, the scattered individual farms or villages of Rhode Island held to their independence and nonconformity, with Newport and Portsmouth fighting Providence and Warwick. However, in 1658 Roger Williams united all the towns under the umbrella of Providence Plantations. Baptists and Quakers lived and worked alongside Anglicans, and by the end of the decade, fifteen Jewish families had arrived in Newport, fleeing the Spanish Inquisition. Roger Williams wrote, "We have long drunk of the cup of as great liberties as any people ever can hear of under the whole heaven."

Portsmouth, New Hampshire, and the surrounding areas boomed throughout the 1650s with sawmills and shipbuilding, trading directly with the Caribbean and southern Europe, sending tall white pines and dried fish, and receiving wine, rum, and salt. To the northeast, treacherous waters around countless islands and long overland journeys around the jagged coastline made governing Maine a dubious prospect for anyone beyond local magistrates. Unlike New Hampshire, there was no central community, and the coastal villages were vulnerable to hostile native and French attacks. The people who settled here were often those who were steering clear of the secular or religious authorities for one reason or another, making them fractious and difficult to control.

Cromwell supporter and Pequot War veteran John Endecott became governor of Massachusetts, and tried his best to annex Maine. In 1658 he was finally successful, at least temporarily, further increasing Massachusetts's power and dominance in New England. Harvard College graduated ministers, and the first mint in the colonies stamped silver coins, taking both the rights of the English church and state to themselves. But Massachusetts's ascendancy was noticed and distrusted by the other smaller colonies.

Plymouth in particular looked askance at their much larger neighbor. Myles Standish died in 1656 and a year later his friend William Bradford followed. He had spent almost four decades as governor of Plymouth, and wrote before he died: "I am refreshed to have seen some glimpse hereof, as Moses saw the land of Canaan afar off." Perhaps it was a blessing that he missed the changes soon to come.

CHAPTER 5

Hanged Quakers and Outlaw Judges

1660s

"It is an hour of the greatest joy," said Mary Dyer as she was escorted to her execution on Boston Common with two other Quakers—William Robinson and Marmaduke Stephenson. A few years earlier, Puritan ministers in Massachusetts had passed a law that menaced both Quakers and Baptists with banishment for evangelism, and with execution should they return from banishment. The Baptists did not make trouble, but the Quakers of the 1650s were still in the passion of their early years, and many felt the need to make their testimony known and to convert others if possible. Over the next few years they suffered the stocks, fines, and mutilation to spread their faith.

Mary Dyer had been one of the dissatisfied people who left the Bay in the 1630s with Anne Hutchinson. Two decades later, while back in England, she had converted to Quakerism, and returned to New England to preach, something allowed in this radical new faith in which ministers did not exist. Expelled from the New Haven Colony, she went to Boston in support of the imprisoned Robinson and Stephenson. They were all deported, but in June the two men were arrested in Boston again. Dyer returned from Newport and was arrested too.

In October of 1659, under the nooses on Boston Common, they tried to speak to the crowd but were drowned out by drums. The two men hanged, one after the other. Dyer was bound and blindfolded and led to the elm tree, but at the last moment an announcement came. She had been reprieved. It was a ploy by the Massachusetts authorities, who apparently did not want to enforce the law and execute a woman. However,

Dyer wasn't going to let it stop her. After wintering on Shelter Island, she returned to Boston, and on June 1, 1660, at 9 a.m. was led to the gallows a second time. The magistrates tried once again to get her to repent, but she preferred death.

Another death would trouble New England even more. Oliver Cromwell had died in 1658, and after more conflict, the monarchy of Charles II was restored just a few days before Dyer was executed. After siding with Parliament during the English Civil War, New Englanders were now in a difficult situation. The king soon passed two more Navigation Acts, which solidified control over colonial trade and allowed the Crown to collect duties. With dread in their hearts, the colonists waited for the king's commissioners to arrive.

As a condition of the restoration, Charles had promised that the only ones to be hanged would be the so-called regicides, including the judges who had signed the death warrant of his father. He made good on his promise with the Act of Indemnity, and the remains of Cromwell were disinterred and hung in gibbets. Two of the regicides, Edward Whalley and his son-in-law William Goffe, escaped to Boston just ahead of their death sentence. Governor Endecott welcomed them and they settled in Cambridge. But by the following spring they had to flee, continuing to New Haven, where a third regicide, John Dixwell, was living under a false name. Goffe and Whalley hid in a jumble of boulders on West Rock for almost a month while a local farmer brought them food. After two years under assumed names in Milford, they fled upcountry to Hadley in the wilds of western Massachusetts to escape the king's commissioners. Dixwell boldly lived to a ripe old age in New Haven under a pseudonym.

The restoration of the monarchy didn't stop Connecticut governor John Winthrop Jr. from sailing for England to receive his fellowship in the Royal Society. While there, he quietly endeavored to get a new charter for the colony—lingering in the corridors of Whitehall, shepherding this document through its elaborate progress of ministers and clerks, paying the fees and bribes. Meanwhile, the colonies pledged their loyalty to the new king, but New Haven's pledge arrived a bit late. Between this and the regicides fiasco, the Crown nullified their charter, uniting it with the Connecticut Colony. It was a better result than it might have been—without the merger, everything west of the Connecticut River might have been granted to the king's brother, the Duke of York.

The duke did in fact nullify the contracts the settlers of Long Island had signed with the Connecticut colonies, even though they begged to remain part of New England. The boundary of West Chester was fixed, too, leaving many unhappy Puritan settlers on the "New York" side. To the north and east, the boundary line was fixed without consulting the Mohegans or other tribes. The new Connecticut charter allowed the election of the governor and officers, giving the colony a nearly complete representative government. The renewed charters to Massachusetts and Rhode Island gave almost as much latitude, and it may have been this generosity of freedoms that later caused the English government so much trouble when they tried to take those freedoms back.

Reverend Davenport and the other New Haveners complained of their new status, but to no avail. Throughout the spring of 1664, arguments nearly came to blows between the two merging colonies. Finally, on September 1, the disgruntled commissioners from New Haven sat down in the Hartford council chambers. One town, Branford, had remained completely antagonistic to the union, and many people there packed up their belongings and left to found Newark, New Jersey.

Meanwhile, the martyrdom of Mary Dyer led to more protests. Other Quakers ran through the streets of Boston and Cambridge in sackcloth or greasepaint, proclaiming the end times. "Thus will the Lord break you in pieces," they screamed. Thirty were fined, imprisoned, or whipped for this behavior, which was considered a public nuisance, but not a hanging crime. Or maybe the Puritan elders had simply lost their taste for it. Most had already started tolerating dissident preachers and congregations, or at least treated them without the hysteria of the 1630s. Orthodoxy over small matters no longer seemed to be as serious as it had been when the colony teetered on the edge of dissolution.

Royal commissioners soon arrived to fix boundaries, chase the regicides, and spy for the king. They also put an end to legal action against Quakers, though local punishments continued. In Connecticut, Governor Winthrop accepted dissident Quakers, and in Rhode Island, Nicholas Eaton soon became the first Quaker governor, in 1674. By then Quakers were allowed to practice in Boston, and even a young firebrand named Cotton Mather became indulgent toward them. He said later that Quakers were not so bad, and it was only the first generation who had been "madmen," easily cured by shaving their heads.

Mather would be one of many to focus on a more insidious threat: witchcraft. Witch trials had cropped up as early as 1647, when Windsor's Alse Young became the first to be hanged for the crime in the colonies. However, while the Quakers specifically set out to disrupt Massachusetts society, most of the so-called witches were simply people who got on the wrong side of their fellow citizens. John Godfrey of Essex County was accused many times by grudge-holding neighbors. Springfield's Mary Parsons was accused as a witch, but was hanged for the more concrete crime of infanticide.

In the 1660s an extensive witch hunt raged through Hartford when one woman accused another of bewitching her, followed by an eight-year-old girl accusing a woman of causing her illness. Accusations quickly spread across the town, fueled by an inheritance dispute, leading to several executions. Near the end of the hysteria, the younger Winthrop commuted the death sentence of Katherine Harrison of Wethersfield for witchcraft, but suggested she leave town for "the contentment of the people who are her neighbors," and more pointedly so they wouldn't take the law into their own hands and drown her in Blackbird Pond.

For the next twenty years the "witch question" would simmer, while war and rebellion occupied the New England colonists. But the end of the old Puritan theocracy had already begun.

CHAPTER 6

Death's Head at the Feast

1670s

SACHEM MASSASOIT WAS DEAD. FOR FORTY YEARS HE HAD KEPT THE truce he signed with William Bradford, living in relative peace with the Plymouth Colony. His eldest son died just a year later, and in 1662 his second son, Metacom, inherited the responsibility for leading all the Wampanoags between the Charles River and Narragansett Bay. He had taken the name "Philip" on his father's death, and bought English-tailored suits in Boston. However, as time passed, he grew more and more disillusioned with the exploitation by the colonists, the disruption of fishing and hunting, and the conversions of fellow Wampanoags. He gathered guns in his village on the Mount Hope peninsula in Narragansett Bay.

There were approximately four thousand converted Indians in New England in the 1670s, at places like Chappaquiddick and Natick, where the Indians used an English-style meetinghouse and lived in wigwams on house plots. Converted Nipmuck Sarah Boston of Grafton, Massachusetts, lived in town, wore English boots and hat, and did the heaviest farm work. She spent her free time reading the Bible and outdrinking everyone at the local ordinary. She and others like her seemed to have found a way around the cultural divide that separated the other hundred thousand colonists and Native Americans living in New England at the time.

In January 1674 a converted Wampanoag named Sassamon, who served as a schoolmaster and preacher in Natick, brought disturbing news to Governor Winslow at Plymouth: Metacom was planning a war. Although colonists had suspected this for several years, Winslow sent Sassamon away. Shortly afterwards, the Natick preacher's body was found frozen under the ice in Assawompset Pond near Middleborough. Six Wampanoags were arrested on the testimony of another who claimed to have seen the murder while standing on a nearby hill. They were tried and executed by a jumbled jury of twelve colonists and six Indians.

Two houses were burned nearby at Swanzey. A few days later, shots sliced through more houses. Soon afterwards, one man was killed, then nine more. During a lunar eclipse on June 26, which seemed a terrifying omen, soldiers gathered in Boston and marched. Near Mount Hope they found a number of Plymouth colonists dead or dying on the road. One soldier, a "stout man," on seeing a man killed in front of him "ran distracted," in shock. Metacom lit Taunton, Middlebury, and Dartmouth on fire, and stripped and scalped men and women alike.

A game of cat and mouse ensued, with the militia searching for Metacom, who burned house after house, town after town. In July the colonists pursued him and his men into the Dismal Swamp, but could not finish him off and retreated. Whether by conspiracy or by popular accord, other tribes joined the rebellion. The Nipmucks of central Massachusetts attacked settlements along the Connecticut River—Brookfield, Deerfield, and Hadley, where, legend has it, the regicide William Goffe led the defense.

So far, the Narragansett Tribe had not joined the fray. But when called by Boston to surrender in order not to be counted among the enemy, they did not appear, possibly because their long-standing enemies, the Mohegan, did. So in December a large force of Connecticut, Massachusetts, and Mohegan troops marched toward the largest Narragansett village in South Kingstown, Rhode Island. A Narragansett traitor led them deep into the swamp to a fort protected by palisades and thick hedges. Many of the officers were wounded in the first assault and the colonists were repelled twice during a brutal three-hour battle. On the third assault they set fire to the wall and part of the village, and the few remaining Narragansetts fled. The militias retreated through falling snow, struggling to get home before the year's end.

It was a victory dearly bought for the colonists—230 were wounded or killed, along with many hundreds more of the Narragansett—for its size, one of the bloodiest battles in American history. It also decided the issue for the Rhode Island tribes, who now firmly joined Metacom in an all-out war against the English. On March 17, 1676, Warwick was burned to the ground, and two days later a group of Narragansetts attacked Providence. Roger Williams walked out unarmed to meet them, pointing to his house, which "hath lodged kindly some thousands of you these ten years." By the time he finished his speech, the house was on fire. In the argument that followed, according to Williams, the Narragansetts said that the colonists had forced their hand, and that God was with them and not the colonists. They were fighting for the preservation of their way of life.

In Maine and New Hampshire, tribes in the Wabanaki Confederacy took the opportunity to satisfy grudges and reclaim their lands, attacking Brunswick, Falmouth, Wells, Kittery, and Woolwich. Eighty settlers were killed and mutilated and their houses burned. Then the Wabanaki hit Oyster River, Salmon Falls, Dover, and Exeter. The Nipmucks attacked Lancaster, and preacher's wife Mary Rowlandson was taken prisoner, her baby dying on the march. At Northampton, Massachusetts, the surprise attack was turned around and the villagers were victorious. But towns like Northfield, Sudbury, Chelmsford, Weymouth, and Eel River went up in flames, with many on both sides killed.

Local militias turned their ire on easier targets—converted Indians who were living peacefully in English-style villages. Some of the Christian converts had "defected" to join Metacom, and those defections made the colonists suspect the rest, even those who fought side-by-side with them in the militia. Some were sent to prison camps on the Boston Harbor islands. In spring, the remaining friendly Indians were hired as guides, which helped somewhat. Troops from Connecticut, which included old allies the Mohegans, counterattacked, with an aging Uncas leading his warriors. Only the western Connecticut tribes remained neutral, though a few eager warriors joined colonist militias.

Metacom's rebellion had developed into a civil war for the soul of New England, a day by day fight in which the fear of impending personal harm was constant and real on both sides. Captain Wadsworth of Milton and 160 militia were ambushed by five hundred Indians; only twenty colonists escaped. Captain Turner of Boston seemed to be more successful, massacring three hundred Indians and destroying food and supplies.

But later that day he was killed in a Greenfield meadow. Wampanoags waylaid an armed party in Pawtuxet, and Nipmucks attacked a church service in Springfield. Women at work in their kitchens and men at work in the fields were shot from nearby bushes. Peaceful and converted Indians feared they would be rounded up and shot, while others were killed at random on the highways. Two Indian prisoners in Marblehead were beaten to death by a crowd of female colonists.

By midsummer 1676 better supply lines and equipment began to give the colonists an advantage. Victories at Marlborough and Providence were matched by voluntary surrenders at Norwich and Plymouth. The Nipmuck chief and two hundred followers surrendered on July 27. Soon enough, a disgruntled Wampanoag showed up. His brother had been killed by Metacom for advising surrender, and he now guided a group of Rhode Islanders to the sachem's hiding place near Mount Hope. At dawn on August 12, Captain Benjamin Church set up colonial militia and Indian guides at intervals in the brush to wait in ambush. A converted Indian named John Alderman pointed out Metacom himself, and the colonist fired. He missed, but Alderman himself fired and hit the Wampanoag chief in the heart.

The rest of the hostile Wampanoag and Narragansett fled to the far north of Maine or to Canada. But the war was not over. The Wabanaki Confederacy continued to attack the settlers in Maine throughout the summer and autumn of 1676. Not one settlement was left between Casco Bay and the Penobscot. Refugees gathered on Monhegan Island before fleeing to Boston. Four hundred Indians went to Dover, New Hampshire, to a treaty meeting, and were tricked into laying down their arms. Half were released and the other half sent as prisoners to Boston. This deception triggered another round of massacres into the winter of 1677 at Wells, Black Point, and Scarborough.

The following spring, attacks continued. All fifty families in Kennebec County fled, deserting homes and farms. Bristol and Biddeford were destroyed. An abandoned Portland was burned to the ground. Skirmishes and burnings continued throughout the year, until April 1678, when the chiefs of the Wabanaki met representatives of the Massachusetts government and signed a truce. If anyone had won the war, it had been them, since Maine had been practically depopulated of colonists, with seven hundred settlers dead or prisoners in Canada and hundreds of houses burned to the ground.

One out of every twenty people in New England, native or European, was dead. Over half the towns in Plymouth and the Bay Colony were damaged or destroyed. The war debt of the Plymouth Colony may have been more than the entire worth of all the personal property of the inhabitants. In Rhode Island only a few hundred Narragansett remained, and the colonial villages had to be completely rebuilt. Over the next forty years, not a single new parish was founded in all of Maine, and abandoned towns were not resettled completely until 1713.

Things were much worse for the Native Americans—peaceful, converted, and hostile alike. At least five thousand were dead and a thousand had been sent as slaves to Bermuda, including Metacom's nine-year-old son. The remaining tribes never again trusted their neighbors, if they ever had, knowing that there was no possibility of living on equal terms. The mediation between cultures that literate, bilingual men like Sassamon, Uncas, and Roger Williams had hoped for now looked naïve. Tens of thousands of settlers who had previously been neutral or even friendly toward their neighbors came out of "King Philip's War" with hate in their hearts. The wilderness had become terrifying again, and they drew together, frightened of Native Americans and of the violence inherent in their own colonial experiment.

After Metacom was killed in the ambush, his body was quartered and left for the wolves. But his hands were sent to Boston, and his head was set on a pike atop the watchtower at Plymouth, rotting into a bone-white skull for the next twenty years. How many children growing up there saw that gleaming skull, high above the town? How many saw their own reflections?

CHAPTER 7

The First Revolution

1680s

AFTER KING PHILIP'S WAR, ECONOMIC AND SPIRITUAL DEPRESSION settled over the land. Homeless colonists in Plymouth and Rhode Island spent their time building new houses. Between acrimonious political disputes, the leaders of Massachusetts created a provincial government for the depopulated wilds of Maine, while their apparent greed for land made all the other colonies nervous. Only Connecticut had come out of King Philip's War with little damage, and continued to grow steadily. However, its leaders spent valuable time bickering with Rhode Island about borders.

These squabbles and disagreements played right into the long-term plan of King Charles II to take tighter control of the colonies. Indeed, it had already begun, with customs collectors serving in every colony now, taking the king's portion of profits. Then, in 1680, the Crown took New Hampshire under direct royal control. Portraits of the king were hung in meetinghouses and widely hated former spy Edward Randolph became the collector of King's Customs at Portsmouth.

Born in Kent in 1632, Randolph had studied at Gray's Inn and Queens' College, but had never graduated. While spying on New Englanders' activities, he had made plenty of enemies, and now he returned with boundless ambition, a talent for political manipulation, and thoughts of revenge. Soon enough, the New Hampshire administration under Governor Cranfield started to become oppressive, and when the legislative council vetoed a tax revenue bill in 1683, Cranfield dissolved the council and proclaimed a direct tax on the people.

On January 27, 1683, Edward Gove of Hampton urged rebellion and rode to Exeter to try to spark a popular uprising. He gathered about a dozen supporters before the local militia arrested him. Cranfield made an example of Gove, sending him to London, where he spent three years in the Tower awaiting execution. This only increased the grumbling of the rest. Both farmers and fishermen refused to pay illegally assessed taxes. In Exeter the women prepared boiling water and hot pokers for Cranfield's marshal, who wisely absconded. Soon enough the royal governor did the same. Randolph moved on to more tempting targets.

In October 1684 the Massachusetts Bay Company was dissolved by the king and the colony's charter revoked. It was just what Randolph wanted, and he continued plotting to consolidate his power. King Charles died a few months later, but his successor, King James II, was more than willing to listen to Randolph and take advantage of the fractious situation in New England. In October 1685 the new king created the position of president of the Council of New England and appointed a man named Joseph Dudley. A native of Roxbury who had attended Harvard, Dudley was in Randolph's pocket, and soon assumed his duties presiding over all the colonies except Connecticut and parts of Rhode Island.

A number of the original magistrates, including the highly respected Reverend Increase Mather, refused to serve on Dudley's council, but to the dismay of many, Edward Randolph was appointed. His ambition had been revealed, but there was nothing they could do about it. Randolph crowed in triumph that the Puritans were wrong in their "opinion that God would never suffer me to land again in this country." However, Dudley had no charter, no truly representative legislature, and thus no ability to raise taxes. He enforced the Navigation Acts, and attempted to extend control over the other colonies. With the blessing of the king, Randolph wrote to Governor Robert Treat of Connecticut, threatening to divide the colony's land between New York and Massachusetts, saying, "His Majesty intends to bring all New England under one government; and nothing is now remaining on your part but to think of an humble submission and a dutiful resignation of your charter."

But Randolph and Dudley were only placeholders. On December 20, 1686, Sir Edmund Andros landed in Boston with a company of soldiers and a piece of paper that gave him control of all New England. All the rights the colonists had earned were now meaningless; they had been relegated to "conquered" states. For his troubles, Edward Randolph became the secretary, continued his duties as customs collector, and kept his hand in anything where money was involved. Boston became the capital of the newly named Dominion of New England, and in January 1687 representatives from each of the five colonies were required to appear in Boston. A new flag flew from ships sailing out of Salem, Providence, and Portsmouth, featuring a red field with a cross of St. George in the canton, punctuated by a small green pine tree in its first quarter.

A lantern-jawed veteran soldier, Andros had already served as governor of New York and had been considered "imperious" by the colonists. He earned that reputation again, consistently ignoring the advice of the New Englanders' advisory council. He raised money with import duties on alcohol and imposed taxes. Officials from towns that refused to cooperate were arrested and fined. The poorer residents of Plymouth could barely afford the high rates. When the Reverend John Wise protested, he was arrested and told, "You have no more privileges left you than not to be sold for slaves."

Soon, town meetings were banned and what press existed was censured. New patents had to be proposed for land ownership, legal fees went up precipitously, and Andros gave chunks of town commons in Lynn and Cambridge to his cronies. Samuel Shrimpton, a powerful landowner with a royal appointment, had Deer Island taken from him. What hope was there for the poor? Many of the more religious residents were shaken by Andros's use of a Puritan meetinghouse for Anglican services when it was not occupied by its members. Other communities were told that they had to turn over their church to the Anglicans or build a new one.

In summer 1687 Andros renewed Randolph's attempt to get Connecticut to surrender its charter, even though the Dominion supposedly superseded it. Sixty grenadiers and Andros himself marched to the Connecticut River, crossed the ferry at Wethersfield, and continued to Hartford, where they were received politely by Governor Treat. Hours of debate in the meetinghouse followed, with Andros demanding the charter and the colonists delaying him. What happened next is shrouded in legend. One story relates that the candles in the meetinghouse were blown out and the charter handed out the window to Captain Joseph Wadsworth, who secreted it in a hollow of the large oak on Wyllys Hill. Or it is possible that Andros was simply given a fake charter. Either way, the Connecticut settlers cleverly prevented him from getting the real one.

The colony was annexed anyway. Andros continued to Fairfield, New Haven, and New London, creating courts and sheriffs and military hierarchy. He tightened control on Rhode Island and Maine. On April 7, 1688, a new commission arrived that extended the Dominion all the way to the Delaware River and authorized Andros to dispose of open lands in this territory at will. He was now the leader of the largest and most populous territory north of Mexico.

Some of the colonists did not believe that the king could possibly be behind these depredations. Throughout early 1688 Reverend Increase Mather gathered signatures of protest and made ready to sail to England. Ever vigilant, Edward Randolph found out and arrested him. At trial Mather beat the charges, but when a second round of charges were leveled, he slipped onto a ship and fled. When he reached England he brought the colony's case against Andros to King James himself, but found his petition largely ignored.

That summer the Wabanaki Confederacy attacked villages in Maine again, part of a concerted effort by the French to consolidate power in the north. Negotiations were attempted, but broke down and Andros recruited a thousand soldiers to lead north. Unfortunately for him, the expedition set out in the winter, and many died from the cold rather than from battles, in which "not one Indian hath been killed." The "Popish" Andros lost even more credibility.

He returned in March 1689 to Boston to hear the first whispers of rebellion against King James in England. Rumors also flew about Andros's failed Maine expedition, and in retaliation he prosecuted two Sudbury men in a widely scorned trial. Then, on April 4, news arrived of the rebellion of Parliament and the landing of William of Orange in England. Opinions and speculation flew and rebounded. Two weeks passed. Then at dawn on Thursday, April 18, the people of Massachusetts began to gather.

At 8:00 a.m. armed groups marched from Roxbury, crossed the river from Charlestown, and appeared in the streets of Boston. They seized known allies of Andros, including Randolph, and threw them in jail. At the town hall, a group that included former governor Simon Bradstreet, Wait Winthrop, and young Cotton Mather formed a Council of Safety. They signed a "Declaration of the Gentlemen, Merchants, and Inhabitants of Boston and the Country adjacent," which praised William of Orange and enumerated Andros's wrongs.

However, Andros himself was safely ensconced in his headquarters at Fort Mary in Boston Harbor. Hundreds of English soldiers were also garrisoned in the fort on Castle Island, and the twenty-six-gun frigate *HMS Rose* hovered ominously in the harbor. But the Massachusetts citizens had prepared well. Drums beat from hidden places and an orange flag flew from the top of Beacon Hill. Twenty companies of militia answered the call, more than enough to deal with the few English soldiers.

Andros was summoned to "surrender and deliver up the government and fortification." Otherwise the rebels would take the fort "by storm." The English frigate in the harbor readied for war, with its commander swearing to "die before she should be taken." He sent a small boat to collect Andros, but it was attacked and overwhelmed as soon as it reached shore. Andros had started down the hill to meet it, and hastily retreated into the fort. The rebels dragged every cannon in Boston to the harbor and pointed them at the *Rose*. The commander of the frigate tried to make a deal to avoid surrender, but Protestants amongst his crew took down the sails and closed the gun ports. Andros was soon forced to send an order to the "castle," and the English soldiers there gave it up "with cursings." He surrendered with a guarantee he would not be executed.

The rebellion had ended without casualties, but the true unhappiness of the New Englanders now became clear as they flooded into Boston, trembling with rage, calling for Andros's head. A story circulated that the tyrant had disguised himself in a dress and bonnet, slipping past two sentries, but was caught when one noticed the men's shoes he still wore. In actuality, he did briefly escape when his servants bribed the guards with liquor. After fleeing to Rhode Island, he was recaptured and kept in solitary confinement.

Joseph Dudley was in Newport when he heard the news of the uprising and hid at a friend's home. But the angry colonists tracked him down and put him under house arrest. Of all Andros's associates, he was in the most danger of mob justice, since in their eyes he was more than a tyrant, he was a traitor. Plymouth also arrested their puppet governor, and Connecticut quietly resumed government under their charter. New York, Pennsylvania, and Maryland followed Boston's lead, and King James's appointees were forced to leave. A ship arrived in Boston, announcing that William and Mary had been crowned, and celebrations spilled into the streets.

In England, Increase Mather presented the joint petition, in which Connecticut, Plymouth, and Rhode Island would "be restored to their ancient privileges." At first, all King William and Queen Mary would promise was that Andros would be removed officially from power. They were still wary of the fractious colonists who had rebelled against a king, despite the fact that they had done the same. After several years of discussions, a compromise was struck. Massachusetts would still have a royally appointed governor, but charterless Plymouth was annexed, as were Nantucket and Martha's Vineyard. New Hampshire kept its status as a Royal Province, and Connecticut and Rhode Island were overlooked and kept their charters.

Once again, the colonists of New England were nominally free to pursue their own destinies. But they would tell stories of the bitterness of tyranny and the sweetness of rebellion to their children and grandchildren. This brief revolution would not be the last.

CHAPTER 8

The Letter of the Law

1690s

ON JUNE 27, 1689, IN DOVER, NEW HAMPSHIRE, TWO WOMEN ASKED for leave to enter the garrison house. The guards opened the doors to a hidden Wabanaki war party, who stormed the small fortress and took bloody revenge on seventy-four-year-old Major Waldron, who years earlier had sold many Wabanaki as slaves. They also killed his son-in-law, took his daughter and grandchild captive, and killed or kidnapped dozens of others. One woman was spared because an attacking Wabanaki recognized her as the person who had helped him escape thirteen years earlier. More battles throughout the summer left many dead and villages burned to the ground. The following year, just north of Portsmouth along the Piscataqua River, isolated family homes were burned down one by one, with almost one hundred settlers massacred. A surprise attack on Salmon Falls, New Hampshire, left thirty people dead and fifty captive. It seemed that King Philip's War had never ended.

A man named William Phips was given command of the Massachusetts forces. Born a poor shepherd boy, Phips had built ships in Maine and then struck literal gold when he salvaged a galleon off Haiti, earning a knighthood in the bargain. With seven hundred men and fourteen ships, Phips promptly sailed from Boston to Port Royal in Acadia, wrecked the town, and returned with prisoners and loot. After this success, he organized a huge expedition to Quebec City, but was hampered by lack of provisions, smallpox, and the terrible October weather of the St. Lawrence River. Phips demanded Quebec's surrender, and the Comte de Frontenac replied that it would come "from the mouths of my cannon and muskets." Boston warships cannonaded the city, but the French fired back and the New Englanders retreated in the face of increasing resistance. Defeated, having lost £50,000—a fortune at the time—Phips sailed to England to join Increase Mather.

By the 1690s most of the first generation of settlers had died, and with them the religious zeal necessary to maintain the "holy community." Increase Mather often mentioned the deaths of the long-lived first generation with dread, fearing that "another and more sinful Generation" would follow. Of course, these children could hardly do more than their parents had done; founding a new civilization is a tough act to follow. But what their sin really was, according to their dying predecessors, was "worldliness." They were victims of their parents' prosperity.

Mather may have considered his own son, Cotton, an exception. Born in Boston in 1663, Cotton had been a stammering, sickly child, and like most others of his generation who grew up during the terrifying war with Metacom, had a severe prejudice against Native Americans. He graduated Harvard at eighteen and was ordained into the ministry at North Church in May 1685. His father warned him that the brutal wars of the 1670s and the despotism of the 1680s seemed to point toward chaos, the end times. He grew up believing that the devil and his servants, witches and Indians, were conspiring to destroy Puritan New England.

At age twenty-five, Cotton witnessed a witchcraft case firsthand in Boston, brought by four children against their family's Gaelic-speaking laundress, Elizabeth Glover. The children barked like dogs and flapped their arms like wings. The Goodwins accused Glover of witchcraft, and called in Mather, who investigated the case, praying and talking with the supposed witch in her jail cell. He tried to teach her the Lord's Prayer in English, but she couldn't seem to learn it, though in Latin she could. Meanwhile, they discovered small dolls that Glover admitted using as magic charms to torment the children. Mather and the rest of the town took this admission of guilt as truth and Glover was taken to be executed, since witchcraft was equal to murder, according to the law. Before she died, she claimed she had made a covenant with the devil and cursed the children.

Spectral evidence, confession, small tokens of physical evidence—these were enough for a conviction in Mather's mind, and for just about everyone else in New England at that time. "Unriddle these things," Mather charged his readers. They could not, and throughout the late 1680s and early 1690s, reports of bewitched houses, possessions, and curses abounded, told over and over to eager listeners. Tales of witchcraft in previous centuries were dredged out of literature, and ships brought reports of devil-born conspiracies in England, Germany, and Sweden.

Salem church's Reverend Samuel Parris often preached about witchcraft, and it seems his nine-year-old daughter was listening. In the winter of 1691, Betty Parris and her eleven-year-old cousin, Abigail Williams, experimented with fortune-telling, trying to predict their future husbands. In January 1692, Betty seemed to be preoccupied, and when her father reprimanded her, she barked like a dog. She screamed during prayer, threw a Bible, and cried that she was damned. She and her friends began to say strange phrases and garbled sentences at odd times, choke on nothing, and have apparent fits.

A local doctor suspected witchcraft, and on February 29, 1692, the adults of Salem interrogated Betty Parris, Abigail Williams, and two other friends, Ann Putnam and Elizabeth Hubbard. They first accused the Parris's slave, Tituba, homeless beggar Sarah Good, and the unpopular Sarah Osborne, all the sorts of women who for centuries were considered likely candidates for witchcraft. They were questioned, Tituba confessed to practicing "witchcraft," and all three were sent to freezing jail cells. But that was not the end of the matter, since the ministers and other adults suspected a larger conspiracy. Soon the girls had a series of "fits," screamed in pain, and reported that another "spectre" was tormenting them.

Throughout March and April more women and men were accused, including minister George Burroughs and Rebecca Nurse, who had bravely tried to defend her sister from allegations. The fever spread from nearby Ipswich to far-off Fairfield, Connecticut, as a general hysteria caused many resentful people, attention seekers, and even the mentally ill to level accusations. Abigail Williams claimed that Elizabeth Proctor's specter had attended a blood ceremony outside the Parris house. She also accused John Proctor and many other "respectable" people, and once it was clear that everyone was fair game, accusations tripled, then quadrupled in number and force.

It was not the first time in New England the testimony of a young girl had led to executions—a Connecticut girl named Anne Cole had caused two sets of hangings years apart when she blamed her seizures on witchcraft. Clinical hysteria, social pressure, attention seeking, a mental virus—the original and continuing motivations of the girls were probably complex. The particular form this hysteria took was natural for the time, since nearly everyone from the English king down believed in witchcraft.

On May 14, 1692, Increase Mather and William Phips arrived in Boston with the new charter in hand. By then 125 people across Massachusetts had been accused and arrested. Phips commissioned a "Court of Oyer and Terminer," with judges he thought could be trusted, like John Hathorne, Samuel Sewall, and Lieutenant Governor William Stoughton. Nathaniel Saltonstall refused to serve, telling the court that spectral evidence was not acceptable. Shortly afterward he was, of course, accused of being a witch.

None of the judges were trained in the law, and in fact no such judges existed in Massachusetts. These were ministers, working with false evidence and an archaic system. And they very quickly became just as hysterical and credulous as the rest of the population. If multiple people accused one lonely old woman, or a handful of teenage girls swore that Satan had come in the form of a local minister, what could the judges do but believe them? "Upon the testimony of many witnesses" were the witches condemned.

Both Mathers, father and son, waffled and equivocated with their advice throughout the trials, cautioning against spectral evidence but not denying it, alternately giving warnings and inspiration. Increase Mather tried to remain supportive of his friends Sewall, Hathorne, and Stoughton, but also questioned the way the trials were conducted. Perhaps the Mathers were smart not to fully condemn the proceedings; when ministers from other towns who did not believe in spectral evidence protested, they found themselves whispered about too.

On July 19 five women were executed, including Rebecca Nurse, Sarah Good, Elizabeth Howe, Susannah Martin, and Sarah Wildes.

Shortly afterwards, on August 1, Governor Phips left to build Fort William Henry at Pemaquid, recruiting Major Benjamin Church to fight the Wabanaki. He left Lieutenant Governor Stoughton in charge, as leader of both courts and government. Stoughton sat as the judge on this court and began to ruthlessly try and execute the legions of suspected witches now sweating in jail.

On August 19, John Proctor and three others were executed. On the hanging ladder, former minister and supposed ringleader of the witches George Burroughs declared his innocence, affecting the crowd with his emotional speech. But he was hanged anyway, and Cotton Mather assured the assembly that "the devil often had been transformed into the Angel of Light." That same month he contradictorily claimed he wasn't so sure that spectral evidence should be used by itself in the trials, since the devil could assume any shape. As the leading judge, Stoughton accepted spectral evidence without question. People were admitting witchcraft, after all. The conspiracy must be real.

On September 19, Giles Corey was crushed to death with stones, after bravely refusing to confess he was a witch in order to save his family's inheritance from forfeiture. On September 22, eight more were executed. Others pled guilty; others were tried and found guilty to await execution. On September 29, Phips returned from the Maine expedition to a Boston ruled by Stoughton with a growing horror, finding hundreds of accusations filling the courts, even against his own wife. The court "must fall," he declared, and dismissed it too late for some, just in time for others. Fourteen women and five men were dead. Fifty had confessed, to avoid being hanged, and another hundred were awaiting trial.

In October, Increase Mather printed his book *Cases of Conscience Concerning Evil Spirits*, cautioning too late that "it were better that Ten Suspected Witches should escape than that one innocent person should be condemned." Sick in bed, his son, Cotton, wrote his own book, *Wonders of the Invisible World*, published in England the next summer. It was a defense of the proceedings, and became an instant best seller. However, it was a public relations disaster—he was then and forevermore associated with the trials. When the publisher cut out Mather's "qualifications and doubts" about spectral evidence, the book marked him forever as the witch-hunter of Salem, even though he never served as a judge or accuser. Indeed, he was only a small part of this failure of the community from top to bottom. Everyone was culpable, everyone had been involved. They believed the evidence because they wanted to believe it.

Judge Stoughton remained unrepentant, and tried to convict eight more "witches" in January 1693, ordering that graves be dug in advance. Phips cleared them by proclamation, and no one else died. Slowly sanity returned. In 1695 a Quaker named Thomas Maule wrote a repudiation that cited Increase Mather's earlier statement, and for which he spent twelve months in jail. Then on January 14, 1696, in Boston's Old South Church, one of the judges, Samuel Sewall, stood up in his pew with a bowed head, declared his guilt, and asked for prayers while a confession of his part in the witch trials was read aloud. For the rest of his life he prayed for forgiveness for his part in the "blame and shame of it," and "for New England."

Over the next few years, those who had confessed retracted their statements as being extorted under duress and pain of death. Thomas Fiske and twelve others who had sat on the juries wrote public declarations and asked for forgiveness. Reverend John Hale of Beverly, Massachusetts, had witnessed and even participated in the mass hysteria, and in a book published after his death he admitted that "such was the darkness of that day, the tortures and lamentations of the afflicted, and the power of former precedents, that we walked in the clouds, and could not see our way." Churches began to reverse their excommunications and petitions were filed for the wrongly accused. Cotton Mather never publicly repented his part in the hysteria, but in his diary he wondered if God would curse his family because he had failed to act against the trials.

One of the group of girls, Ann Putnam, came clean in 1706, saying that she had not done it "out of any anger, malice, or ill will," but rather that "it was a great delusion of Satan that deceived me in that sad time, whereby I justly fear I have been instrumental, with others, though ignorantly and unwittingly, to bring upon myself and this land the guilt of innocent blood." It was about as close to a confession as could be hoped for. Many of the others lived in shame, according to Governor Hutchinson, "abandoned to all vice," while others "passed their days in obscurity and contempt." Still, Stoughton and Hathorne never recanted and remained pillars of the community. Betty Parris married a shoemaker, had four children, and lived until 1760 in quiet and peace.

The new generation had failed—just not in the way that Increase Mather had expected. Instead of a lesson about religious backsliding, the witch trials became a lesson about righteous overreach, about the dangers of linking hearsay and law, and about the fragility of human reason. It became a warning to future generations, unfortunately to be repeated over and over again in different ways, forgotten, and repeated again. "If truth were everywhere to be shown," a descendant of Judge John Hathorne wrote many years later, "a scarlet letter would blaze forth on many a bosom."

CHAPTER 9

A Mutual Possession

1700s

ON MARCH 5, 1697, A MOTHER OF EIGHT CHILDREN, HANNAH DUSTIN, was kidnapped, along with her infant and a nurse named Mary Neff. The baby was promptly killed, and Dustin found herself on a nightmarish journey into the wilderness. One night while her Native American captors lay asleep around the fire, Dustin woke up two other prisoners, Mary Neff and a young boy named Samuel Lennardson, and the three of them killed the entire raiding party as they slept. Dustin sawed off hunks of their hair and skin, stole a canoe, and paddled downriver to Haverhill, Massachusetts. The scalps were worth fifty pounds sterling, and she promptly cashed them in.

This was one of the last incidents of King William's War, which had been smoldering throughout the 1690s. Peace was declared in Europe that September, though raids and skirmishes with the Wabanaki continued until 1699. Just a year later, in 1700, rumors spread among both Indians and English that each was going to wipe out the other, but luckily cooler heads prevailed, and a few precious years of peace followed.

However, conflict between the colonies and England had flared again, and the charters seemed constantly in danger of being revoked. During the 1690s the "impressment," or kidnapping, of colonists onto British ships became more and more common, and was widely resented, not only by the men forced to labor for months or years on the decks of English frigates, but by New England merchants who lost potential seamen and families who lost husbands and sons.

On July 14, 1702, a Royal Navy vessel called the *Swift* sent a gang onshore in Boston to impress sailors, threatening death to the men they kidnapped. A group of town elders protested this loss of liberty, and when the captain vulgarly refused, the lieutenant governor ordered the fort in Boston Harbor to fire on the ship. The *Swift*'s captain responded to warning shots by saying, "Kiss my arse, you dog." The third shot was not a warning. It smashed into the top of the capstan, killing one sailor and leaving five others wounded. One of the impressed men, Edward Storey, grabbed the anchor and grounded the ship. The captain was relieved of duty and the impressed men were let go.

The English government under Queen Anne ignored both the colony's complaint and the death of the sailor. However, that same year the Queen appointed Joseph Dudley as governor of both New Hampshire and Massachusetts. He had helped the hated Edmund Andros during the brief Dominion of New England thirteen years earlier. Now governor again in 1702, he spent the next thirteen years unsuccessfully trying to take a salary from the resentful colonists, intriguing to destroy the charters, and vetoing the election of councilors who opposed him.

A year earlier a new European war had erupted over the succession to the Spanish throne, and a reluctant New England tried to stay out of it, meeting with the Wabanaki at Casco and exchanging letters with the governor of Quebec. But shortly afterwards, bands of raiders, with or without the permission of their leaders, began to attack and plunder eastern Maine. On August 10, 1703, a combined force of French and Abenakis attacked Wells, striking from the forest in a series of coordinated attacks. Thirty-nine colonists were killed or taken prisoner. Soon multiple settlements were aflame, and 150 colonists were dead. The French sent ships to sink New England fishing vessels and disguised assassins to kill Governor Dudley. But he survived, and organized a war against the French and Wabanaki, sometimes successfully, sometimes less so.

On February 29, 1704, a large group of French soldiers under Jean-Baptiste Hertel de Rouville swept into the unsuspecting town of Deerfield, Massachusetts. Held at gunpoint, Reverend John Williams witnessed the death of two of his children and Parthena, their female slave. The other five children, his wife, Eunice, and he were bound as captives. House by house fell, with half the colonists killed or taken prisoner. Over one hundred hostages marched through deep snow up the Connecticut River Valley toward Montreal. Williams watched as his wife collapsed from exhaustion and was summarily tomahawked.

In response, Major Benjamin Church and five hundred volunteers sailed up the coast of Maine and raided Grand-Pre and Pisiguit in Acadia, capturing prisoners to exchange for the Deerfield captives. During King Philip's War, the bulky but agile Church had taken part in the Great Swamp Fight against the Narragansett. Over the preceding thirty years, operating independently in small, mobile groups, his moccasin and buckskin-clad soldiers had adopted many of the tactics of native tribes, becoming effective and ruthless along the bloodstained borders of what the settlers called civilization. Church and others like him were a new kind of settler, a new kind of warrior, adapted to the dense forests and marshes of their new home.

That home was still hotly contested, though, and the Penobscots, Micmac, and other tribes along the border continued to defend their territories. The French armed them and sent other help, like the Jesuit priest Father Sebastian Rasle. In 1694 Rasle had built a mission in Norridgewock along the Kennebec River, and worked on converting the Maine Indians to Catholicism, living in a wigwam and learning their languages. He had his own vision for northern New England, and he would spend three decades fighting for it with every fiber of his being.

In 1707 an expedition against Port Royal in Acadia was mounted, but failed miserably. Negotiations for prisoner exchanges went on, sometimes successfully, though returned captives were often mistrusted by their former neighbors. Reverend Williams was eventually freed, but his youngest daughter, Eunice, stayed with her captors. She was rebaptized Catholic as Marguerite, married a Mohawk named François-Xavier Aronsen, and lived for the rest of her long life as a member of that tribe.

A winter expedition against Father Rasle's snowy outpost at Norridgewock found no one home, and the Massachusetts soldiers consoled themselves by burning his chapel. Hannah Dustin's hometown of Haverhill was attacked again in 1708, and fields remained fallow throughout New Hampshire and northern Massachusetts due to fear of attack. New

Englanders holed up in their forts and waited. Finally, in October 1710, a combined force of English and colonial soldiers laid siege to Port Royal and captured it.

Flush with this success, a large expedition of colonial and English forces set out to take Quebec in 1711. But in the St. Lawrence River ten ships smashed on the rocks and nearly a thousand people drowned, most of them colonists. A force of New York and Connecticut soldiers heading north to take Montreal heard of the disaster and turned back at Lake Champlain. The disgraced admiral tried to put the blame on Massachusetts, and once again friction arose between New and Old England. The impressment of colonial sailors had been officially banned in 1708, but it may have only been constant war with the French that kept England from tightening the screws of parental discipline even further.

The war stumbled on. Once again Maine was almost depopulated of English colonists, but this time the eastern Wabanaki lost a third of their own people. Skirmishes and sieges between local French and Indians and the British and Massachusetts forces continued for several years in the land now called Nova Scotia. Finally, in 1713, peace was declared in Europe, and at a conference in Portsmouth, Dudley made a separate treaty with the Wabanaki Confederacy. It wouldn't last. Parent and child, neighbor and neighbor, Catholic and Protestant, all were fighting for the New England they imagined.

Decades later, Marguerite Aronsen and her Mohawk husband visited her birth brother, Stephen Williams, in Longmeadow, Massachusetts, for a "joyful, sorrowful" meeting. She camped in the apple orchard and their children played together in the fields. He implored her to stay, but though she visited several times, she always returned to her home in Canada. A brief reconciliation was possible, but their paths had diverged long ago.

CHAPTER 10

Mine Early Home

1710s

EVERY SPRING, EACH SMALL TOWN IN CONNECTICUT HELD ELECTIONS, and in May representatives took these votes to be tallied in Hartford. After the election sermon, everyone walked to the town hall, and once the votes were counted, a guard fired his gun before evening festivities. The few small inns and taverns did not have enough beds, so electors stayed overnight at various houses, eating large portions of frosted "election cake." A formal ball was held the next day, and the celebration "brightened the whole year." In the words of innkeeper and traveler Sarah Knight, Connecticut was full of "Sociable people, and I hope Religious too: but a little too much Independent in their principals." Knight criticized the colony's laws against young people kissing, but she did enjoy the oysters.

What Sarah Knight found in her travels from Boston to New York was no longer English culture; it was something brand-new, with new customs, foods, and laws. The century spent in North America had changed the character of these people, as they staked claims in the pine tree hills and rocky dells. Many of the settlers had already been outcasts in Europe, but now even the culture of Puritanism was leaking away. People were simply no longer willing to sit through a three-hour sermon or a two-hour prayer, and they took pleasure from a touch of color in a scarf, a flash of brass button, or the exclamation of a scrimshaw pin.

A booming economy had caused some of these changes. Small dams were built at every waterfall, and mills ground corn or sawed lumber. Ironworks, saltworks, and mines sprang up throughout the region. The colonies had postal service as early as 1639, and by the time an Act of

Parliament in 1710 required post offices, Boston and New York had regular monthly delivery. On November 5, 1715, Elisha Cooke and a few companions opened the first public bank in Boston. The Bible forbade taking interest on loans and the Puritans had preached that, if not always practiced it. But a bank meant that the sway of the more pious preachers was over.

Politics, too, had changed the culture. Ejection from church membership made it less likely for someone to hold office, but not impossible. Each community could make bylaws through "selectmen" and their constituents gave them instructions, not the other way around. The colonies needed to interact peacefully or not with the French, the Indians, and all the other colonies. Individually and together they developed strategies for dealing with the faraway English government and their trading partners in the Caribbean. Foreign policy requires compromises, distasteful to many of the original Puritans. Their grandchildren, though, were learning to swallow them.

A fleet of merchant ships now sailed from every port, connecting New England with a wider world. In the 1700s, raspberry leaf "tea" was put on the back shelf, and imported tea took its place. Wealthier families could afford Spanish leather and Chinese silk, writing paper and coaches with glass windows. New styles of homes were built—the wood-shingled houses with steeply pitched, side-gabled roofs and massive chimneys were transformed by gambrel roofs and saltbox shapes, and by more elaborate front doors and cornices. The small, diamond-paned windows through which a boy or girl peered out at the world grew bigger, with twelve-paneled, rectangular, double-hung sashes.

The self-reliance forced upon many settlers had changed women in particular. Mothers and daughters spun wool or flax into thread and yarn, then wove this into clothing. They spent hours pleating, stacking beats of flax or hemp, carding wool, and ironing linen. They bleached thread with buttermilk and scoured pewter plates. But they also participated in the social and economic life of the community in ways undreamt of by their European counterparts, giving opinions at town meetings and organizing community events like quilting bees, corn huskings, and barn raisings.

Meanwhile, their husbands and sons had diversified their professions; New England now had dozens of dedicated saddlers, gunsmiths, and hatters. Tin peddlers walked purposefully down the lanes, a yeast man called his wares, and a meat wagon delivered door to door. Fishermen kept weaving their nets with gnarled hands, making daily forays into the waters off the coast, filling swift whaleboats with slippery cod, splitting and salting it, and selling it at markets.

Cod joined mackerel, shad, and salmon on dinner plates next to johnnycakes and apple pie. Suppers of porridge or broth during the week might include salt pork and molasses, or preserves made from currant bushes and pumpkin patches. On Sundays, women in calico gowns and men in great coats walked to the church after a breakfast of hot chocolate and doughnuts. As people had more opportunities for leisure and religious rules relaxed, games playing and feats of strength became common. Sinful activities like circuses and theater performances were still banned, but the new craze for smoking took off. Clay pipes full of Virginia tobacco were in the burn-scarred hands of tinsmiths and even the callused fingers of midwives.

By the early 1700s the old house-based ordinaries had disappeared and every settlement had a licensed inn or tavern where you could taste a tall mug of flip or a short of rum. Another drink that began to come into use was the "syrup of soot," better known as coffee. In larger towns, this drink was also available in "coffee houses," which were alternately lauded and condemned. Some made temperance pledges against both alcohol and caffeine, but it wasn't until over a century later that the New England reputation for dry living came into full force.

Education had become more important. The first continuously published newspaper had appeared in Boston in 1704, taking its place alongside bookshops and pamphleteers. In 1695 Harvard had been reorganized, and a second college had been founded in 1701. By 1718 this second school had moved to its permanent home in New Haven and was named "Yale" after one of its benefactors. Over the next few decades, library societies, schools, and newspapers would be founded in every town, even in the rural areas of New Hampshire and Maine. Confident that more education would increase peoples' belief in God, ministers everywhere in New England supported the creation of these institutions.

Despite the exodus of many of the Indians in the late 1600s, the region maintained ethnic and religious diversity. The standout was Rhode Island, which included Quakers, Baptists, Anglicans, Jews, and Sabbatarians, whose habit of working on the "Lord's Day" annoyed even the most tolerant neighbors. Rural New Hampshire included Scotch and Irish, while Maine and Nantucket still had majority native populations. There were Anglicans in western Connecticut and non-Christian Mohegans in the east. Ben Uncas and John Mason III remained as cautiously friendly as their ancestors had been, and when in 1714 the tribe complained that two Englishmen "set up the frame of a house within the land of the Mohegan country," Governor Saltonstall arrested the colonists.

The urban slaves of New England experienced leniency of movement that rural plantation slaves did not, hiring themselves to other masters, often earning enough money to buy their freedom. European settlers and Africans mingled in both taverns and churches, and though intermarriage was not common, it did exist in both cities and rural areas. More often the diminishing Indians and increasing Africans found common bonds and affections.

Including about five thousand Indians and five thousand Africans, there were a hundred thousand people living in Massachusetts now, thirty thousand in Connecticut, and about nine thousand each in New Hampshire and Rhode Island. Most of Nova Scotia was also a British Province, included in the provincial charter of Massachusetts, but most of Maine and what is now Vermont remained contested territories. Immigrants continued to arrive from Europe but there were also movements from colony to colony, out into the wilderness and back into the cities. As early as 1636 the Massachusetts General Court proclaimed that no new plantations could be made without magistrate approval, but many ignored these sorts of orders, and assembled new towns until a monopoly in land or resources developed. Those not prospering would then move and build a new town.

But they could no longer truly be called settlers. They had grown up in the wood-framed farmhouses by village greens to the ringing sounds of blacksmith hammers, the cries of seagulls, and the swish-clop of horses' hooves on the packed-earth paths. They knew the savor of hasty pudding and the smell of white pine and the feel of hemp rope. This corner of North America was the only home they had known, no longer an idea in the mind of John Winthrop and the Puritans, but a breathed reality. They were New Englanders.

CHAPTER 11

Ninety-Eight Notches

1720s

In 1721 a homemade bomb flew in the elderly Cotton Mather's window in the dead of night. Was it a belated missive from the relative of someone hanged as a witch thirty years earlier? No, it was a protest from someone upset by his campaign for combating smallpox. Earlier that year an outbreak had swept over New England, with 844 deaths in Boston alone. Mather had promoted the new scientific method of inoculation, and out of 287 people who tried it, six had died. The *New England Courant* called Mather a "baboon."

That same year, for the first time since the 1660s, settlers pushed into the interior and eastern areas of Maine. It was a contested territory between France and England, and still occupied only by the tribes of the Wabanaki Confederacy. Four Catholic missions stood in the four largest native villages, including Father Rasle's long-standing home at Norridgewock. Massachusetts built forts downriver at the mouth of the Kennebec to protect the settlements. At a meeting with Governor Shute of Massachusetts at Arrowsic, the Wabanakis protested this incursion. Shute refused to hear their demands, citing the treaty with the French, which had ignored the Indian claims. The Wabanakis stole livestock from the new settlers, but also offered Boston "hostages" to guarantee good behavior. Shute protested the presence of Rasle at Norridgewock, fearing that the French were using the Wabanakis to press their own interests.

There was indeed some truth to that, because Father Rasle was displeased about the offer of hostages, and so was Governor Vaudreuil of Quebec. He had been supplying the Norridgewocks with bullets and expected something in return. Letters and threats flew back and forth. Soon the Norridgewock Tribe took English prisoners from Merimeeting Bay as their own hostages. Then Brunswick was burned. Massachusetts recruits marched toward the Penobscot. Five hundred Abenaki attacked the fort at Arrowsic Island. An abandoned Catholic chapel and Indian fort at Oldtown near Bangor were burned. The St. Francois Indians moved down from Quebec, and the Wabanaki raided into southern Maine and New Hampshire.

Massachusetts soldiers raided Norridgewock in 1722, but Rasle escaped into the forest. The soldiers took a strongbox from his wigwam and found inside letters that apparently confirmed their suspicions that Father Rasle was an agent of Quebec. That same year another Jesuit priest led the Penobscots and Medunic Tribes in a siege of the colonists at Fort St. George. The Micmac laid siege to Annapolis Royal in Nova Scotia and Arrowsic, Maine. Rasle and the Norridgewock Tribe helped against Arrowsic, and attacked Fort Richmond as well. The forts held, but all the new houses were burned to the ground.

Finding as many problems as his predecessor had with the Massachusetts Assembly, Governor Shute sailed to England in disgust, leaving Lieutenant Governor William Dummer in charge. The following spring of 1723, Thomas Westbrook led an expedition up the Penobscot, but found Norridgewock as eerily empty as they had two decades earlier. The Wabanaki made fourteen more raids throughout the summer and autumn, and ten more the following year, including a daring raid on a sloop that ended in a massacre of all the sailors. Canoe attacks captured two dozen whaleboats and fishing vessels in just a few weeks. The Micmac attacked settlements and forts throughout Nova Scotia, including a deadly raid on Annapolis Royal on July 4, 1724.

But on August 22 things started to turn the way of the New Englanders. Jeremiah Moulton and Johnson Harmon took two hundred trained rangers stealthily up the Kennebec, taking care not to be seen. At Norridgewock half the men ran straight for the village and the others surrounded the cornfields. At 3 p.m. they were spotted as they entered the wigwam village with its small chapel. A large group of warriors ran out shooting, but the orderly Massachusetts troops fired simultaneously with deadly effect. The warriors followed the women and children into the river, where many were shot or drowned. The rangers searched for Rasle, with orders to take him alive, but upon finding him in a wigwam loading a musket, Lieutenant Benjamin Jacques shot and killed him. His scalp was taken back to Boston in triumph.

The French took full advantage of Rasle's martyrdom with a touching story of how he died under the cross he had built himself, but that was the end for the Norridgewock, and the survivors retreated into Quebec. The Penobscot made peace the following year and many left the area. However, the war had already spread to the west, with tribes under Chief Paugus and Chief Gray Lock raiding in New Hampshire and western Massachusetts. Gray Lock had attacked Northfield and Rutland the previous summer, and in response William Dummer constructed a fort west of the Connecticut River, the first permanent English settlement in what would become Vermont.

A colonist from New Hampshire named John Lovewell led three expeditions into the White Mountains, pushing Chief Paugus and the Pequawkets back, establishing a fort northeast of Lake Winnipesaukee. On May 9, 1725, in Fryeburg, Maine, they snuck up on what they thought was a lone Abenaki warrior, leaving their packs in a clearing. Sneaking behind the colonists, Chief Paugus and his war party set up their ambush near the packs. Lovewell was wounded by the lone Abenaki, and as his men helped him back to their equipment, Paugus sprung his trap. Lovewell and eight others were killed immediately, but so was Chief Paugus.

Meanwhile, Gray Lock led raids along the Connecticut River, killing people at Deerfield, Hatfield, and Westfield. Fort Dummer was attacked in October 1724, and the following autumn a scouting party was ambushed. Fighting went on in Nova Scotia until summer 1726 when the tribal chiefs there signed a peace treaty. The next summer, all the northern tribal leaders other than Gray Lock reconfirmed a lasting peace. But he stopped his raids, and faded into the forests, and into legend.

That autumn a terrific earthquake shook New England. "The air never more calm, the sky never more fair," wrote Cotton Mather. And then, "a horrid rumbling like the noise of many coaches together driving on the paved stones" and "a most awful trembling of the earth that rocked houses." Flames of light rent the atmosphere and fissures cracked the earth. A bell tower rang and rang in Newcastle, New Hampshire, and terrified citizens huddled together in churches from Nantucket to Maine. But no one was killed, and as the days passed, people noticed that wells had more water and marshes had been raised up into tillable land. Was God punishing them? Or rewarding them? Mather tried to reconcile science and religion, saying, "Let the natural causes of earthquake be what the wise men of enquiry please, they and their causes are still under the government of Him that is God of nature."

He died a few months later, long before he was vindicated for his stance on inoculation, if not his many other sins. His fellow New Englanders had an easier time praising Native Americans; only a few years later, one described a chieftain of the Saco admiringly: "He Hercules-like had a famous Club, which he always carried with him, and on which he had made Ninety-Eight notches, being the number of English-men that he had killed with his own hands." Chief Gray Lock had a mountain named after him; Chief Paugus earned a mountain and a bay. Even Father Rasle received a granite monument at Norridgewock. It was easy enough to admire the enemy after he was dead.

CHAPTER 12

Great Awakenings

1730s

JONATHAN EDWARDS CHOPPED THE WINTER WOOD HIMSELF, WIELDING his axe deftly. He used these rare moments to speak to God, to ruminate on problems of theology, to bring together his head and heart. In many ways a typical stoic and sober New Englander, Edwards often declared his desire to live a simple life. And yet, like many others over the centuries, he also felt a mystic ambition welling up in his heart. Unlike Roger Williams or Anne Hutchinson, he had little interest in mixing politics and religion. But something must be done to save peoples' souls from the modern preoccupations with moneymaking and leisure. There must be a new birth of faith and conviction.

A descendant of Puritan pioneer John Cotton, Edwards was born in Windsor, Connecticut, in 1703, one of eleven children. He listened to his sisters and mother read from the Bible and, as early as age nine, he planned prayer meetings for local children. Four years later he had already entered the colony's new Collegiate School, which by his junior year had been renamed Yale College. He learned the philosophy of John Locke and the theology of the Puritan elders, suffering "great and violent struggles" with his faith and serving as the college butler. In the seemingly secular culture of 18th-century New England, dominated by militia training and moneymaking, he felt himself to be an anomaly and never more so than in that college dormitory, surrounded by drunk and indolent classmates.

In 1726 he became a junior pastor under his grandfather Solomon Stoddard at a church in Northampton, Massachusetts. Stoddard had nearly been killed in an ambush during King Philip's War, and his stepdaughter had been kidnapped by Abenakis in 1701, but he had risen above these events to become a staunch defender of Indian rights in the 1720s. When Stoddard died in 1729, Edwards found himself responsible for a formidable legacy, and over a thousand souls. He woke at dawn and worked thirteen-hour days, suffered anxiety attacks, and questioned his own abilities. He asked himself how could the people of his parish, and of New England, return to a more spiritual life?

On Thursday, July 8, 1731, he presented a public lecture in Boston, stressing the "mere and arbitrary grace" of God in the working of salvation. He also preached on the necessity of virtue, the value of community, and the meaning of true love—to make others happy without thought for ourselves. His efforts worked, and throughout the winter of 1733 and 1734 the Northampton church experienced a spiritual revival so intense that people neglected to sell their crops or make preserves.

Diphtheria epidemics had swept through New England over the past few years, with ninety-nine children dying in Portsmouth alone, along with thousands of others across the region. People in New England were desperate for solace. By 1735 Edwards's revival began to spread up and down the Connecticut River, but quickly turned toward religious mania rather than conversion. That summer many people were so convinced of the logic of their own damnation that they turned to despair, and even suicide. Edwards's own uncle, Joseph Hawley, killed himself. It had been three decades since the horror of the last witch panic, which everyone now agreed had been a disaster, and people were wary of inciting hysteria.

Things quieted down for a few years, while Edwards wrote a thorough and exciting study of the revival, titled *A Faithful Narrative of the Surprising Work of God in the Conversion of Many Hundred Souls in Northampton*. In 1737 food shortages became famine in the rural areas of New England. Some in northern New Hampshire and Maine starved to death, something that had rarely happened since the 1630s. Diphtheria, famine, the earthquake of 1727—to many these were all signs of displeasure from God, and once again people felt they had to do something.

Edwards's book had been published in Great Britain and found an advocate in preacher George Whitefield, who began a full revival tour of America in 1739. The suicides of four years earlier were forgotten, and a new wave of tens of thousands of conversions swept the land. Benjamin Franklin printed Whitefield's tracts, and preachers throughout the colonies read them aloud from pulpits. Whitefield arrived on Edwards's doorstep in October 1740 and thanked him for giving the theological underpinning on which his emotional style of preaching could rest. When Whitefield preached at the Northampton church, Edwards felt so moved that he wept.

More preachers followed, but they were less successful. One itinerant minister who was supposedly inspired by Whitefield advocated book burning and attacked unconverted ministers. He was found to be insane and deported. With the inspiration of Whitefield's emotional style, Edwards himself continued his own ministry, giving a July 8, 1741, sermon at Enfield, Connecticut, exactly ten years after his celebrated Boston lecture. The vivid imagery and inexorable logic of "Sinners in the Hands of an Angry God" caused a "great moaning and crying" as parishioners begged him to save them from the torments of hell.

Edwards's sermons were repeated by ministers around the region, and often caused a great stir in congregations. That winter of 1741/1742 was one of the worst in memory, with giant drifts of snow snuffing out travel and killing thousands of farm animals. The ice along the southern coast allowed one foolhardy man to travel by sledge from Cape Cod to Manhattan. In March the snow remained three feet deep, and on April 1 the few travelers who ventured out found they could still cross most rivers on foot. "God has sealed up the hand of every man," wrote John Bissell of Bolton, Connecticut, finding evidence for theology in this natural disaster. Around the region, churchgoers convulsed, groaned, and danced through services. In Durham, New Hampshire, people saw visions of angels and bright lights. Some churches collapsed, others saw huge increases in attendance. The new birth of conviction and faith was here.

It did not last, and even in Northampton conversions decreased throughout the following decade. In 1750 Edwards was expelled from his frustrated congregation, partly for his overeager attempts to censor profanity and to ban books. In Stockbridge he preached to Indians and colonists and continued to write theology before being named president of the new College of New Jersey, where he died from a smallpox inoculation. Around New England the fervor subsided, replaced by a different kind of fervor for independence. Its people continued to develop secular traditions and to separate church and state.

The theocratic society imagined by the settlers of the 1630s, or even the perfect community under God imagined in the 1730s, might have been too ambitious, even for New Englanders. But Edwards's combination of logic and zeal would echo in the words and deeds of Henry Alline of Rhode Island preaching in the Canadian Maritimes in the 1770s, Lyman Beecher of Connecticut taking Congregationalism to Ohio in the 1830s, and William Miller of Massachusetts sparking the Adventists in the 1840s. Crusaders and enthusiasts from this small region would continue to spread their intense, passionate faiths to the far corners of the earth.

CHAPTER 13

Triumph and Disaster

1740s

IN 1741 THE BRITISH NAVY ATTACKED CARTAGENA, COLOMBIA, AS PART
of a concerted effort to capture Spain's main ports in the Caribbean. Parliament had already involved the American colonies when it legalized
privateering, encouraging many in New England to take up the flag of
piracy. Now with a huge army that included thirty-six hundred colonial
soldiers of the "American Regiment," the British landed on the mainland
of South America. Back in Newport they rang the bells and lit bonfires
in celebration of inevitable victory. Unfortunately, the most competent
commander died of dysentery, and delays, rains, and yellow fever began
to take control. A hapless English general ordered assaults without siege
engines, and soldiers died in the thousands. Sailors were treated to the
image of their comrades floating naked in the harbor, being devoured
by sharks. An astonishing 90 percent of the colonists who volunteered
did not come home. It was another disaster that did not endear the New
Englanders to the Old.

Due partly to constant warfare and partly to the frigid winters of
the Little Ice Age, New England had lost its population advantage to
the rest of the North American colonies. Nevertheless, the region was
still prosperous, growing without interruption since Father Rasle's War
in the 1720s. Falmouth, Maine, swelled with immigrants from around
Massachusetts Bay and soon surpassed Portsmouth as an anchorage.
Scotch-Irish immigrants dispersed throughout New Hampshire to farm
lots along the rivers, tapping maple trees, fermenting apples for cider, and
breeding livestock.

Most of the struggles were internal. Massachusetts tried to collect from tax evaders and wrangled with timber pirates in its "private colony of a colony," Maine. The Molasses Act of 1733 led Connecticut and Rhode Island sailors to learn the gentle art of smuggling, when they weren't arguing about their own borders. Merchants soon avoided custom houses and import laws, trading with the Caribbean, Portugal, and French Canada. Splits amongst the ministry during the Great Awakening became greater, dividing churches into "New Lights" and "Old Lights." Preachers spoke against each other from their pulpits.

New Hampshire fought Massachusetts over both governance and borders until the Crown settled the dispute, appointing Benning Wentworth as governor in 1741. Benning's father, John Wentworth, had served for over a decade as the New Hampshire Royal Governor, encouraging settlements and commerce, and now his son did the same, remaining for twenty-five years, the longest-serving governor in colonial history. Ruthless, nepotistic, and willing to use the office to make himself rich, Wentworth also loved New Hampshire, and his political machinations established its equality with the other colonies.

But mere politics would have to wait. On May 3, 1744, word of a new European war reached the French at their fortress on Cape Breton Island. They acted quickly, taking the Nova Scotian port of Canso on May 23 and attacking Annapolis Royal. French privateers began capturing New England fishing vessels, pretending to be ships in distress and then turning their guns on the Good Samaritans. Massachusetts's flagship, *Prince of Orange*, was sailing off Cape Cod when another ship appeared under British colors. But Captain Edward Tyng was no fool, son and grandson of veterans against the French and Spanish. Ready when the other ship struck its false colors, he smashed the French with a full broadside of cannonballs. After a chase, the damaged French ship turned in a last-ditch effort to engage hand to hand, but Tyng's men were too quick with the cannon, and the *Prince of Orange* was victorious.

This was the first of several New England victories, and soon an attack on the huge Louisbourg fortress was proposed. The problem was that the Massachusetts General Court had no permission or support from England, and the proposal passed by a margin of only one vote. The people were much more eager. One hundred fishing captains pledged to transport colonial militia to Cape Breton Island and various ambitious men volunteered to command this daring invasion. However, the governor of Massachusetts chose instead a reluctant leader, the respectable William Pepperell of Kittery, Maine. He wanted nothing to do with it, knowing that if they lost, he would be ruined. But he finally accepted, and volunteers flooded to the cause from across Massachusetts, Connecticut, Maine, and New Hampshire. The mid-Atlantic colonies declined to send soldiers, though New York and Pennsylvania sent ships and weapons.

On Sunday March 24, after church, thousands boarded small vessels in Boston Harbor. As Parson Samuel Moody of York, Maine, walked up the gangplank, he held up his axe, which he called the "Sword of the Lord and of Gideon," saying that it would be used to cut down the symbols of "papal worship" in the French fort. Though he and other preachers blessed the enterprise, the fleet was immediately hit by a nor'easter, complete with snow, and the flotilla scattered all over the North Atlantic. Some ships found shelter amongst the Maine islands, others rode it out in the great ocean swells. Only sixteen years old, Connecticut's Solomon Wales fell off his ship and was forced to swim through the icy waters to safety. On April 4, Pepperell sailed his icebound ship into Canso Harbor and promptly retook it. Within a week the rest of the ragtag fleet arrived, and on April 19 the armies of New England reached Louisbourg as the sun came up over the eastern sea.

It was an impressive sight, with earthen walls enclosing an entire town and part of the harbor. The colonial troops lacked large cannons to take such a fortress, and the troops consisted mostly of farmers, indentured servants, and clerks. Many Native Americans from southern New England had also joined the fight, eager to do something of consequence in a culture that did not value them. Each militiaman carried a smoothbored, ten-pound musket that fired round lead balls that settled loosely in the bore. The black gunpowder created so much smoke that battlefields were often covered in dense fog.

Pepperell blockaded the harbor and even drove off a French frigate, his small, maneuverable colonial ships swarming the larger foe. They captured some big cannons from the Grand Battery, and though they had been spiked, gunsmith Seth Pomeroy was able to drill them. Soon some Royal Navy ships arrived, having decided that the "savage" colonials needed help. Luckily, the commander was an old friend of Pepperell, and when a frontal attack was rumored, the company captains all voted against the idea. That they were even asked was a far cry from the British military's usual enforced discipline. Already the New England soldiers disliked the navy due to its policy of impressment, and this was exacerbated when a French ship slipped past the British blockade. The colonists dealt with it themselves by creating a "fire ship" that sunk it.

The New Hampshire regiment heroically dragged captured cannons through swamp and rocks, using large trees and giant sledges. A brisk exchange of cannon fire erupted. Skirmishes on the outskirts led to the slaughter of a group of twenty-one men from the Third Massachusetts. A failed attack on the island battery that protected the docks led to 60 dead and 119 captured. But all the while, Richard Gridley, the chief engineer, brought their trenches closer and closer. The Americans lobbed heated shot and exploding mortars over the walls into the fortified city.

Some of the French soldiers began to complain about their living situation. One deserted, another met with the gallows. A French fleet arrived, but after a fierce sea battle it was turned back. The Americans finally knocked out the Island Battery with properly placed cannons. Now the big ships could move in and shell the city. The French citizens begged the commander to surrender. On June 17, just before the New Englanders were about to start a general attack, the French sent a flag of truce. Parson Moody did his duty with his axe, and preached a sermon amidst the wreckage.

Everyone seemed surprised and happy that the colonies, with little help from England, had mounted a successful campaign against the power of France. And yet, despite these successful efforts, the Royal Navy continued kidnapping Americans. In November 1747 Commodore Charles Knowles arrived in Nantasket, and his press-gangs grabbed dozens of men from boats and docks. A mob of Bostonians seized three Royal Navy officers and forced their way into the governor's office. In return, he called out the militia, but they refused to stop the mob. Indeed, many of them were the mob, and the rest swelled its numbers. Now several thousand people demanded the release of the impressed men.

The situation was temporarily defused when the Massachusetts Council condemned the uprising but arranged the release of the sailors. Shortly afterward, a young editor named Samuel Adams released a newspaper called the *Independent Advertiser*, on January 4, 1748. "We are ourselves free, and our Paper shall be free—free as the Constitution we enjoy—free to Truth, good Manners, and good Sense, and at the same time free from all licentious Reflections, Insolence, and Abuse . . . to state and defend the Rights and Liberties of Mankind." Many of the editorials of this newspaper criticized the British government. Adams and his fellow writers began by debating the latest impressment controversy, and continued in full force when Louisbourg was returned to the French in the Treaty of Aix-la-Chapelle.

It felt like a slap in the face. Massachusetts had lost 8 percent of the adult male population in this war, and the treaty was resented by every man who had laid siege to Louisbourg, every woman who lost a husband or son, and every merchant who lost his investment. What was it all for? Why were they fighting the battles of a faraway king? Adams's paper said as much, and was instantly suppressed. Soon afterwards, a bill was passed prohibiting riots and unlawful assemblies. Adams and other disgruntled writers, merchants, and soldiers began to meet in secret. When town firefighters were confronted with the flaming house of a man who had helped pass the law, they let it burn.

One fine April day three decades later, Solomon Wales and his two sons heard the bells ringing in Connecticut, and marched toward Lexington. A month later, in Philadelphia, Samuel Adams nominated the younger brother of a man killed at Cartagena to be commander-in-chief of the Continental Army. Two days after that, sixty-nine-year-old gunsmith Seth Pomeroy borrowed a horse and rode to a hill north of Boston to take his stand at a redoubt built by his old friend, sixty-five-year-old engineer Richard Gridley. They shook hands and turned to face down a force of British redcoats.

CHAPTER 14

Into the Heart of Story

1750s

THE LAST WOLF IN CONNECTICUT WAS DEAD. KILLED BY ISRAEL PUT-
nam in a cave by torchlight, she would soon become a symbol of the
victory of civilization over the wilderness. And few could argue that New
England was not civilized now, while sitting around the tavern fire on
straight-backed, rush-seat chairs, waiting for bread from a beehive oven
while sipping a pewter mug of carefully prepared brandy-milk punch or
fortified wine straight from Madeira. "Wits" met to recite poetry or play
games, and some inns even featured performances of plays like *Othello*,
though the sinful profession of acting had not yet become entirely
respectable. More often, people gathered to hear a story told well, and
those stories were more often not from Europe. Like the tale of Putnam
and the wolf, they focused on legendary feats achieved in the recent past,
here in this small corner of North America.

Any given town hosted cattle drovers and pig farmers, brewers and
meat packers, millers or tanners. Dockworkers packed slabs of bacon
and pickled hooves in barrels for export to Europe, and unloaded cotton
clothing and rum casks for sale in nearby stores. Townspeople gathered
around the village green to buy vegetables on market day or to throw
apples at a criminal in the stocks. The white birches and towering pines
had been cut back, and green, pleasant fields of clover and hay stretched
for miles along every roadside.

By 1750 coach building had become a New England industry, and
regular coach routes were established. Anyone with a little extra silver
or paper money could pay to take a "stage" from Boston to New York,

passing milestones and watering troughs, watching foxes and rabbits dash across the road. Harassed by local children and penny-pinching travelers alike, farmers collected tolls for the turnpikes and sold refreshments. In the winter, sleighs carried passengers over the frozen ground, wrapped in their greatcoats, bearskin caps, and fur-lined overshoes.

Connecticut's population had tripled in the past three decades, to reach 130,000, and had grown more tolerant of other religious groups like Baptists and Quakers. Anglicans now dominated Fairfield County. However, in the eastern part of the state, the Native American belief systems kept shrinking with their territories. Sachem Ben Uncas of the Mohegan had recently become the first leader of his people to convert to Christianity, in an effort to stave off private and public land claims. Other tribes consolidated and moved west and north, passing farther and farther into alien lands.

In contrast, Portuguese Jews heard tales of Rhode Island's freedom to worship and many crossed the Atlantic to join the long-established Jeshuat Israel congregation in Newport. Aaron Lopez arrived in 1752 and introduced methods of processing sperm-whale oil, soon to become one of New England's most valuable products. He created a monopoly, making Newport richer than ever, and himself one of the richest men in North America. The Jewish community in Newport began building the Touro Synagogue a few years later, and Lopez laid the cornerstone. But he needed to cross the border to Massachusetts to get his citizenship; Rhode Island was no longer as tolerant as tales had claimed.

The other unhappy change was that, despite being the first to ban the practice in 1652, Rhode Island's towns of Bristol and Newport had booming slave markets. They were not alone—New England had become a center of slave trafficking and was economically dependent on it due to the triangular Atlantic trade. Originally this had involved shipping raw materials to Europe, manufactured goods to Africa, and slaves back to North America. That pattern was now shifting to exclude Europe, with slaves sent from Africa to the Caribbean colonies, which sent sugar to New England, which in turn sent rum and other goods directly to Africa. Few local ships made the entire triangular circuit, but the new economy depended on it.

Starting in the 1750s, free and enslaved men throughout the Northeast created African governors elections, as an attempt to integrate into political culture. One such leader was a slave belonging to Colonel George Wyllys named Quaw, elected for the first time in Hartford in 1760. Although such elections came complete with grand inaugural balls and the responsibilities of leading a community, they did not mean that slaves like Quaw were freed from bondage. Some slaves in New England chose instead to run away, having more opportunity to join free communities in nearby cities or to become privateers and soldiers.

Those opportunities opened in 1754 when word came that England and France were once more at war. Representatives from Maryland, Pennsylvania, New York, and all the New England states met in Albany to discuss options. Though the main topic of conversation was how to approach a treaty with the powerful Iroquois Confederacy, Boston-born Benjamin Franklin encouraged unifying the colonies with a "President-General" in charge. The suggestion was tabled, but both the plan and the conference itself became important models over the next few decades.

This colonial unity did not help much the following year. A Virginia expedition to the Ohio Valley met with disaster, and Nova Scotia started deporting French-speaking Acadians. The governor of Quebec procured a copy of the New York campaign plans and built Fort Carillon on Ticonderoga Point. Then on November 1 a massive earthquake destroyed Lisbon, Portugal, and sent shockwaves across the Atlantic, jolting New England's wood-frame homes. In Salem, Connecticut, Colonel Samuel Browne's enormous domed house, eighty feet across its front, cracked and collapsed. People were less inclined to see portents than they used to be, but it was still taken as a bad sign.

Most of the fighting had moved west and north of New England now, but New Englanders still served on the front lines. In New Hampshire, John Stark of Londonderry had been captured by French allies in 1752 while on a fishing trip and taken prisoner to Canada where he was forced to run a gauntlet of stick-wielding warriors. However, he kept his wits about him, learned their methods and, after returning to New England in a prisoner exchange, became one of the savviest forest trackers. When this new war started, he served as a lieutenant to Robert Rogers of

Dunbarton, and the two men and their company of Rangers skirmished in the white-pine forests along the frontier with Canada.

On October 2, 1759, the Rangers crept all the way up to the home base of the French-allied Indians on the St. Francis River. They waited patiently until a wedding concluded and then killed two hundred drunken men, stole the collection plate from the Catholic church they worshipped at, and set fire to the town. Supposedly burned amongst the huts were six hundred scalps the St. Francis Tribe had taken in recent years. On the long march back down the Connecticut River, they took more; Rogers and Stark lost forty-nine men to the vengeance of the remaining Canadian Indians.

Although many British regulars had been shipped across the Atlantic to fight alongside colonial militias, the colonists did all the work provisioning those armies. One of the merchants who learned to handle that intricate and frustrating task was hawk-nosed Jonathan Trumbull of Lebanon, Connecticut. Born in 1710, he had graduated from Harvard with the intention of becoming a minister but, after the deaths of his two brothers, came back to his home of Lebanon to run the family store. Now he supplied troops from Connecticut that joined New Yorkers on assaults up the Hudson Valley toward Canada.

Those assaults stalled, but in 1758 Fort Louisbourg was conquered again by British regulars, this time for good. That victory opened up the St. Lawrence River to the navy, and General Wolfe sailed up and attacked the walled city of Quebec in 1759. After a battle on the Plains of Abraham, it fell, and Montreal collapsed a year later. English-speaking colonists now held sway over nearly all of eastern North America. The war would rage in Europe for another three years, but other than a few small raids and skirmishes, it was over for New Englanders.

Unlike earlier wars with Canada, this one united the colonies in new ways. It helped create connections between someone like Jonathan Trumbull and other merchants from the Carolinas to Maine, all of whom came out of the war disenchanted with their parent country. In Trumbull's home state, the towns of Stamford and Norwalk had been used to quarter English troops, who regularly insulted both their hosts and the colonial militia. Provisioning debts to thousands of homeowners and shopkeepers throughout the colonies went unpaid. Men who had joined the war due to the promises of military recruiters found that many of those promises went unfulfilled.

One more result of the war was the Crown Point military road over the Green Mountains—the first road of any kind to cross the range. Without the direct threat of the French and their Indian allies, the untapped region between the Connecticut River and Lake Champlain seemed less frightening. At the end of the decade, Governor Wentworth of New Hampshire took advantage of the situation and made land grants to build an astonishing 130 towns in this new territory. Eager settlers moved west from Portsmouth and north from Hartford, and vales between the mountains filled with the sound of axe strokes and the smell of cooking fires. The story of the last New England state was about to begin.

CHAPTER 15

This Is the Place to Affix the Stamp

1760s

DRINK IN HAND, SAMUEL ADAMS SAT IN A WOOD-PANELED BOSTON tavern with a group of tanners and tailors, speaking about liberty. Two decades earlier he had written his master's degree thesis on "Whether it be lawful to resist the supreme magistrate, if the commonwealth cannot be otherwise preserved?" And it seemed that he had never stopped talking about it to everyone he met, including every farmer, sailor, and shopkeeper, despite the fact that since 1756 he had served as tax collector for the city of Boston. It was a political appointment no one else wanted and was usually the sort of job that got one hanged in effigy. How then was he able to get along so well with these tavern-goers? He had a fine solution to the problem: He refused to collect taxes from them.

The job also won him friends in high places in "the Christian Sparta," as he called Boston. Poor himself, in one incident he convinced his friend John Hancock, who was rich, to pay for the drinks of men who would listen to his arguments. They listened, and many were convinced by the inexorable logic. The population of the American colonies was now half that of England, but they had no representation in Parliament. Therefore, the decisions of that Parliament in which America had no representation were by their very nature tyrannical.

Boston was not the only hotbed of such ideas. In Connecticut, Oliver Ellsworth had been kicked out of Yale College for drinking wine and protesting unjust laws, and after transferring to the College of New Jersey he formed a pro-republic society with Aaron Burr and other young firebrands. Many college graduates from Yale and Harvard, as well as the newly chartered Dartmouth College and College of Rhode Island, would go on to join the Sons of Liberty, "shadow government" Councils of Safety, and colonial militia. By the 1770s a full one-half of the officers in Connecticut's militia would be Yale graduates. College alumni served as ministers throughout the colonies, preaching liberty at the pulpits. Many also joined the Freemasons, creating a network of connections and promoting antimonarchist policies.

Both merchants and common people were easier to convince after Parliament levied the Sugar Act in 1764. After all, duties on luxuries like molasses, raw sugar, and wine meant that fewer could enjoy what little free time they had. Some products were only allowed to be sent to Great Britain, like raw silk or iron. And if New Hampshire and Rhode Island exchanged coffee or pimentos they had to pay a duty too. Many gave up the West Indian trade entirely, with even wealthy John Hancock writing that "times are very bad." Of course, duties made sense from Parliament's perspective, since the Seven Years' War with the French had left England with even more debt than its American colonies. Were not British men-of-war protecting the trade that Boston grew rich from?

That same year Parliament outlawed paper money in the colonies, though New England's had been gone for over a decade. Samuel Adams's father had been ruined by that earlier decision, and he wrote protest pamphlets with increasing fury. Then, on March 22, 1765, the king signed the Stamp Act, which taxed all paper documents in the colonies. Unlike the duties imposed earlier, it was not an "invisible" tax, but a direct one, and the people rose in protest. In Boston, the king's agent Andrew Oliver was hanged in effigy. Boycotts followed against lamb and tea, and in December merchants signed a formal agreement not to import any English goods, soon followed by similar procedures in Salem, Plymouth, and other ports. Liberty poles were raised in almost every town.

The act was even less popular in Connecticut, where the Yale president, Napthali Daggett, attacked it openly in the *Connecticut Gazette*. In New London they burnt a "stamp man" in effigy, and one protestor railed at the crowd that "being called Englishmen without having the privileges of Englishmen, is like unto a man in a gibbet, with dainties set before him, which would refresh him and satisfy his craving appetite." When

Jared Ingersoll of Milford was appointed as stamp agent by the king, he found a crowd of people surrounding his house, demanding he resign. He rode to Hartford to gain protection from the governor, but on Wethersfield's town green a group of five hundred mounted men surrounded him and escorted him to a nearby house. "The cause is not worth dying for," Ingersoll said, writing out his resignation and accompanying the protestors to the state assembly.

Governor Thomas Fitch had wisely opposed the Stamp Act but declared that the law was the law, and on November 1, 1765, he tried to get the Council of Assistants to take an oath to uphold it. Speaker of the state house of representatives, Jonathan Trumbull, and three other members refused and walked out. Tavern keeper, farmer, and storied veteran of the most recent war Israel Putnam threatened the governor with more direct action, saying that his house would "be leveled with the dust in five minutes." In the following year's election Fitch was voted out, and Trumbull became governor. A religious man, he believed that rebelling against wicked leaders was a sacred task and failure to do so would bring the wrath of God.

By then Parliament had rescinded some of the acts. Merchants were happy again and smuggling dropped to its lowest point since the 1730s. But the Sons of Liberty had gained thousands of new members, and in 1767 they called town meetings, and both women and men signed blacklists of duties items. In February 11, 1768, the Massachusetts House of Representatives sent a circular letter to the other colonial assemblies to suggest boycotts and petitions. Drinking sassafras and Labrador tea, wearing locally made watches and shoes, colonists discussed and argued and signed their own petitions, printed on locally made paper whenever possible. The problems of trade and the problems of personal liberty had become inseparable, not just for merchants but for everyone.

Meanwhile, Parliament tried a new approach, passing the Townshend Acts in 1767, strengthening the various duties and establishing a more powerful customs organization. Designed to curtail smuggling, they only increased boycotts, including one by John Hancock, who would not attend public events alongside customs officials.

On April 9, 1768, two of those officials in Boston Harbor tried to go below deck on Hancock's ship, *Lydia*. He refused them permission on the grounds they did not have a search warrant. The officials tried to file charges, but since Hancock had broken no laws, there was nothing they could do. The following month Hancock's sloop, *Liberty,* arrived with a shipment of wine in the evening. However, when officials inspected it in the morning, they found only one-fourth of the carrying capacity of wine filled, which Hancock dutifully paid. A customs agent swore that nothing had been unloaded the previous night, but a month later changed his story, saying that he had been forced to allow Hancock to unload wine. British officials seized the ship.

Already angry about the various acts, as well as the renewed policies of impressment by the British navy, Bostonians rioted, but with little effect. Samuel Adams wrote petitions to England and letters addressed to the other colonies, where he found many sympathetic ears. Angered, the king sent troops to Boston. The *Liberty* was used to enforce British law until angry Rhode Islanders burned the ship to the water.

Neighboring New Hampshire did not join in many of these protests, mostly because it was more agricultural and the governor was a strong supporter of the king. Besides, they were stuck in their own conflict with New York. After Wentworth had given grants for over a hundred towns on the west side of the Connecticut River, New York sent counterclaims. Settlers threatened surveyors with violence. While in Albany, a young man from Connecticut named Ethan Allen told a group of New Yorkers, "The gods of the hills are not the gods of the valley." The New Yorkers were not amused. Allen traveled back to Bennington and in Fay's Tavern held the first meeting of the Green Mountain Boys. A few years later, the Boys burned down the house of a New York surveyor.

These were not the only colonies fighting over land in the late 1760s. In 1754 the Susquehanna Company of Connecticut had bought large tracts of land in northeastern Pennsylvania, a disputed area for which both colonies held charters. John Durkee of Norwich had fought hand to hand against the French during the recent war and had barely survived the siege of El Morro Castle in Cuba. He joined the Sons of Liberty and was one of the leaders of the band who assaulted tax collector Jared Ingersoll. In 1769 he crossed the Hudson and the Delaware to settle the upper Susquehanna River with two hundred other eager New Englanders. He named the town Wilkes-Barre, after two supporters of colonial rights, and built Fort Durkee.

On November 14, 1769, the fort was attacked by angry Pennsylvania militia, and Durkee was thrown in prison. In the bitter winds of winter, families were driven out of their new homes. The following February the valley was retaken by the "Yankees" and more Connecticut settlers arrived in what they called Westmoreland County. For the next decade, the so-called Yankee-Pennamite Wars would simmer and flare in both the courts and in the forests of the upper Susquehanna.

Meanwhile, in Boston, effigies of English tax collectors hung from an elm tree just off the Common. The house of the lieutenant governor was vandalized and plundered. Then, on March 5, 1770, several small incidents erupted into violence, though later no one could quite agree how things started. It may have begun when two probably drunken soldiers wounded two youths in the street near Doctor Loring Corner. It may have begun when Samuel Atwood asked if the soldiers were going to murder people, and they hit him with a club. Or it may have begun when a boy poked a guard outside the Custom House on King Street and was given a smack with the rifle butt for his effrontery. Certainly, things had already progressed when a large group gathered outside the Custom House, harassing and taunting the guards. The incensed crowd of several hundred was soon confronted by a large force of English soldiers under Captain Preston. The mob yelled and threw snowballs—some with hidden rocks—at the bayonet-wielding soldiers. They raised their muskets and fired, wounding many and killing five, including freed slave Crispus Attucks, shot through the lungs and liver.

The next day, Samuel Adams and thousands of other angry Bostonians attended a meeting at the Old South Meetinghouse, with more spilling into the streets outside. After discussion, Adams paraded over to the acting governor, Thomas Hutchinson, and demanded he remove the soldiers to the fort in the harbor and out of the city. Hutchinson agreed to take one of the two regiments out. Adams returned to the protestors with the governor's terms, telling everyone he met: "Both regiments or none." The vote was unanimous, with Adams's words echoing off the houses of Boston in loud shouts. Adams issued the ultimatum, and his friend John Hancock claimed that ten thousand militia stood ready to invade the city if the soldiers did not agree. Hutchinson and the British soldiers backed down.

News of this "Boston Massacre" spread throughout the land. In New Haven, a young apothecary named Benedict Arnold wrote: "I was very much shocked the other day on hearing the accounts of the most wanton, cruel, and inhuman murders committed in Boston by the soldiers. Good God, are the Americans all asleep and tamely yielding up their liberties, or, are they all turned philosophers, that they don't take immediate vengeance on such miscreants?" Men joined the local committee of safety, filled a powder horn, and hid the silver.

A grand jury indicted Captain Preston and his men, who now under Massachusetts law faced the death penalty. Risking mob justice himself, Samuel's younger and less magnetic cousin John Adams decided to take the case, convinced that everyone deserved a fair trial. First, he defended Captain Preston, and easily persuaded the jury that no order to fire had been given. Then came the more difficult matter of the soldiers who had fired on the mob. His self-defense argument was so nuanced that it pleased almost everyone. "Facts are stubborn things and whatever may be our wishes, our inclinations, or the dictums of our passions," Adams said, "they cannot alter the state of facts and evidence." The mob was at fault, not the soldiers, but the mob was merely a result of the unreasonable policy of quartering soldiers in the town. Six soldiers were acquitted and two convicted of manslaughter; they avoided imprisonments by having their hands branded with the letter M.

Adams stuck by his choice to defend the British soldiers, pointing out that "judgment of death against those soldiers would have been as foul a stain upon this country as the executions of the Quakers or Witches." Surprisingly, no riots followed the verdict, but something was definitely different now. When speaking of the English, whether government or soldiers or citizens, many New Englanders no longer used "we" but rather "us" and "them." In a letter to Thomas Jefferson decades later, John Adams wrote, "What do we mean by the Revolution? The War? That was no part of the Revolution. It was only an Effect and Consequence of it. The Revolution was in the minds of the People."

That revolution had already begun.

CHAPTER 16

The Hour of Darkness and Peril and Need

1770s

ON NOVEMBER 5, 1773, A BOSTON TOWN MEETING MODERATED BY JOHN Hancock agreed that any person who supported the new monopoly-creating British Tea Act was now an "Enemy to America." A few weeks later, on December 16, a small party of Sons of Liberty dressed as Mohawks slipped aboard three tea-laden East India Company ships and over the course of several hours dumped the cargo into the murky water of Boston Harbor. The act was repeated over and over again, and not just in the big cities. In the village of Old Lyme, Connecticut, a merchant arrived in March 1774 trying to sell a hundred pounds of tea. The local constabulary arrested him, and the local chapter of the Sons of Liberty burned the tea on the village green. Housewives across New England refused to serve tea to their guests, and when someone asked, she was treated with suspicion.

This response brought stricter laws from Parliament, including the Boston Port Act of 1774. Future trials of offending colonists were set to be held in England, far from help or friendly lawyers. Boston Harbor was blockaded on June 27 and four thousand troops under General Gage were quartered in the city. Hancock stood up on the anniversary of the Boston Massacre and spoke against the British troops, who were there "to enforce obedience to acts of Parliament, which neither God nor man ever empowered them to make." Committees of Correspondence in nearby towns and states gathered supplies, the Continental Congress met in Philadelphia, and almost all the members of the Massachusetts government moved their operations to Concord. Militia drilled all over New England.

The spring of 1775 came early, and the grass was high on the evening of April 19 when British troops marched toward Concord with instructions to imprison the rebel leaders and collect their weapons and supplies. But the revolutionaries had been watching the occupiers carefully. Paul Revere and several others rode out from Boston to warn the surrounding countryside, allowing militia to remove provisions and guns just ahead of the soldiers' arrival. Bells rung in the dark of pre-dawn, and by 4 a.m. the British knew they had lost the element of surprise and sent for reinforcements. At Lexington they found a small band on the town green, and somebody took a shot. Driving the Massachusetts's militia away, the British forces were joined by new regiments and marched confidently toward Concord.

Meanwhile, hidden companies of militia were moving in great numbers toward Concord. At North Bridge they confronted the British regulars, who spread out and fired sloppily at the advancing double file of colonial soldiers. When the band of patriots was fifty yards away, they fired and drove a wounded group of British soldiers back into town. They continued to retreat toward Boston, harassed and crippled as shots sang through the trees and high grasses to wound and kill them. The redcoats turned to fight, and again and again got the worst of the fighting. Increasingly outnumbered and outmaneuvered, with only one unwounded officer remaining, they were rescued from complete disaster at Lexington by reinforcements, but continued to suffer as they retreated to the city.

Swift riders carried the word west, and the following morning fifteen thousand militia from all over New England surrounded Boston. Hour by hour each town heard the news and sprang into action. In Brooklyn, Connecticut, Israel Putnam supposedly set down his plow and galloped to help. Benedict Arnold rode from New Haven and joined Vermont's Ethan Allen in a swift raid on Fort Ticonderoga that caught the garrison in their pajamas. Portly bookstore owner Henry Knox snuck out of Boston with his wife while British soldiers looted his shop and, without a military commission, started fortifying the American positions with the tactics he only knew from reading.

In Rhode Island, an untried merchant named Nathanael Greene, with asthma and a bum leg, was elected by his peers to lead their army.

Brought up a Quaker, he quit when they wouldn't let him read books, which he often bought from fellow bibliophile Henry Knox. When the British blockaded Boston after the Tea Party, he wrote, "Soon, very soon expect to hear the thirsty Earth drinking in the warm blood of American sons." He had only been a private in the local militia when the war started, but now he was a general. It was one of the strangest and most fortuitous decisions in American military history, because he turned out to be a tactical genius.

But while gathering supplies in Rhode Island, Greene missed the next battle. After learning that the British would try to take the hills around Boston, colonial militia had fortified Breed's Hill, north of Charlestown. On June 17 British forces landed on the peninsula and with fixed bayonets marched toward the ragtag militia. Veteran warrior John Stark of New Hampshire arrived just in time, filling a gap in the lines and placing a stake a hundred feet out as a marker. As overall commander, Israel Putnam did much the same, telling the men not to fire "until you see the whites of their eyes." They waited, and shot, and shot again. Line after line of redcoats fell, but their discipline held. They kept coming, and finally the Americans fled to Cambridge.

The British had taken Breed's Hill and then Bunker Hill, but at a terrible price, losing twice the number of soldiers the Americans did, over a thousand men, including ninety-two officers. "I wish we could sell them another hill at the same price," said Greene. George Washington arrived in Cambridge on July 2 in the rain to meet Greene, Putnam, Knox, Stark, and the other New England leaders. John Adams managed to get Knox a commission and Washington sent him to bring the cannons over the snow-covered mountains from Ticonderoga.

As the Siege of Boston dragged on, the question of what to do with thousands of people loyal to the king became a crisis. To some of the revolutionaries, every one of these loyalists was a potential spy or turncoat, and they had reason to be concerned. Dr. Benjamin Church was caught spying that autumn and imprisoned. John Stark's former commander Robert Rogers had declined to join the army, but then belatedly asked for a command. Instead, he was arrested as a spy and, after escaping, served against his old comrades with the Queen's Rangers. The following year he would assist in the capture of the Americans' first spy, Coventry, Connecticut's, Nathan Hale. In nearby Hebron, a clergyman named Samuel Peters pled for the Lord to "deliver us from anarchy." When neighbors discovered a cache of weapons in his house, he was summarily kicked out of town. Loyalists to the king like Peters were not as numerous in New England as they were in some of the other colonies, but they still made up a sizable percentage of the population. Neighbors began to spy on each other, and many tragedies resulted—some with loyalists leading British forces into their New England hometowns and some with townspeople tarring and feathering innocent men.

The royally appointed governors of the colonies were quickly removed. Benning Wentworth's thirty-year old nephew, John, had succeeded his uncle as governor of New Hampshire in 1767, but he remained loyal to the Crown. On June 13, 1775, a crowd of armed men surrounded his house and forced him to flee. Joseph Wanton of Rhode Island declared his neutrality and was removed but allowed to keep his house. The only governor of any American colony who remained in place at the revolution, Connecticut's Jonathan Trumbull, began handing out salt pork and oats from his own family store in Lebanon to militia marching toward Massachusetts. Soon that tiny store became one of the headquarters for the entire war, hosting nine hundred meetings over eight years, the focal point of supply for the northern armies. Ration schedules were instituted for luxuries like coffee and butter, and clothing quotas assigned to each town.

Meanwhile, in an epic logistical achievement, Knox hauled sixty tons of brass and iron cannons on ox-drawn sleds across Lake George and over the Berkshire Mountains, pulling them out of ice-choked rivers and struggling to find help amongst snowbound locals. Six weeks later, he arrived to break the Siege of Boston. Setting the cannon on Dorchester Heights, the Continental Army began to shell the city. On March 16, 1776, in what seemed to be a stunning victory for the Americans, the British boarded their ships and fled.

But they would be back, arriving on Long Island in the summer of 1776 with overwhelming force, smashing the Americans with their army, their navy, and tens of thousands of hired Hessian mercenaries, driving them out of New York City and into New Jersey. Earlier that spring, an invasion of Canada had failed, with Ethan Allen taken prisoner in Quebec. Loyalists had been exiled from Newport, but in autumn 1776 the British navy swept in and occupied it, controlling both ends of Long Island Sound. The Continental Army kept retreating, all the way to Pennsylvania. It looked like hope was lost. There were already thousands of New England soldiers kept prisoner on ships in New York Harbor, and with the rest of the army scattered to the four winds, it would mean a full-scale occupation of the Northeast by the British. It meant death or bondage for countless soldiers, as well as John Hancock and everyone else who had signed the Declaration of Independence that summer.

George Washington knew this. On Christmas Day 1776, after a year of defeats, Greene and Knox boarded boats at McKonkey's Ferry, Pennsylvania, in the late afternoon. "Shift that fat ass, Harry," Washington said to Knox. "But slowly, or you'll swamp the damned boat." With sleet freezing their oars and poles, they crossed the Delaware River. That night, outside Trenton, Greene grabbed the first outpost while Knox set up his cannons, raining grapeshot onto a squadron of Hessian mercenaries as they stumbled out of their barracks. "The storm of nature and the storm of the town," Greene noted, "filled the mind during the action with a passion easier conceived than described." Over a thousand prisoners were taken and only four Americans wounded in the first of the reversals that the revolutionaries needed to keep their spirits alive.

The next year continued to go poorly for Washington, Knox, and Greene, as they were pushed out of Philadelphia to Valley Forge. Back in New England, things went a little better. On April 25, 1777, British forces landed on the Connecticut coast and marched to Danbury, intent on destroying the supply depot there. Messengers like Sybil Ludington rode to get help, and militia from Connecticut and New York gathered in nearby Redding under commanders Silliman, Wooster, Huntington, and Arnold. As the redcoats returned from burning Danbury, they met harassing forces under Wooster, who was shot and mortally wounded. Then at Ridgefield they exchanged fire with troops under Arnold. Trapped underneath his horse, he coolly shot a soldier with his pistol and escaped to the woods. The Americans drove the British to their ships with many losses.

But the real attack that year would come from the north, as General John Burgoyne led a large army down from Montreal along Lake Champlain. After retaking Ticonderoga, in early August he sent Loyalists, Native Americans, and Hessians into Vermont to capture supplies. General John Stark, Seth Warner, and the Green Mountain Boys met them ten miles outside Bennington with an overwhelming force. On the morning of August 16, Stark gathered his men and gave a speech, telling them, "There are your enemies, the Red Coats and the Tories. They are ours, or this night Molly Stark sleeps a widow!" Using the ruses he had learned in the forest warfare of his youth, he surrounded the Hessians and chopped them to pieces, capturing or killing nearly a thousand invaders.

Reduced by Bennington and other skirmishes, Burgoyne's army met the northern Continental Army on September 19 at Saratoga. After a hard-fought, indecisive battle, the Americans continued to delay, and reinforced by Massachusetts's General Lincoln and two thousand militia, the army attacked at Bemis Heights on October 7. General Arnold urged a group of Connecticut troops forward, "Now come on boys; if the day is long enough, we'll have them all in hell before night!" His leg was hit with a bullet and his horse was shot from under him again, but the day was won. The entire British Canadian army, more than seven thousand men, was captured. On hearing the news, that winter the French joined the war on the side of the Americans.

In 1778 the Connecticut settlers along Pennsylvania's upper Susquehanna were massacred, and their homes were destroyed by the Tories and their Iroquois allies. Their home state lived in constant fear of attack, with batteries and fortifications dotting the coast to protect against the ever-present British fleet. Throughout the war, the careful planning of Governor Trumbull and his sons saved Washington's army, with clothing, guns, salted shad, and cattle, including at Valley Forge and Morristown. Trumbull lost his wife, his daughter committed suicide after seeing the "horrible realities" of war, and his eldest son overworked himself as commissary general and died. He continued, earning Washington's praise: "Few Armies, if any, have been better and more plentifully supplied than the Troops under Mr. Trumbull's care."

The summer of 1778 changed things for the better, with Knox and Greene helping win, or at least draw, the Battle of Monmouth Courthouse. They were learning an important lesson while fighting an essentially defensive war—stalemates and harassments were almost as good as victories. Still, a victory would be nice, and on July 28 one seemed at hand when a French fleet anchored off Block Island to help retake New England's only occupied town. Militia gathered from all over New England, and Greene rode like a whirlwind from New Jersey, covering the distance in three days. He arrived in time to kiss his wife and take command of ten thousand troops gathered at Tiverton on August 5, standing side by side with Paul Revere and John Hancock. Four thousand French marines landed at Jamestown, Rhode Island, and their ships began to cannonade Newport. British soldiers began burning their own few ships so that they would not be captured.

Then the real British fleet arrived. The marines returned to their ships, and the French sailed out to maneuver against the enemy. A storm battered the militia and many slunk back to their homes in nearby towns. Even Hancock and Revere left. The occupying forces in Newport, so recently ready for defeat, now gave chase. On August 29, Greene finished his breakfast, called for his horse, and took command of the disaster, driving the bayonets of the redcoats back to the walls of their fortifications. The New Englanders had not retaken Newport, but at least they had the pleasure of seeing the enemy run away. Another draw would have to suffice.

The following year the British finally left Newport of their own accord, but the Connecticut coast remained at a slow boil. An invasion of Greenwich in February 1779 surprised sixty-year-old General Israel Putnam while he was shaving. He made a daring escape, gathered reinforcements, and returned to drive the invaders out of town. Kidnappings and raids across Long Island Sound had been common since 1776, and on the morning of May 2 armed men snuck across to kidnap General Silliman from his Fairfield home in the middle of the night. Then on July 5 forty ships anchored off of West Haven and were sighted from the Yale College chapel tower. Alarms rang as fifteen hundred British soldiers landed at Savin Rock and began to march toward New Haven. They captured

Yale's impetuous former president, Napthali Daggett, smashing the old man's skull with a rifle butt. After a running firefight, the redcoats reached the green and looted the town. But they were soon surrounded by militia from nearby towns, including sharpshooters on the cliffs of East Rock, and they boarded the ships and apparently retreated. However, the invaders were not done yet, sailing west to Fairfield, plundering the houses, and burning the town center. Two days later, they landed again at Norwalk and razed it. Connecticut troops counterattacked across the Sound and into West Chester, burning forts and capturing hostages, but the damage was done.

Meanwhile, Paul Revere and a fleet of forty-four ships under Commodore Dudley Saltonstall sailed from Boston to Penobscot Bay to attack "New Ireland," which is what the British had begun calling eastern Maine after taking it a month earlier. Revere and Saltonstall landed troops on the Majabigwaduce Peninsula and attacked the British forces at Fort George. A three-week battle ensued, with Saltonstall delaying action and the defenders holding out until a British fleet from New York arrived on August 13. They destroyed the entire American flotilla, and the American soldiers had to march through the forests to return to Massachusetts in defeat. Saltonstall was dismissed as "ever after incompetent to hold government office or state post," and Paul Revere was accused of cowardice and dismissed, though he was later cleared. The British held New Ireland until the end of the war.

Though the small French army camped in Rhode Island, and the large French navy in the Caribbean seemed to hold some hope, the revolutionaries of New England and the rest of the American colonies met the new decade with uncertain hearts. Two years later, Nathanael Greene would put it this way: "We fight, get beat, rise, and fight again." Perhaps that was better than any mere victory.

CHAPTER 17

Union and Its Discontents

1780s

ON SEPTEMBER 24, 1780, GENERAL BENEDICT ARNOLD FLED WEST Point when his conspiracy with the British was uncovered. A year later, after sacking eastern Virginia and fighting against his former comrades in the Continental Army, he returned to New London, Connecticut, and burned his neighbors' houses to the ground while soldiers under his command massacred a small group of unprepared defenders across the river on Groton Heights. He became the most hated man in America, a symbol of betrayal, corruption, and evil that allowed the rest of the colonists to see themselves as a virtuous, united people.

Arnold's attack on his home state came too late for the British. The French general Rochambeau had already left Rhode Island, marched across Connecticut, and joined George Washington, Henry Knox, and the Continental Army for one of the longest sneak attacks in history. Assisted by a squadron of French ships, they surrounded the British army at Yorktown and won the war. Skirmishes and small battles continued for another two years, with Nathanael Greene taking back town after town in the South, and thousands of English loyalists fleeing to Canada. A treaty seemed inevitable, and it was finally signed in Paris in 1783 by John Adams, Benjamin Franklin, and other representatives of the new United States. All across New England veterans planted victory elms and watched them grow.

Another nation had won its freedom too. During the chaos of the revolution, Vermont had declared its independence on January 16, 1777, though at first they called their country "New Connecticut." This was changed later in the year to Vermont, since New Connecticut was already the name of a territory on the upper Susquehanna River. They remained a self-governing republic throughout the 1780s, abolishing slavery, coining money, and flirting with the idea of joining Canada. Ethan Allen's sway over what he considered his private domain faded, though, and his reputation cratered when he targeted Christianity in his 1785 book, *Reason: The Only Oracle of Man*. He helped his birth state's claims against Pennsylvania along the Susquehanna, and negotiated with the Canadian governor for Vermont's possible return to the British Empire.

Even before the end of the war, debate raged as to how the rest of the colonies would be united, since the 1777 Articles of Confederation had proved themselves woefully inadequate to the task. Many New Englanders called for a new contract. For governor Jonathan Trumbull's many services, George Washington called him the "first of patriots," and after the war, he supported the creation of a strong central government to unite the colonies. "They are men," Trumbull wrote, "who from interest, affection, and every social tie, have the same attachment to our constitution and government as ourselves." The idea of a national or federal government soon became a popular opinion across the region, but when Trumbull actually used the government's power to levy a tax to pay the veterans of the war, he became much less popular. Hardest hit by the tax, small farmers in Connecticut promptly voted the war hero Trumbull out.

In the 1780s, 70 percent of New England farmers lived at subsistence level or had a small surplus that allowed the purchase of items like nails and salt. Although crop rotation and fertilizer were well-known, most stuck firmly to tradition and practiced a poor sort of agriculture without commercial aspirations. Other people were tied to the land too: Even a clockmaker might also own a small farm to fall back on and trade clocks for a nice fat pig instead of money. Merchants were the ones who really hated the English and their laws, and they were the ones to gain most from the revolution. The farmers and fisherfolk who sold directly to the merchants also profited, but the others did not. So although New England had been the most eager of all the North American regions to break from its parent country, not everyone benefited from the new order.

Lawsuits against debtors rose precipitously in the mid-1780s. In Connecticut, a full 20 percent of the state's taxpayers were taken to court by creditors in the single year of 1786. Vermont governor Thomas Chittenden complained that such suits were "so numerous that there is hardly any money sufficient to pay for entering the actions, not to mention the debts." The chain of debt reached from the British banks to large merchants to the owners of country stores to the farmers themselves. Soon property was seized and this seemed to be the very thing their grandfathers had fled Europe from—mere tenancy on the land of the rich, with a threat of debtor's prison if they had nothing to give. One hundred forty-five men were jailed in Worcester, Massachusetts, over a two-year period for small debts, almost all of them rural farmers and laborers.

Captain Daniel Shays had fought at Bunker Hill and Saratoga. But after the war he was broke, selling the sword given to him by Lafayette to pay the mortgage on his farm in Brookfield, Massachusetts. Local newspapers urged action, and legal petitions were sent to Boston. However, popular feeling was against lawyers, who were seen as vultures that preyed on people already struggling. Tax collectors were sometimes attacked as they had been before the revolution; what difference if those taxes were going to a faraway government or a nearby one? Only the Rhode Island legislature did anything about this crisis, issuing paper money and somewhat relieving the emergency. A secession movement in Maine was forestalled by placating protesting farmers with a hundred acres of land. But the rest of New England had no extra land to give. Shays and his fellow farmers, calling themselves the "regulators," began cleaning their guns.

On August 29, 1786, Shays and a crowd of fifteen hundred people showed up in Northampton, halting the courts. Over the next two months more of these protests took place; wearing sprigs of evergreen on their hats, groups of angry farmers crowded judges, compelled sheriffs to stand down, and forced lawyers to stay home. The courts ground to a halt. Merchants thought them "madmen" for threatening property rights, but that is just what they were concerned about. Soon, the common people of Boston united behind them. Others suspected a Tory uprising, including the British themselves, who began to start a gleeful round of "I told you so."

New Hampshire took quick legal and military action, but Colonel David Humphreys of Connecticut could muster only a hundred men. Militias in western Massachusetts refused to help at all. Finally, the merchants themselves agreed to subsidize government troops, and former general Benjamin Lincoln of Hingham, now at an impressive postwar weight of three hundred pounds, led a force of three thousand men toward Worcester.

At first this merely inflamed the farmers, and Shays pushed for open rebellion against the state. He approached iconoclast Ethan Allen for help, but Allen declined, despite an offer to make him "king of Massachusetts." Farmers snuck into Springfield, took control of roads, and raided shopkeepers who had prosecuted many of them for debt. On January 25 a small army of fifteen hundred men marched toward the arsenal through deep snow. The officer in charge of the cache, General Shepard, warned them of what would happen, but they continued to advance. He fired warning shots with cannon, but they kept coming. Finally, the guards at the arsenal fired grapeshot into the ranks, killing four and wounding twenty. The rest scattered.

Shays led the retreat to Petersham, raiding local shopkeepers for supplies, and even taking hostages. On the night of February 3, 1787, General Lincoln led his men through a blinding snowstorm, arriving on the next morning to completely surprise the rebels. Many were captured, others fled home to their farms, but a small group continued grimly on westward to raid Stockbridge. Former Continental Army officer John Ashley gathered eighty men and attacked Shays's larger band on February 27 in Sheffield.

Desperate and angry, Shays's regulators used prisoners as human shields, but lost the battle anyway. As spring approached, stores of all sorts were burned to the ground. Some regulators tried to capture Benjamin Lincoln while he bathed in New Lebanon's hot spring. General Shepard's farmlands were burned and his horses were mutilated, eyes dug out of their heads. But public feeling turned decidedly against the rebels now, and surrounding states moved to help. Even the recalcitrant Ethan Allen called the Shaysites "criminals." Those farmers who could move out of the area did, some all the way to the Ohio Valley. Shays fled from the state and hid in the forest.

By the next year the economy recovered as the balance of trade improved. Four thousand former rebels signed confessions in exchange for amnesty; eighteen ringleaders were convicted and two of them hanged. Shays himself was pardoned and returned to his farm. With a small pension that finally arrived from his years in the army, he was able to survive, but lived in relative poverty, turning to drink, a pariah to most of his countrymen. He had a legitimate complaint, but he went too far, and people died.

Meanwhile, during the summer of 1787, representatives of the confederation of states were meeting in Philadelphia. Originally, they planned only to fix the articles, but soon realized that a completely new constitution would be needed. Throughout the long, hot summer, they listened to the reports of committees and debated. One of the sticking points was the representation in the legislature, with large states preferring to apportion delegates by population and small states preferring to do it equally. Roger Sherman, William Samuel Johnson, and Oliver Ellsworth of Connecticut forged a compromise in which a bicameral legislature could include both a Senate and House of Representatives. The plan was modified and the Constitution was written by five people, including Oliver Ellsworth and Massachusetts's John Gorham. It resulted in the "partly national, partly federal" government that we still have today.

In October, Connecticut's Noah Webster, the young, popular writer of the *American Spelling Book*, wrote a pamphlet called "Leading Principles of the Federal Convention," which convinced thousands that the new Constitution was essential. Massachusetts governor John Hancock had been on the fence but, by 1788, called the Constitution "indispensably necessary to save our country from ruin." Other writers followed, declaring support, and throughout the following year the states voted, one by one, for adoption.

Ethan Allen did not live to see it. In February 1789, while crossing the frozen Winooski River, he observed that "it seems as if the trees are very thick here," before being struck ill and dying. His adopted country, the Republic of Vermont, had been convinced to give up its claims to land west of Lake Champlain and east of the Connecticut River, and New Yorkers still angry about Vermont's independence finally withdrew their own claims after a $30,000 sweetener. The Vermont General Assembly authorized a convention, which met in Bennington and voted to join the "Union of the United States of America" by 105 to 2. A few weeks later, on March 4, 1791, the Republic was dissolved and Vermont was admitted to the Union as the fourteenth state.

It had been a long road since the Siege of Louisbourg in the 1740s and even longer since the First Revolution in the 1680s. New Englanders had proved to be the most patriotic, the most committed to independence from Great Britain, the most supportive of creating a new nation. And yet, the region had also produced Ethan Allen, Daniel Shays, and Benedict Arnold—those who rejected it, protested it, even betrayed it. Perhaps it was something contradictory in our character, a stubborn, refractory quality. Perhaps it was a struggle between the "we" and the "I," the community and the individual.

Whatever the case, New England would now have to search for answers to questions like this as part of the United States of America.

CHAPTER 18

Great Necessities

1790s

EVERY MORNING, JOHN ADAMS ROSE, DRANK A TANKARD OF HARD CIDER with breakfast, and set to work on piles of papers. Then he walked to Congress and listened to Oliver Ellsworth and the rest of the senators argue the latest law. Adams had already made a grievous error defending a more "aristocratic" title for President George Washington, and the senators had taken to ignoring his occasional harangues. But he would in fact cast more tie-breaking votes than any other vice president in history. After the session, Adams sat down to a dinner of corn pudding, with molasses and butter, bacon, mutton, and boiled vegetables, followed by a sweet whipped syllabub.

He wrote letters to his wife, Abigail, begging her to join him. After all, the road from Boston to New York could be passed by a stagecoach in just three days. "I am warm enough at night," he told her. "But cannot sleep since I left you." At their home in Braintree, Massachusetts, called Peacefield, Abigail Adams was running the forty-acre farm, tending to her flower garden, and expanding the house from a "wren's nest" to one with a large parlor, attic, and study. Like the wives of other politicians, sailors, prospectors, and merchants of the 1790s, she was left to her own devices for months or even years at a time. Duty and happiness were often incompatible.

Along with running farms and tending shops for absent husbands, in the late 1780s women spun flax, knitted, and embroidered samplers or fine lace. Often it was farmers' wives who were willing to experiment, trying new crops like peaches and planting mulberry trees as food for silkworms. They sometimes had strong, growing sons to help them with the labor, but in the 1790s many of those sons were leaving for the more plentiful resources in the West.

Western New York welcomed New Englanders throughout the decade, followed by western Pennsylvania and northeastern Ohio, the "second New England." John Chapman of Leominster, Massachusetts, had been born just before the revolution, and in 1792, at age eighteen, left for Ohio. He apprenticed in an apple orchard, beginning a lifetime of planting the fruit throughout the Midwest while he preached the gospel, passing into legend as "Johnny Appleseed." Settlers from Granville, Massachusetts, founded Granville, Ohio, in 1805, choosing a spot that seemed like their old home valley. They praised God and began work clearing trees and building houses. Two hundred years had passed, but their ancestors would have recognized almost everything about the scene but the buckskin pants.

Connecticut had ceded its lands along the Susquehanna, but it still held claim to the "Western Reserve" along Lake Erie. Moses Cleaveland left to divide the region into townships, founding the largest city. In 1792 the western end of the reserve was set aside as the "firelands" for those whose homes had been destroyed by the British in the revolution, though very few of those people ever made it there. At the end of the decade, Connecticut ceded these lands, too, but people from the Northeast would continue coming here, and would use Ohio as a staging area for further settlements in northern Indiana, Illinois, Michigan, and Wisconsin. All around the south edge of the Great Lakes, small towns sprang up that looked suspiciously like the clapboard villages of New England.

Others had taken to the sea, bringing resources back to northeastern ports. Groton, Connecticut's, John Ledyard sailed with Captain Cook in the Pacific before attempting to hike across Asia and Africa. His tale of the fur trade in the Pacific Northwest inspired Captain Robert Gray of Tiverton, Rhode Island, to sail the *Washington* around Cape Horn, sell fur pelts in China, and buy tea to bring home to Boston Harbor. He became the first American to circumnavigate the globe carrying the new stars and stripes. These voyages launched the Chinese export trade, and soon tea returned to the cupboards and porcelain adorned many tables.

But the most important resource New Englanders brought back was the oil of the sperm whale. Nantucketers had been harpooning whales since the 1600s, and since 1712 when Captain Hussey first killed a sperm whale, they had been going after its perfect blubber and spermaceti, which could light the dark winter nights better and truer than candles or other oils. By the 1790s they had reached the Arctic and South Atlantic in their pursuits, and now salty Quaker captains began to round the capes of Africa and South America. New Bedford's sailors joined this dangerous new profession, soon creating the fourth busiest port in America. Warehouses on the salt-crusted wharves were piled with casks and hemp rope. Fish-chowder taverns rang with the toast: "Death to the living / Long life to the killers / Success to sailor's wives / And greasy luck to whalers." The sea kept many hostages out beyond the rocks and beach roses, but the need for, and price of, oil kept rising.

In 1796 John Adams succeeded George Washington as the first of many American presidents from New England. The margin of victory was narrow, and his main opponent, Thomas Jefferson, became his vice president. He was inaugurated on March 4, 1797, in a ceremony that he compared to a play in which he played a part, dressed stoically in unadorned gray broadcloth. "Extravagant popularity is not the road to public advantage," he wrote. He was willing to be unpopular in order to do the right thing, ignoring the fact that a democratic voting process makes popularity somewhat necessary.

Once again, he asked Abigail to join him. "I must go to you or you must come to me. I cannot live without you." Adams's mother died in April 1797, and Abigail joined him in May to assuage his grief. John rode out of the city to meet her and then spent a blissful afternoon on the banks of the Delaware River. That summer when he was confronted with the prospect of war with France, he was able to please nearly everyone by building up the military but keeping the nation out of war. He and Abigail spent two precious months at Peacefield before he had to return to the venomous political climate of Philadelphia.

It was a delicate time for American government, with precedents being created and broken every few days. The newspapers had been printing shocking and untrue things for decades, but as parties began to split

American politics, it became much worse. At Peacefield, Abigail had to open letters full of death threats and newspapers full of lies. She remained imperturbable about her duty, and her husband's. She had written in 1775, at the outset of the revolution, "Great difficulties may be surmounted by patience and perseverance," and both she and John tried to hold to that.

Peace commissions to France met with requests for bribes, and negotiations broke down. Adams was attacked as incompetent, but when the papers were released detailing the French greed, many called for war. Prompted by his cabinet, he instead signed the Alien and Sedition Acts, which targeted French immigrants and made publishing "false, scandalous, and malicious writing" against the government a crime. No deportations were ever signed by Adams, but indictments against newspapers followed, with ten convictions, including Congressman Matthew Lyon of Vermont, sentenced to four months for criticizing the president.

When a French privateer captured an American ship in May of 1798, the people cried again for war. Adams knew this would be a mistake but that it would be the popular thing to do. As he did when he defended the soldiers at the Boston Massacre, Adams made the unpopular but right choice. He agreed to build up the army and navy, but delayed entering a war against their former ally, France. To pay for the military overhaul, Adams and Congress passed a direct tax, the first in American history. Citizens in Pennsylvania refused to pay and threatened federal tax collectors. The army stepped in and arrested John Fries and two other leaders, who were sentenced to hang. Adams pardoned them, to the chagrin of his fellow Federalists.

The Adamses spent much of 1799 at home, and soon afterwards Abigail noted that "Electioneering is already begun." Adams's vice president and onetime friend, Thomas Jefferson, was running against him in the first party-nominated election in the United States. Adams moved to the slave-built White House in the new federal city on the mosquito-ridden Potomac River, and just as quickly returned to Peacefield in disgust at both the place and the politics. The bitter campaign went beyond gossip to accusations of treason and personal attacks on the "senile" Adams and the "howling atheist" Jefferson from supporters of each. Though Adams himself stayed out of the public furor, Jefferson hired a "hatchet man" named James Callendar, who smeared Adams in propaganda newspapers throughout the continent. After the election, Callendar went to jail for slander, but by then it was too late. Adams had lost.

Keeping out of war may have cost Adams his second term. Or perhaps it was the ruinous Alien and Sedition Acts, which eventually would be deemed unconstitutional by the Supreme Court. Or it could just be that Adams was too stubborn to be popular, too iconoclastic to be president. Anxious about the future of his country, he nevertheless conceded the White House to a political enemy who had tried to destroy him. It was a bold move, almost without precedent in the history of the world. But it was the right one.

Adams left before the inauguration, reaching Abigail's side at Peacefield just as a nor'easter struck, stranding them inside together for days. They must have been very happy.

CHAPTER 19

From Farmstead to Factory Floor

1800s

THE NEW ENGLAND STATES HAD NOT ONLY SACRIFICED LIVES FOR THE revolution, they had also drained resources like ship masts and iron ore. Little farms and rivers exhausted themselves providing the salted beef and shad that kept the Continental Army afloat during the brutal winter camps. Add to that the struggling economy of the nation and the departure of thousands of English loyalists, and the region languished throughout the 1780s and 1790s. The larger farms west of the Appalachians settled by New Englanders quickly became rivals of the small plots of the home states. Seemingly overnight there was no rivalry at all.

There had been emigrations before, to Vermont and Long Island, but combined with the losses caused by the revolution, this one was particularly demoralizing. Apples rotted on the ground for lack of pickers and beech trees crept down the hillsides into fallow fields. In some ways New England farming never recovered from this disaster, turning to specialty crops like peaches, cheese, and silkworms, which one by one failed in turn. With fewer profits coming from the land, coastal cities turned more and more to whaling, and continued a lopsided trade with Europe.

Others began to make things. A long history of small crafts had established a practice of homespun labor, while sawmills and shipyards fostered a tradition of mechanical industry. Shoemakers, clockmakers, and silversmiths like Paul Revere created profitable consumer goods for the Atlantic trade. Then in 1790, at Pawtucket Falls, Rhode Island, an immigrant named Samuel Slater built a water-powered textile mill. He had apprenticed in the cotton mills of England and brought with him knowledge of new spinning and carding machines, ready to break the monopoly of his former country. He hired whole families, moving them into a small village that included cottages, shops, and the obligatory church. This was going to be bigger than the small artisan workshops of the previous century. It was production on a huge scale, "mass" production.

These budding textile mills were helped immeasurably, if indirectly, by an invention of a man from Westboro, Massachusetts, named Eli Whitney. As a child, Whitney had crafted chairs, reconstructed a pocket watch, and even built a violin from scratch. By the time he was twelve, his sister claimed that he had "more general knowledge than men considered of the first standing in the country." As a teenager during the revolution, he forged nails. When the English flooded the market, he switched to hatpins, then to walking canes.

After attending Yale College, Whitney went south to teach, as part of the "intellectual capital" New England was sending from its colleges to the hinterlands. While at his tutoring job in South Carolina, he invented a small machine that separated cotton from its slippery seeds and, like a good Yankee merchant, swiftly marketed this "gin." The design was just as swiftly stolen from him, and lawsuits had little effect in a nation without patent rights.

Back in New Haven, a despondent Whitney looked for work, and the "quasi-war" with France in 1798 created an opportunity. Guns were already being made in Springfield, Massachusetts, at one of the two national armories created by George Washington. So, with the help of his friend Oliver Wolcott, secretary of the treasury, in 1798 he entered into a government contract to build ten thousand muskets. Never mind that he had no money and no factory yet. Like many others, he believed in new technology, new methods, and in his own powers of invention and salesmanship.

Whitney built a two-story factory on the Mill River in Hamden, Connecticut, applying Samuel Slater's new ideas of division of labor, "mill village" housing, and waterwheel power to increase his yields. Shortly afterwards, he added the even more radical idea of interchangeable parts. A few had tried this before in complicated products like watches and even guns, but none had succeeded completely. The lock of a musket required precise calculations, and the consequence of getting it wrong could be the death of the operator. Taking what had always been the art of skilled craftsmen and turning it into a regulated, methodical process, using not only interchangeable parts, but division of labor, was still considered risky or even insane. "I find that my personal attention is more constantly and essentially necessary to every branch of the work than I apprehended," he wrote in near despair.

It was a haphazard process, and though he struggled to achieve true interchangeability, he had enough success to justify his contracts. At the beginning of the decade, he traveled to Washington to meet with incoming president Thomas Jefferson. With the entire cabinet watching, Whitney gathered a collection of gun parts on the table. Eyes closed, he grabbed random pieces and assembled a gun, encouraging the others to do the same. Jefferson was immediately sold on both the viability and future possibility of this method, and soon the US government would require all its weapons to be made with interchangeable parts.

Whitney also added modern accounting methods and machine tools to the factory. "In short," he wrote, "the tools which I contemplate are similar to an engraving on a copper plate from which may be taken a great number of impressions exactly alike." By 1801 he had already developed a drilling machine, a boring machine, and a screw machine, versions of which are still used in factories today. These types of machines were rare, but after the trouble with the cotton gin he did not pursue patents and gave away designs freely, something that would be considered business suicide today.

By the end of the decade his factory finally worked properly, and would produce fifteen thousand guns during the War of 1812, using well-seasoned pine boxes to ship weapons over a century before this became common practice. He built a water-driven cutting machine, and the first true milling machine in the country, in what was called a "revolutionary technological advance." He gave away the plans to his barrel-turning machine and trip-hammer. Professor Benjamin Silliman at Yale noted that his inventions were present in "every considerable workshop in the United States."

Machine tools, division of labor, interchangeable parts, factory housing, modern accounting methods—Eli Whitney was not the first to try any one of these things, but he was the first to put them all together. He would not be the last. Others soon did these things bigger, faster, better. The Springfield Armory would increase its production to record levels after the War of 1812. In the following decade, Maine's John Hall and Connecticut's Simeon North began to take interchangeable parts to new heights of precision, normalizing a system that has since become a model for the world.

The radical changes of method and production were not only in firearms. Francis Cabot Lowell and Nathan Appleton further integrated the division of labor in textile manufacturing, hiring young women and housing them in company boardinghouses along the Merrimack River, constructing Slater's "mill village" on an epic scale. Farther up the same river, in New Hampshire, Samuel Blodgett and Benjamin Prichard created the "Manchester of America." Eli Terry and Seth Thomas applied interchangeable parts and mass production to clock making along the Naugatuck River. Hats and axes, shoes and shovels all began to be produced faster and better than ever before.

If New England could not compete with the agricultural production of the Midwest or South, it could certainly compete in industry. Second sons who might have otherwise left for the frontier opened factories. Men and women who might have become farm laborers walked through those factory doors. Rural populations continued to decrease throughout the 19th century, but towns and cities continued to grow. New England had found a new calling in the sound of the factory bell.

CHAPTER 20

The Decade without Summer

1810s

IN 1811 THE FEDERALIST PARTY OF MASSACHUSETTS LOST AN ELECtion. Control of the state government passed entirely into the hands of Democratic-Republicans, with Governor Elbridge Gerry presiding. The legislature stuffed the courts with appointees and changed electoral boundaries according to partisan vote counts. In Essex County, one of these strange boundaries looked like a salamander, leading to a political cartoon that called it a "Gerry-mander." However unethical, this highly unusual redistricting worked, and though Gerry was ousted in the next election, the state Senate remained in Democratic-Republican hands.

Meanwhile, President James Madison placed an embargo on English goods, and then declared war. Ostensibly because of the continued annoyance of British naval impressment, the war also appealed to many who wanted to take over the rest of North America. Madison chose Elbridge Gerry as his running mate, and the Federalist Party of George Washington and John Adams lost yet another election. The idea of war was always popular, especially since everyone was confident of victory. US militia members alone outnumbered the entire population of Canada, and according to former president Thomas Jefferson they could certainly just "walk" there and take it over.

The US navy was also more formidable now than in 1775. In 1804 Commodore Edward Preble of Portland, Maine, had taken the *Constitution* to Tripoli and forced the Barbary pirates to surrender. The ship carried a bell, spikes, and copper sheathing all made by an aging Paul Revere. Now in the same ship, Captain Isaac Hull of Derby, Connecticut, outpaced a British squadron, captured three merchant ships, and defeated the British warship *Guerriere*. Many of the cannon shots from the enemy simply bounced off the metal hull, and the ship became known as "Old Ironsides," continuing to more victories throughout the war.

However, not everything went so well for America. The Democratic-Republican Party had disbanded the national bank, and the private banks of New England refused to finance "Mr. Madison's War." Indeed, the war was so unpopular in Massachusetts that two representatives who supported the war were insulted and hissed, while another was kicked through town by an angry crowd. After all, the economy of Boston and the other northeastern ports depended on trade, and the first thing the British fleet did was blockade them. Smugglers snuck goods back and forth to Canada through Maine while former merchants added cannons to their ships, ran up their flags, and attacked foreign merchant vessels as privateers.

Much of the naval war took place far out on the Atlantic swells, although on June 1, 1813, the *Chesapeake* was soundly defeated within sight of disappointed crowds at Boston Harbor. Other naval battles raged on the Great Lakes, with Rhode Island's Oliver Hazard Perry, sailing under his handmade blue flag emblazoned with "Don't Give Up the Ship," leading a resounding victory over the Royal Navy, the first time an entire squadron of British ships surrendered. "We have met the enemy, and he is ours," he reported of the action, which secured Ohio and opened Canada for invasion.

The war didn't touch New England shores until May 1814 when a fleet of British ships managed the sandbars at the mouth of the Connecticut River and, after a round of drinks at the Griswold Inn, red-coated soldiers burned the ships at Pettipaug, later called Essex. In July, Thomas Hardy and two thousand men took Eastport, Maine, without firing a shot, forcing townspeople to swear allegiance to the king or leave. Two months later, three thousand more British troops occupied all of the territory east of the Penobscot River, giving it the name "New Ireland," as they had four decades earlier during the revolution. Another group of British ships under Hardy shelled the small island of Stonington for four days in August with less impressive results. As cannonballs clattered through houses and along the streets, the local militia returned fire with two small eighteen-pound cannons from the tip of the island, killing ninety-four sailors and taking between zero and three casualties themselves.

Larger battles continued to rage in the far south and west, with alternating victories and defeats. The British burned the White House in Washington; the Americans won the Battle of Plattsburgh on Lake Champlain. By that time, both sides were eager to end the conflict. The Americans had not simply walked into Canada as Jefferson had predicted, and business continued to be bad for everyone, not just New England. Son of former president John Adams, John Quincy Adams, had been serving as an ambassador in St. Petersburg during Napoleon's invasion and now left for Ghent, where he and two other delegates negotiated a peace that returned everything between England and America to prewar status.

Meanwhile, the New England–based Federalists had also decided they had enough of the war. Connecticut's Assembly declared the drafting of soldiers unconstitutional and a group of Boston merchants led by George Cabot called for a formal convention. On December 15, 1814, representatives of all five New England states met in Hartford to decide, as they thought, the future of New England. Some actually wanted to secede from the Union, but others discouraged this radical course. Instead, they agreed to call for an amendment to the Constitution requiring a two-thirds vote for war, and ask for the federal government to protect and aid New England's damaged economy. These were reasonable demands but were poorly timed, being read into the US House and Senate records just as news of the Treaty of Ghent reached the capital. New Englanders were ridiculed and even branded traitors in the nation's newspapers, while the Federalist Party practically dissolved overnight.

Later that year a massive hurricane smashed directly into Old Saybrook, Connecticut, the first to make landfall on New England's coast in 180 years. This "Great Gale" wiped out shoreline villages on Long Island Sound, with storm surges that inundated farms with seawater, and winds that destroyed every ship from New London to Providence. The autumn crop of corn was blown to pieces and vineyard grapes tasted like salt. The hurricane was the least of New England's problems though. Halfway across the world, Indonesia's Mount Tambora had been spewing out ash since April, and though for the moment the farmers of New Hampshire and merchants of Boston were blissfully unaware, the following year they would experience one of the most terrifying summers on record.

In March 1816 farmers began to plant crops as usual, and watched as the young plants died in April. Dry, cold fogs reddened the mornings and darkened the afternoons. In May, frost crackled over the farms of New Hampshire and Vermont, killing everything. "Weather backward," wrote Massachusetts's Sarah Snell Bryant. Snow fell in June, frosts continued in the hills until August, and farmers wore mittens and hats to check their failing crops. Food shortages caused by the war and the hurricane increased dramatically, and both people and animals died by the thousands for lack of sustenance. Sometimes called the "poverty year," the "year without a summer," or more poetically "eighteen hundred and froze to death," its effects were devastating. More and more people left for Ohio, carpetbags bulging with possessions. Farms sold for a penny on the dollar.

Maine experienced some of the worst weather, with fifty-degree swings in temperature and nine inches of snow in June. Starving wolves broke into chicken coops, and people began to talk of witches. Perhaps not coincidentally, they also began to talk about separation from Massachusetts. They had been considering this idea since at least 1785, when they had almost voted to break away before Shay's Rebellion had killed the taste for it. Every few years they took another vote, but the "separation question" always failed. Merchants wanted to stay, and people in York County wanted to join New Hampshire rather than create an independent state.

But something had changed. Maybe their time as "New Ireland" had inspired a more independent streak. Maybe it was the weather, or witches, or the fact that by now the "District" of Maine included five newspapers, banks, and Bowdoin College. The Mainers were also not firm Federalists, and the debacle of the Hartford Convention may have driven many to reconsider their previous positions. In December 1817 the legislature began to debate, and two years later preparations were made for a statewide ballot. On July 19, 1819, voters approved independence from

Massachusetts by a wide margin, and politicians began to put together a state constitution.

The following year statehood was unceremoniously jammed into the so-called Missouri Compromise, a bill designed to keep parity with the slave states in the US Senate. Mainers didn't like it, and neither did many other New Englanders. Five Maine congressmen voted against their own independence if it came at the price of expanding slavery, and wrote that if the bill passed, Americans "shall deserve to be considered a besotted and stupid race, fit, only to be led blindfold; and worthy, only, to be treated with sovereign contempt."

The Missouri Compromise passed anyway, and a sixth New England state took its place at the American table. But after a decade of disasters, the dinner that followed must have tasted like ash.

CHAPTER 21

My Soul to Take

1820s

AT SEVEN YEARS OLD, JOHN QUINCY ADAMS HAD WATCHED THE BATTLE of Bunker Hill. Forty-nine years later he became president of the United States in an uncertain tripartite election, only winning after a second vote in the House of Representatives. However, he was well-prepared to do his duty—over the previous decades he had served as senator, secretary of state, and ambassador to six countries, engaging in diplomacy under the most grueling conditions. He had been nominated to and approved for the Supreme Court, though he declined the honor. Now in the White House, he woke before dawn as his father had, and lit his own fire with a tinderbox. Despite his age, before his daily duties he often swam across the Potomac River. Even in the winter. In the dark.

His sharp-nosed good looks had hardened into bald severity, he refused to wear the queue of long hair or knee breeches of previous presidents, and he pledged his oath of office on a book of constitutional law. He kept a disciplined diary every day. From his parents he had inherited a sense of public service and a love of his country for which he often sacrificed his relationships, his free time, and his meager wealth. His long-suffering, British-born wife, Louisa, protested every time "Quincy" took another government job, wishing that he could have just settled into private law practice and made a little money instead.

Adams had voted against his fellow New England Federalists many times, had served under his father's "enemy," Thomas Jefferson, and had countered public opinion whenever he thought it right to do so. And yet he had already accomplished great things, from the treaty ending the War of 1812 to the one allowing for the purchase of Florida. As secretary of state he had negotiated with England for a border at the 49th parallel, helping to establish the less contentious and eventually friendly relationship between the countries. He had also outlined a policy to keep European powers out of the Western Hemisphere, which became known as the Monroe Doctrine for the president he served.

But now, because he had no mandate, it seemed the whole country was against him. He ignored this fact, and immediately called for huge federal infrastructure projects needed to unite the physically and culturally fractured nation. After all, his predecessor had recently built the "national road" over the Appalachian Mountains, and "canal fever" was sweeping the country.

The frenzy had been recently sparked by the success of the Erie Canal, built by the "father of American civil engineering," Benjamin Wright of Wethersfield, Connecticut. But it went back even further to 1803, when the "Incredible Ditch" from Lowell to Boston had helped foster Massachusetts's industrial revolution, while other small canals helped power factories and transport goods. Now dozens more were being built; one from Casco Bay to Sebago Lake raised boats 267 feet above sea level, and another stretched all the way from New Haven, Connecticut, to Northampton, Massachusetts. Wright himself designed the Blackstone Canal, which connected Worcester and Providence.

Travelers navigated some of these canals in the old-fashioned way, with mule and towline, but others turned to the miracle of steam power. Connecticut inventor John Fitch had built the first steamboat in the country in 1787, demonstrating it for the assembled politicians at the Constitutional Convention in Philadelphia. Granted a patent for this mechanically successful device in 1791, he was not able to make a profit and eventually took an opium overdose to end his life. But in the new century, others combined the mechanical and financial elements more successfully, and by the 1810s steamboats had started to replace sailboats for both people and goods. A regular service from New York to Bridgeport began in 1815, and the strange, smokestack vessels began chugging around Boston Harbor in 1817. Canals and the steamboats grew together, and eager entrepreneurs dredged rivers and harbors around the region.

By the end of the decade puffs of steam dotted the coastlines, with passengers huddled in unheated rooms lit by whale-oil lamps, conversation drowned by the roar of the paddles.

But these changes would be overshadowed by another steam-powered device—the railroad. People had been experimenting with gravity-powered rails for years, including ones on Beacon Hill in Boston, but the new century inspired more ambitious projects, and the first commercial railroad in the United States began operating on October 7, 1826, to carry stone from Quincy quarries to the nearby river. Horse powered, the "Granite Railway" pioneered switches, turntables, and double-truck railroad cars. Soon steam-powered engines would transport people and products between factories, towns, and ports; by 1835, Boston, Lowell, and Providence had been fully connected by rail.

Everyone was excited about these infrastructure projects, though few wanted the federal government involved. So Adams tried to connect the nation in other ways, but every time faced severe resistance from states opposed to any centralization, even if it directly benefited them. Many in the South believed that despite Adams's loyal service to several slave-owning presidents, he was secretly an abolitionist. In fact, he was, but nonpartisan ideas like establishing a national university, a naval academy, and a uniform system of weights and measures were dead on arrival due to this suspicion. He tried to balance the country's western expansion with the rights of Native Americans, expand trade with Europe and Central America, and tried to make agreements with South American nations. He was stymied at every turn.

It was a difficult time for him personally. His wife had experienced numerous miscarriages, two young sons were dead and another was killing himself with drink. His beloved mother had passed away in 1818, and his father died on July 4, 1826, the same day as his sometime friend and rival Thomas Jefferson. For the junior Adams, the sublime coincidence of this event seemed unimportant. "I feel it is time for me to begin to set my house in order and to prepare for the churchyard myself," he wrote. But his chief problem was political, not personal. He used big words and spoke in complete sentences in several languages, which the aristocrats of Europe had appreciated and his Brown and Harvard students had loved.

But his humorless speeches confused and angered the illiterate voting public. He was an excellent public servant and a terrible politician.

Other New Englanders were doing a better job of weaving the federal fabric together. Gilbert Stuart and John Trumbull painted an American mythology, while Noah Webster finished his epic American-language dictionary. And another Webster, no relation to Noah, was galvanizing the nation with his speeches on national unity. When he was not milking cows at Marshfield, Senator Daniel Webster of Massachusetts spent his time rhetorically welding New England to the other states, creating a national identity that may have briefly existed during the revolution, but had since fragmented through politics, religion, and culture. "Liberty *and* Union, now and forever, one and inseparable," he argued on the floor of the Senate, in a powerful rebuke to the idea that states could nullify federal laws.

Webster was one of Adams's best allies in Congress. But he was one of very few. Adams's vice president, John Calhoun, had been angry about the "unholy bargain" of the election in 1824, and Adams's antislavery attitude no doubt leaked through. Calhoun opposed his own president at every opportunity. The loser of the 1824 election, Andrew Jackson, had begun to run for the next election almost immediately afterwards, and other enemies, like Martin Van Buren, organized against Adams. His allies lost seats in the midterm elections, and for the first time in American history, a majority in both House and Senate opposed the president's policies.

"My career has attached no party to me precisely because it has been independent of all party," he wrote. Unfortunately, this eventually meant that, as he put it, "all parties disown me." The coalition of these enemies doomed Adams in the 1828 election, particularly since his hatred of party politics allowed Andrew Jackson's new Democratic Party to control many of the newspapers and local organizations. And more importantly, the war hero Jackson was too popular. Adams lost the election, becoming a one-term president, just as his father had been.

Upon learning the results, he took a long horse ride to cool off. That night he knelt by his bed and just as he did every night of his life, crisply and clearly said the prayer from the *New England Primer* his mother had taught him:

Now I lay me down to sleep,
I pray the Lord my soul to keep,
And if I die before I wake,
I pray the Lord my soul to take.

Less than two years later, friends from his home district convinced him to run for the US House of Representatives, and against all tradition he accepted this lesser office, where he would perform even greater services to his nation. The Lord wasn't finished with John Quincy Adams just yet.

CHAPTER 22

The Swiftness of Thy Course

1830s

BEFORE THE 1800S, YOUNG BOYS IN NEW ENGLAND HAD FEW CHOICES beyond the farm. Now it seemed they had too many. As Ralph Waldo Emerson put it: "A sturdy lad from New Hampshire or Vermont, who in turn tries all the professions, who teams it, farms it, peddles, keeps a school, preaches, edits a newspaper, goes to Congress, buys a township, and so forth, in successive years, and always like a cat falls on his feet, is worth a hundred of these city dolls." Character was becoming more and more important in a fragmented world, and New Englanders seemed to have it in abundance.

However, to find a matching abundance in the world, many needed to leave the confines of the seventy thousand square miles of their homeland. "Go west, young man," said Vermonter Horace Greeley to Joseph Grinnell, who left New Haven to found a college in Iowa. He wasn't the only one. A young Alphonso Taft told his father that Vermont was "a noble state to emigrate from," and hurried to Cincinnati to found his dynasty. Vermonter John Deere built his tractor empire in far-off Illinois. And it was not only gold they were seeking. Joseph Smith Jr. had left in 1817 to found Mormonism, now flourishing in Ohio. He published the *Book of Mormon* in 1830, inspiring fellow Vermonter Brigham Young to join him. Hundreds of New England congregations sprang up throughout the Midwest and beyond, seedbeds for new American theologies. Massachusetts missionaries Asa and Lucy Goodale Thurston set sail to bring small, white clapboard churches to the Hawaiian Islands.

Many New Englanders continued to find their callings and occupations on the sea itself. Captain Nathaniel Palmer became the first American to see the Antarctic continent, and Captain John Davis became the first to set foot on it. Mathematical genius Nathaniel Bowditch of Salem, became a captain's clerk, and during a journey across the Pacific found eight thousand errors in the standard navigation manual. Now, everyone used his *Practical Navigator*, an American book that was so good the British navy was forced to buy copies.

Maine shipwrights designed ultrafast clippers to hunt the giant sperm whale and ships set out from Newport, New Bedford, and New London for the far ends of the earth, so that households in North America could beat back the darkness with whale-oil lamps. In the 19th century, African Americans and Native Americans made up more than 20 percent of the whalers, finding a sort of equality with European Americans aboard that they seldom found on land. They risked everything on the vast ocean in small whaleboats, lancing the huge mammals and using great try-pots to melt and purify their blubber into oil. "There she blows!" was the cry of many a happy masthead, and many a Greek Revival mansion was built on the ensuing profits.

Young girls had fewer options than young boys in the 1830s. And yet, as visitors often pointed out, New England women were stronger and more opinionated than those of other states or nations. When Lyman Beecher read Jonathan Edwards's "Sinners in the Hands of an Angry God" to his young wife, she stood up furiously, declaring, "Dr. Beecher, I shall not listen to another word of that slander on my Heavenly Father!" Women were being taken more seriously in both the newspapers and the living room.

Their ideas were also getting new venues in the new century. New England had been sending male teachers south and west since the 1700s, but as fewer families had farms to run and men moved into factories or out to sea, women began to find new purpose in teaching. In the early 1800s, city and village schools alike began to open to female children, and the educated women now became teachers themselves. Later in the century a French researcher found that almost every teacher in America, male and female, had come from east of the Hudson River.

Given this opportunity, women quickly became leaders in the field. Connecticut's Catherine Beecher founded the Hartford Female Seminary in 1823 and a decade later took the idea west. She spent the rest of her life creating an education system designed to train women to be the primary educators of children, which she saw as their natural place in the universe. Born to two teachers in Bilerica, Massachusetts, Elizabeth Palmer Peabody was also destined to be an educator. She taught throughout the 1820s and 1830s, and in 1839 opened a bookshop and press in Boston. Two decades later she would create the first English-speaking kindergarten in the United States.

Another one of these "schoolmarms," Mary Lyon founded Adams Academy in Derry, New Hampshire, in 1824, then Ipswich Seminary in 1828, and in 1834 began fundraising and networking to create the first permanently endowed institution of higher education for women in the country. The fruit of her labors, Mount Holyoke Seminary, enrolled eighty students in 1837, and provided a model for women's colleges throughout America.

Others who previously had been overlooked also deserved an education, and when Samuel Gridley Howe's New England Asylum for the Blind opened in 1829 in Watertown, Massachusetts, it became a model for the local philosophy of practical benevolence. "All the wondrous physical, intellectual and moral endowments, with which man is blessed, will, by inevitable law, become useless, unless he uses and improves them," Anne Sullivan said at the school in her valedictorian speech in 1886, before going on to become a miracle worker for her protégé Helen Keller.

Until now, Boston and the smaller cities of New England had not been centers of culture like Philadelphia or London. There had been brief blossoms, like the Puritan poets and the Hartford Wits. But now things heated up. The combination of wealth and learning created music halls, libraries, and literary journals. Publishers like Ticknor and Fields and art galleries like the Wadsworth Atheneum began to curate the culture for the general public. The first civic lyceum had been created in Millbury, Massachusetts, in 1826, and five years later there were over a hundred in New England. Soon there were thousands across America, sponsoring organized debates, scientific demonstrations, and lectures by distinguished speakers. These public forums were not sowing seed corn or building machines, they were farming for ideas and pioneering the spirit.

European critics had begun to take American culture, or more precisely New England culture, seriously. In 1837, using a noctograph and slowly going blind, Harvard's William Prescott published *Ferdinand and Isabella*, the first accurate and thoroughly researched history written in America. The same year, Henry Wadsworth Longfellow moved into the Craigie House in Cambridge, where historian Jared Sparks, orator Edward Everett, and even George Washington had briefly lived. In that house, Longfellow would write the first poems from America that would touch the entire world.

His friend and fellow Bowdoin graduate Nathaniel Hawthorne walked the streets of Salem with his flyaway hair, piercing eyes, and romantic eyebrows, dreaming about the ghosts of the past. Descendant of Judge Hathorne of the witch trials, he crafted new ideas of sin and morality with his pen. The most popular poet in America, Lydia Sigourney held court in Hartford, and Connecticut's Fitz-Greene Halleck was on his way to becoming the "American Byron." Over the next decade, America's first foreign correspondent of either gender, Margaret Fuller, began to write her searing essays, while Charles Lyell and Louis Agassiz would add the sciences to the arts at Harvard. Benjamin Silliman did the same for Yale, and the growing number of New England colleges followed suit—Williams, Bowdoin, Dartmouth, Amherst, and Brown.

Meanwhile, in Concord, Ralph Waldo Emerson had made the decision to resign as a minister, preferring to remain an independent thinker, composing essays to read aloud to the Boston elite. The Boston intelligentsia scorned him, but he kept writing, year after year, changing a few minds every time. With a tomahawk nose, blue eyes, and gray-blond hair, he sat on a rocking chair in his Concord study, listening to an Aeolian harp and shoveling coals into the hot fire of self-reliance, trying to forge a new philosophy for America with his words.

By the 1830s, New England had clearly become a birthplace for the greatest explorers, the deepest thinkers, the most biting ideas. But the idea that was fermenting in the cellar was a simpler one—enslaving other human beings was wrong. In the first decades of the 19th century, New

Englanders had been fairly silent on this "peculiar institution," with a few notable exceptions. After all, the cotton mills needed cotton, and the merchant seamen needed trade. Although slavery was slowly disappearing from the area, it was becoming more and more entrenched in the South, and a senator like Daniel Webster, whatever his personal feelings on the matter, did not want the country to split apart.

New England's free and enslaved African Americans had fought in every war over the past two hundred years, from the Battle of Louisbourg to the Battle of Rhode Island. Many had become farmers, like Venture Smith, stolen from West Africa and enslaved in Rhode Island and Connecticut. He bought himself out of slavery and then bought a farm in East Haddam. Primus Collins of Rhode Island served as an "African governor" during his enslavement to Colonel Richmond of Little Compton, and afterwards he farmed the land and joined the voter rolls. Others became small-business owners, like Mary and Eliza Freeman, who owned rental properties in Bridgeport, or James Scott, who ran a clothing store in Boston. They were also contributing to the world of culture and ideas, with David Walker and Maria Stewart using the lyceum system to lecture on their experiences to sympathetic audiences. It was no accident that New England featured the first female African American poet, Phillis Wheatley; the first female African American novelist, Harriet Wilson; and the first female African American playwright, Pauline Elizabeth Hopkins.

And yet, the mingling of the African Americans with European Americans decreased as the 19th century went on, as both federal laws and political friction increased racism and its accompanying restrictions. In Canterbury, Connecticut, Quaker schoolmarm Prudence Crandall started one of the many schools for girls, and in 1831, when she read a copy of William Lloyd Garrison's antislavery *Liberator,* she was inspired to admit a member of the local church, Sarah Harris, who happened to be "colored." Other parents protested and removed their children. Crandall promptly transformed the school into an "all-colored" one, advertising for applicants from all over New England. The girls were threatened, Crandall was arrested, and someone set the school on fire. In July 1834 the state Supreme Court ruled in her favor, but she had not won the hearts of the villagers, who dumped poison in the well and attacked the school with clubs and rocks. When Samuel Noyes built a similar school in Canaan, New Hampshire, the following year, he received much the same treatment.

Throughout the 1830s mobs throughout the Northeast attacked abolition meetings. In 1835, at a meeting for ladies in Boston, William Lloyd Garrison barely escaped a brickbat-wielding crowd with his life, was locked in a cell, and was forced to leave the city to "tranquillize the public mind." The press was against him, the mayor was against him, and the businessmen were against him. "The disease is deeper," John Quincy Adams wrote sadly, "than can be healed by town-meeting resolutions."

On the floors of the US Congress, Adams himself was spending his old age fighting for the liberties of all. He had called slavery "the great foul stain" destroying America, and now he used petitions to Congress as a means to draw attention, delivering them to the increasingly annoyed House of Representatives, "at the hazard of my life," as he put it. The Southern representatives passed a "gag rule" to stop him, and soon made it a standing rule. No one was allowed to talk about slavery in Congress. Adams was a veteran politician though, and used every trick in the book to keep the discussion going, including presenting a petition from a group of slaves asking to be *protected* from abolitionists.

Then, in April 1839, Sengbe Pieh and fifty-two other Africans turned on the slave traders of the *Amistad*, and after the ship was captured, they were brought to New Haven. Community leaders raised defense funds for the Africans, and as the case proceeded through the courts, New England lawyers Lewis Tappan and Ellis Gray Loring turned to Adams. For four hours the former president defended Pieh and his shipmates in front of a hostile Supreme Court, showing clearly how the Fugitive Slave Law had no bearing on the transatlantic trade. On March 9, 1841, the Africans were freed in a huge blow to the slave-owning states. The war of ideas had begun in earnest.

CHAPTER 23

Castles in the Air

1840s

IN 1841 THE SON OF A PENCIL MAKER NAMED HENRY DAVID THOREAU was hired by Ralph Waldo Emerson as a gardener, editorial assistant, and tutor for the children. Short and lean, with wiry muscles and chestnut hair, Thoreau seemed Emerson's "natural man" made flesh. As he surveyed the fields and forests, birds literally landed on his shoulders. He had gone to Harvard, but refused to pay five dollars for the diploma; worked as a schoolteacher, but refused to administer corporal punishment. He opened his own school in Concord, with radical ideas about education, but it closed when his brother died of tetanus. Meanwhile, Emerson had encouraged this promising youngster to submit work to *The Dial*, their transcendentalist magazine, and suggested he keep a journal.

At Emerson's house, the walking sticks of the greatest minds of the age gathered in the hall. A year earlier, Bronson Alcott had moved to Concord with his wife and daughters, including the precocious Louisa May, specifically to be close to the best intellectual atmosphere in the world. Emerson, Alcott, and Thoreau walked together through the oaks and hemlocks every Sunday, humming Persian songs or throwing stones across Walden Pond, where Emerson owned a woodlot. There was gold in these woods, and not just the golden autumn leaves.

It was no accident that New Englanders took new interest in rural life and nature during those years. After all, we only begin to appreciate things when they are in danger. And the pastoral life certainly seemed in danger, as factories multiplied like rabbits, machines took jobs, and trees fell at an alarming rate. Eli Whitney's son had taken control of his father's old factory, improving percussion rifles, decarbonized steel, and drilling machines. Samuel Colt, the Remingtons, Ames Manufacturing, and more continued the nearly annual revolutions in weapon-making throughout the region. The cotton mills were bigger than ever, and by the 1840s working conditions for the mill girls in nearby Lowell had become measurably worse, with longer hours and increased production speeds.

Everything seemed to be moving faster and faster. Elias Howe of Spencer, Massachusetts, had just invented a better sewing machine that used needles with an eye at the sharp point, creating a "lock stitch" at the rate of 250 a minute. In Pittsfield, Allen B. Wilson would soon perfect the two-motion feed that allowed users to change the direction of the seam, and eventually create the four-motion feed still used today. These wonders allowed twelve shirts to be sewn in the time it had previously taken to sew one.

One reaction to this industrialization was to "go back to the land" as farmers. During these years, George and Sophia Ripley founded the utopian Brook Farm in West Roxbury. Everyone worked the farm equally and shared in the profits in an early version of what they called "socialism." It did not work out as intended. A couple of years later, Bronson Alcott tried to found another of these communities just west of Concord, which he called Fruitlands. Despite avoiding some of the radical ideas of Brook Farm, he tried new ones, such as banning meat, root vegetables, coffee, alcohol, milk, leather, cotton, silk, wool, and warm baths. Alcott's wife and daughters were not amused.

After helping to found and then becoming disillusioned with Brook Farm, Nathaniel Hawthorne and his wife, Sophia Peabody, joined Thoreau and Emerson in Concord. Despite a similar commitment to transcendental philosophy, neither had time for such communal experiments, but believed friendship with a select few could lead to great things. Hawthorne, Emerson, and Thoreau walked and talked and wrote. One day, the three men put on ice skates and bladed down the frozen river. Sophia described how her husband skated: "like a self-impelled Greek statue, stately and grave," while Emerson was "half lying on the air," and Thoreau performed "dithyrambic dances and Bacchic leaps on the ice."

People had been inspired by nature for millennia, but these friends were finding something new there, part science, part spirit. Emerson had led the way with his groundbreaking essay on the subject, but Thoreau took it further, describing nature not as a frightening, savage place, nor as a romantic Arcadian paradise, but as itself. It was valuable not for its symbology, nor its timber, but its own special being. "A match has been found for me," he wrote. "I have fallen in love with a shrub oak."

To most New Englanders, nature was something to be used, to be manipulated, to be improved. At age thirty-two, the wiry five-foot-tall Charles Goodyear had gone bankrupt selling hardware. Born in New Haven, he had briefly flirted with becoming a minister, and kept a Puritanical zeal throughout his life. If Thoreau's true love was a shrub oak, Goodyear's was the rubber tree. The milky, oozy substance from South American trees had intrigued inventors from every country, who coated things with it or flavored it for chewing. But it melted in the sun, cracked in the cold, and stank like an outhouse.

Goodyear had faith that he could do more and, in the shed behind his small New Haven cottage, experimented with chemicals and additives. His clothes stuck to the furniture, his beard and hair stank, and his wife, Clarissa, fed their children scraps. "I have pawned my last silver spoon to pay my fare to the city," he told one companion. He was "ruining" his family and earning the hatred of former friends. They tried an intervention, but failed.

In 1839 he finally tried mixing raw rubber with acid, sulfur, and fire, finding nearly by accident that the rubber had "perfectly cured." Left out in the cold, the rubber remained flexible. It didn't melt; it didn't stink. Then it was a matter of repeating and improving the miracle, which took the practical form of cross-linking rings of sulfur with the slick molecule chains of rubber, forming tougher three-dimensional covalent bonds. What were the bonds of family or friends to such alchemy?

He worked on the method in New Haven, Naugatuck, and Boston. Finally in 1842 he moved to Springfield, where he found all the tools needed to perfect it. Two years later he patented "vulcanization" and began licensing its use to make rubber shoes, rafts, combs, furniture, and tires. Senator Daniel Webster took a break from his presidential ambitions to defend Goodyear's invention of rubber at a patent trial, thundering, "Is there a man in the world who found out that fact before Charles

Goodyear? Who is he? Where is he? On what continent does he live? Who has heard of him? What books treat of him? Yet it is certain that this discovery has been made." Goodyear won the suit, but continued to obsess about his miraculous breakthrough.

Meanwhile, a different kind of obsession led Thoreau to the shores of Walden Pond. In March 1845 he borrowed Bronson Alcott's axe and built a small house there. What he was doing was not unusual for the time or place and had been the practice since at least William Blackstone, that first resident of Boston who left for the solitude of the woods. No, it was the reason Thoreau did it that was revolutionary. He was not becoming a self-reliant recluse, he was simplifying, giving himself space and time to think and to write. He took his baths in the pond and read the *Bhagavad Gita* in the snow.

The railroad went right by Walden Pond, and he enjoyed "all its raw edges," saying, "I am refreshed and expanded when the freight train rattles past me." But he was not as sanguine about the factory system, saying of the nearby mills that "the principal object is, not that mankind may be well and honestly clad, but, unquestionably, that corporations may be enriched." He also questioned how technology was changing human beings, writing, "Our inventions are wont to be pretty toys, which distract our attention from serious things. They are but improved means to an unimproved end." It was the dependence on such things that was the real problem, and he despaired of the technology-loving man who "lays much stress on railroads, telegraphs, and such enterprises" and "does not go below the surface of things."

He was not against capitalism, but was against consumerism. He was not against taxes for roads and education, but against taxes to support wars and slavery. He was not against killing animals to feed others, but was for the protection of wild areas where they could roam free. A philosophy was developing inside his brain that he called "economy," a classic New England virtue that he now applied to the whole of existence. "Most of the luxuries and many of the so-called comforts of life," he wrote, "are not only not indispensable, but positive hindrances to the elevation of mankind."

He made an effort to practice what he preached. While at Walden Pond he refused to pay six years of poll taxes, saying that he opposed what they would be used for: the Mexican-American War and the propagation of slavery. For that, he spent a night in jail, until an anonymous donor paid. He and the other Concord philosophers had taken a stand against slavery, and most of the Boston intellectuals were beginning to agree. In the next decade Thoreau would participate in the Underground Railroad, write defenses of John Brown, and lecture against this human evil.

Some of his philosophy came from Emerson and Cicero, some of it came from woodsmen and Native Americans. Some came from muskrats and box turtles. It was in nature that he found a path to get below the surface of society and find the deep marrow of life. The written result of his labors, *Walden,* featured prose like a river over pebbles but made as little splash as his other works. New England, like the rest of America, had other things on its mind. But those who did read it were changed by its new set of ethics, partly ancient stoic and partly modern transcendentalist, partly rooted in the soil and whispered on the wind. And as the years went by, his writings echoed outward to touch every corner of the world and every aspect of human culture—from the creation of national parks to the tactics of the civil rights movements, from the true value of hard work to the importance of solitude in an overpopulated world.

Just before the Civil War, Charles Goodyear died from the toxins he had spent his life handling. He had eventually made money, but gave it away to friends or family. He was after something else, and achieved it, sparking the plastics revolution and contributing to the rise of American manufacturing. But Thoreau was after something else, too, and as his philosophies of conservation, iconoclasm, and economy of living resonated with succeeding generations, they became an antidote to the many poisons produced by that industrial world.

CHAPTER 24

Mrs. Stowe's War

1850s

ON FEBRUARY 21, 1848, JOHN QUINCY ADAMS COLLAPSED ON THE FLOOR of the House of Representatives, muttering, "This is the end of earth, but I am composed." He lived a few days longer, then died. "Where could death have found him but at the post of duty," Thomas Hart Benton wrote. Adams was taken back to Quincy and buried with his parents, three of the most patriotic New Englanders to ever walk the earth.

In despair over losing their champion, the abolitionists of Massachusetts turned to the state's other great orator, Daniel Webster. But the same year Adams died, Webster had expected the nomination for president, and when he didn't get it, he seemed to change his tune. He served as secretary of state to Millard Fillmore and then championed the so-called compromise bill of 1850, which he claimed would save the Union. However, the bill included the Fugitive Slave Act which, among other injustices, allowed for the kidnapping of African Americans from northern states.

His allies were appalled at this "treason," as Senator Charles Sumner called it. John Greenleaf Whittier, from Haverhill, Massachusetts, put it more poetically, saying, "All else is gone; from those great eyes, the soul has fled; when faith is lost, when honor dies, the man is dead." Whether Webster had switched sides due to his ambition, or because he truly believed that preserving the Union was the right thing to do, he took part in creating one of the worst laws ever passed in the United States. At least he took a side; many of the Senators from free states who could have stopped the law from passing stayed home and hid.

The Fugitive Slave Law cost many human lives and gave questionable returns to slave owners, since the money expended far exceeded the $100,000 worth of "property" recovered during the first six years. But the law united the moderates in a way never seen before, in part because it involved every person as a potential slave catcher, a revolting thought even to those indifferent to slavery itself. Antislavery candidates were elected all over the North. Lawyers like Robert Morris defended runaway slaves and presented challenges in court. In Boston, Sumner stood up in front of four thousand cheering men and women and told them, "The public conscience will not allow a man, who has trodden our streets as a free man, to be dragged away as a slave." Less than two decades earlier, William Lloyd Garrison had nearly been killed by a mob for saying the same thing.

Webster spent the next two years calling abolitionists who refused to follow the law "traitors," over and over during his speeches. And then in 1852 he presented himself at the Whig convention as the natural candidate for president, the only one able to compromise. He was soundly ignored by the Southerners he had helped, and the New Englanders gave him only six votes. He died of cirrhosis of the liver only a few months later, muttering, "I still live."

Secret committees were formed and escape tunnels under homes were constructed. Former slave Lewis Hayden had traveled on the Underground Railroad to Boston, opened a clothing store and lectured on his experiences. He quickly turned his own home into a boardinghouse for runaway slaves. Other free African Americans fled New England for Canada, while still others armed themselves. Wanting to help, some abolitionists donated rifles and powder, while others took up the pen.

Born in Litchfield, Connecticut, in 1811, Harriet Beecher had grown up in the shadow of her older sister, Catherine, and her minister father, Lyman, whom she joined in Cincinnati in 1832. In neighboring Kentucky, she witnessed the captivity of African Americans firsthand and saw a pro-slavery mob attack her father's seminary. "No one can have the system of slavery brought before him without an irrepressible desire to *do* something," she wrote, "and what is there to be done?" She returned to New England with her husband, Calvin Stowe, and in 1849 they moved to Brunswick, Maine, with their children. When the Fugitive Slave Act was passed she "was all on fire with indignation," and her sister-in-law told her, "Now, Hattie, if I could use a pen as you can, I would write something that would make this whole nation feel what an accursed thing slavery is."

She scribbled a first chapter, but realized she was in some ways out of her depth. Writing to Frederick Douglass for help, she gathered the stories of former slaves and tried to "make a picture that shall be graphic and true to nature in its details." The result was *Uncle Tom's Cabin*, which ran as a serial story for a year in *National Era* magazine, then was published as a book in 1852. It sold three thousand copies the first day, and printers on both sides of the Atlantic struggled to keep up with demand.

No novel, before or since, has had such immediate and profound impact on peoples' thinking. Rather than focusing on moral outrage as so many abolitionists had done, she had written a sentimental and engaging narrative that humanized African Americans by focusing on them as individuals. Because readers cared about Uncle Tom as a character, they felt his death in a way that only art can achieve. Free African Americans were cautious about the novel, but Frederick Douglass called it "a work of marvelous depth and power." When slave owners protested that the novel was unjust, former slaves declared that it didn't go far enough to show the cruelty of plantation conditions.

The book spoke most clearly to women, focusing on the breakup of families. "I do not think there is a mother who clasps her child to her breast who would ever be made to feel it right that that child should be a slave," she wrote. Women began taking a more active part, gathering signatures for petitions, convincing their husbands and friends of the injustice of slavery. Queen Victoria loved the novel, and nudged Canada to keep its borders open to runaway slaves.

In the midst of this literary furor, in 1853, former New Hampshire senator and brigadier general in the Mexican-American War Franklin Pierce was elected to the presidency. He was a friend of friends of Stowe, having gone to college with Nathaniel Hawthorne at Bowdoin. He had the same romantic, long-haired look of Hawthorne, and was the son of a revolutionary soldier who had spent that terrible winter at Valley Forge. Just after he was elected, his eleven-year-old son was crushed in a train accident in front of his parents. The nation united behind this sympathetic leader who promised that the slavery issue was "at rest" and focused on reforming government institutions.

But two years later, Pierce's Kansas-Nebraska Act of 1854 threw all that into doubt, reneging on the Missouri Compromise and allowing Kansas to "choose" whether it was "slave" or "free." This time many northern businessmen were against the act, and so were the clergy, the farmers, and the hundreds of thousands of people who had read *Uncle Tom's Cabin*. In response to the passage of the bill, a group of thirty House members held an emergency meeting and formed the Republican Party. In Kansas, mercenaries poured over the Missouri border to take control for slave owners. Some New Englanders raised money for the cause, and others emigrated there with guns ready. Torrington, Connecticut's, wayward son John Brown was in the thick of it, attacking pro-slavery settlers, believing his cause to be just and righteous, as convinced as the Puritans of old that he was building a new Jerusalem.

On May 19, 1856, Massachusetts senator Charles Sumner gave a speech in the Senate about the "rape of a virgin territory"—Kansas. After his speech, the furious Preston Brooks of South Carolina walked up to Sumner, and in a cowardly sneak attack beat him with a cane, stunning him to the ground and crushing his body. Another representative from South Carolina urged him on and, with a gun, warned away a Kentucky senator who tried to stop the beating. Brooks was lauded throughout the South and given testimonials, like a gold-headed cane from the students of the University of Virginia. He was fined a mere $300 and left to go on his way.

Tainted and electorally vulnerable, Pierce was not renominated for the presidency by the Democrats that year. Meanwhile, a dramatization of *Uncle Tom's Cabin* played to sold-out theaters in all the major cities. Through Lewis Hayden, Stowe met with fugitive slaves, and toured Europe to cheering crowds of antislavery audiences. But she also received death threats in the mail on a daily basis from readers in both the North and South. The Fugitive Slave Act and Kansas-Nebraska Act had divided the nation even further, and people everywhere were asking "which side are you on?"

No one had to ask which side John Brown had chosen. A young abolitionist named Franklin Sanborn brought the now-famous guerrilla warrior to Concord, where he dined with Thoreau and Emerson. Brown gathered two hundred rifles in Massachusetts and a thousand pikes in Connecticut, financed by men who thought he was taking them to Kansas. Instead, he met with Harriet Tubman, who agreed to help him find recruits for a raid on the armory at Harpers Ferry, Virginia, hoping to spark a slave revolt. Brown also asked Frederick Douglass, who did not think the raid was a good idea, and in fact actively discouraged African Americans from helping Brown. On October 16, 1859, with a tiny force of only eighteen men, Brown cut the telegraph wires, took the armory, and tried to barricade himself in the engine house. One of his sons died in the attack and another was mortally wounded. The slaves from nearby had not risen to help as Brown had hoped; in fact, there were only a few living in the area. Soldiers under Colonel Robert E. Lee broke in and knocked him unconscious.

Douglass fled to Canada, and those New Englanders who had financed Brown's expeditions became fugitives. Franklin Sanborn was briefly captured in Concord, but the entire town, including Ralph Waldo Emerson, was deputized and prevented the arrest. He was let off on a technicality. The rest struggled for years with the ethical and legal questions of their conspiracy. John Brown went to the gallows, after leaving a note saying that he was "now quite certain that the crimes of this guilty land: will never be purged away; but with Blood."

He was right about that, at least. That same year, Charles Sumner, brain and spine damaged, took his seat alongside twenty-three other Republican senators. The following year an unknown lawyer from Illinois would win the presidency, and the divided nation would be plunged into the worst conflict it had ever known. At the height of the war, on Thanksgiving Day 1862, Harriet Beecher Stowe met President Lincoln. As the story goes, he greeted her by saying, "So you're the little woman who wrote the book that started this great war." It may have been a slight exaggeration, but for the growing millions of readers of *Uncle Tom's Cabin* it had the ring of truth.

Considered by many to be the worst and unquestionably the most hated of the New England presidents even then, Franklin Pierce remained unrepentant, calling abolitionist preachers heretics and attacking Abraham Lincoln. In 1863 his wife died, and his old friend Nathaniel Hawthorne helped him grieve. The following May the two men traveled to the White Mountains together, sharing a meal at the Pemigewasset Hotel in Plymouth. In the middle of the night, Pierce woke to find Hawthorne motionless, having died peacefully in his sleep. Taking his friend's body back to Massachusetts for the funeral, Pierce was forced to sit with the family while Hawthorne's other friends, including Emerson, Longfellow, and Alcott, served as pallbearers.

Everyone had taken a side, and for those who chose the wrong one, there would be no compromise.

CHAPTER 25

The Hopes of Future Years

1860s

ON APRIL 15, 1861, GOVERNOR JOHN ALBION ANDREW OF MASSACHU-
setts received a telegram asking for troops to be sent immediately to save
Washington. Originally from Windham, Maine, Andrew had been fighting the evil of slavery his whole life, first as an abolitionist lawyer in Boston and later as an organizer of the antislavery Republican Party. Now,
as governor, he quickly put together militia into regiments, scrambled
them onto trains and sent them south. The Sixth Massachusetts arrived
in Washington on April 19, the anniversary of the Battles of Lexington
and Concord. The troops crossed the Potomac and set up camp on the
heights, taking control of Robert E. Lee's farm. The abolitionists were not
"all talk" after all.

The quick action of Governor Andrew probably saved Washington from being overrun in the first weeks of the war, and maybe saved
Lincoln from early defeat. Other New England troops followed, with
Maine enlisting more soldiers per capita than any other state. Some predicted an easy victory over the "dam' rebels." However, it was not to be.
In a defeat at the Battle of Big Bethel on June 10, Theodore Woolsey
Winthrop, descendant of Governor John Winthrop of Puritan fame, was
shot through the heart, one of the first officers killed in the war. Armies
maneuvered in Virginia, waiting for the first major confrontation.

On a calm summer night, July 14, 1861, Rhode Island's Sullivan Ballou wrote a letter to his wife, Sarah Hart Shumway, telling her that he and
the other men around him were enjoying their last good sleep "perhaps,
before that of death." He continued, saying, "I have sought most closely

and diligently, and often in my breast for a wrong motive in thus hazarding the happiness of those I loved and I could not find one." He feared that the war would "burn to ashes the hopes of future years, when God willing, we might still have lived and loved together and seen our sons grow up to honorable manhood around us." However, he remained resolute in both his duty and his love for her. "Never forget how much I love you, and when my last breath escapes me on the battlefield, it will whisper your name."

On July 21, at the catastrophic Battle of Bull Run, that moment came when a cannonball took Ballou's leg. Shortly afterwards, the body was dug up out of its shallow grave, beheaded and burned. Rhode Island's governor, William Sprague, railed against this apparent atrocity on the floor of Congress, and many people who had sympathized with the Confederacy turned against it. As battle after battle took the lives of friends and family, more and more New Englanders and others from the North who had been wary of supporting a war to end slavery now supported a war to avenge the fallen.

The handsome features of Massachusetts's Joseph Hooker and the distinctive facial hair of Rhode Island's Ambrose Burnside were soon seen above general's uniforms. The wealthy sometimes bought substitutes, but others, like sewing machine inventor Elias Howe, served proudly in the ranks, eating hardtack and sundried mule meat. New Englanders like secretary of the navy Gideon Welles were in Washington making sure the right policies were in place, and others like Charles Francis Adams were in the courts of Europe making sure no foreign power helped the Confederacy.

Women had played vital roles in the lead-up to the war, and continued during it. Dorothea Dix from Hampden, Maine, had worked diligently to reform insane asylums, and now established a Women's Nursing Bureau, despite the prejudices of an all-male military. From Oxford, Massachusetts, Clara Barton organized a supply distribution service for both hospitals and front lines, bringing vital assistance as the "Angel of the Battlefield." Concord's Louisa May Alcott was one of many who served as a nurse, spending every day within "the sight of several stretchers, each with its legless, armless, or desperately wounded occupant," until she caught typhoid and barely survived herself.

They bandaged the wounds of men like Ezra Day Dickerman of Connecticut, shot in the cheek at Roanoke Island, in the leg at Chancellorsville, and finally in the temple at Peach Tree Creek in Georgia. After each wound, he kept reenlisting, believing that the "holy cause," as he described it, was worth the sacrifice. Maine's Walter Stone Poor told a friend that the crusade to end slavery was "nobler even than the Revolution for they fought for their own freedom while we fight for that of another race." Even so, during the early years of the war, members of that "other race" wanted to join the war effort and were prevented from doing so.

Thousands of free African Americans had fought already in the revolution and the War of 1812. But decades of propaganda about their unfitness as soldiers had taken hold of even some of the most antislavery Northerners. Others feared giving them guns to shoot "white" soldiers, even enemy ones. Governor Andrew, Abraham Lincoln, and Frederick Douglass began to plan a way to counter this and bring the many eager freeborn and former slaves into the Union army. On January 1, 1863, the Emancipation Proclamation was the first step, and a few weeks later Andrew was authorized to begin raising the first African American regiment, the Massachusetts Fifty-Fourth.

Douglass and others like Pastor Leonard Grimes called for recruits from the African American churches and communities. Men flooded into Massachusetts from all over the Northeast, including two of Frederick Douglass's sons, Lewis and Charles. Sergeant William Carney had escaped slavery to New Bedford, protected from the slave hunters by his neighbors. Now he and others like him risked their security and freedom to fight for the freedom of the slaves left behind. They gathered in Readville, Massachusetts, and learned how to work and fight together, while donated clothing, flags, and guns arrived from around New England.

The commander had to be carefully chosen—an abolitionist, an experienced soldier, and a scion of the best families of Boston. Andrew asked the twenty-five-year-old Robert Gould Shaw to accept the task. Shaw had read *Uncle Tom's Cabin* as a teenager and, like so many others, had learned to hate slavery. He was polite, competent, and had served at the

Battle of Antietam. After he accepted, he and other officers of both colors trained the soldiers throughout the spring, and on May 18 they marched through the streets of Boston, pausing at the spot where Crispus Attucks had fallen in 1770 during the Boston Massacre. Governor Andrew addressed Shaw and the rest, saying, "I know not, Mr. Commander, when, in all human history, to any given thousand men in arms there has been committed a work at once so proud, so precious, so full of hope and glory as the work committed to you."

The regiment was sent to the islands off South Carolina, where abolitionists and freed African Americans were already attempting to create postwar communities. An African American teacher named Charlotte Forten had tea with the officers of the Fifty-Fourth on July 6, finding in their "noble" and "gentle" company an equality she had never experienced. They participated in a few minor actions, including a skirmish on James Island in which they lost forty-two men.

Shaw had just married his sweetheart in May, and told a friend, "If I could only have a few weeks longer with my wife and be at home a little while I think I might die happy; but it cannot be; I do not believe I shall live through our next fight." But when the orders were given to spearhead the assault on James Island's Fort Wagner, "all the sadness had left him" and he seemed confident and serene. As the soldiers of the Fifty-Fourth assembled on the beach, Shaw reminded them that the nation would judge them for their actions on that day, and that any "colored soldier" would be shot on the spot or sold into slavery by the rebel troops. In formation, they marched, then ran, through heavy fog along the sandy spit toward one of the most strongly fortified places in the entire South.

A few hundred yards out, the cannon shells began to explode around them. As they kept on, grapeshot hurtled through the air, knocking them down in heaps. Others leaped over their dead comrades. They splashed through a deep water-logged ditch and up a slope toward the parapets, with gunfire and grenades blasting them back. A few reached the top, fighting hand to hand with bayonets and swords. The color sergeant planted the flag on the rampart before he was killed. Sergeant Carney grabbed it and held it for a full fifteen minutes while men around him died. Lewis Douglass was blown off the slope by a grenade. "Swept down like chaff," the wounded Douglass later wrote his father, "still our men went on and on." Captain Appleton used his revolver to kill an entire gun crew. Simpkins and Russel reached the inner fort before they fell. And Shaw, shouting, "Rally, rally!" was shot through the heart.

The supporting regiments from Connecticut and New York were pinned down and couldn't make it past the ditch to help. The momentum of the Union troops faltered amongst the sand and corpses. They retreated, and Fort Wagner remained untaken. Over half of the Fifty-Fourth were dead or missing, and another thousand Union soldiers lay with them. Wounded and bleeding, Carney brought the flag back to the Union lines. "Boys, I only did my duty; the old flag never touched the ground." When asked about Shaw, a Confederate officer evidently said, "We have buried him with his niggers."

The intended insult became a rallying cry across the North, and a symbol of sacrifice, redemption, and brotherhood. The battle became a new Bunker Hill, and helped solidify the Union's resolve. Another 180,000 African Americans joined the army over the next two years, working to crush the rebel states that kept them enslaved. In New England and the rest of the North, public opinion, already greatly changed in the past ten years, now shifted even further. "New antislavery friends are becoming as plentiful as the roses in June," wrote Lydia Maria Child wryly. "I merely marvel at their power of keeping it a secret so long." The war would be won, and a new day of freedom would seem to dawn for African Americans, a new day of redemption for the nation that had accepted their enslavement.

Years later, in a studio in New Hampshire, a young sculptor named Augustus St. Gaudens began designing a monument that would become one of the enduring symbols of the war, of Boston, and of America itself. The thin, mustached figure of Robert Gould Shaw on horseback, accompanied by soldiers of the Fifty-Fourth, each one a bronzed human figure, a sacrifice on the national altar of racism and greed, an exclamation point on the sentence of slavery abolished. At the unveiling, in 1897 on Boston Common, an aged William Carney carried the flag, and Harvard philosopher William James, whose brother Garth had been one of the officers wounded at that battle, gave the oration. "There on foot go the dark out-casts, so true to nature that one can almost hear them breathing as they march," he said of the soldiers on the monument. "There they march, warm-blooded champions of a better day for man." Few who know the story can stand before them without weeping.

CHAPTER 26

Tell It to the Hills

1870s

IT SEEMED THAT EVERY NEW ENGLAND PARLOR HAD A DAGUERREOTYPE on a dark walnut table with the image of an absent man. Emerson wrote that "the energy of the nation seems to have expended itself on the war." He was half right. Before the Civil War, women's groups had sprung up in every city, town, and village, and the conflict had given them new energy and purpose. In the 1870s they helped raise monuments on every village green and in every city park, with a mustached soldier in Union garb above the names of the honored dead. And they raised their voices on issues they cared about like suffrage, spirituality, and temperance.

The fight for universal suffrage had been rolling along since Abigail Adams chastised her husband for leaving women out of full citizenship, but in the 1840s larger numbers of women and some men had jumped aboard. Lydia Maria Child from Medford, Massachusetts, had become an acclaimed author at age twenty-six, and four years later she wrote *The Frugal Housewife*, which made her a national name. Rather than parley it into more wealth, she used that fame to fight for the rights of slaves, Native Americans, and women. When war between the states loomed ever closer, she and everyone like her focused their efforts on the great battle against slavery.

But the two New Englanders that defined the suffrage movement in the 19th century were Lucy Stone and Susan B. Anthony. Born in 1818 in West Brookfield, Massachusetts, tiny Lucy Stone was neglected by her parents due to her "inferior" gender and turned her anger to good purpose, often speaking from her brother's pulpit with dignity and determination.

In 1855 she and her husband, Henry Blackwell, refused the "obedience" part of the wedding vows, and she became one of the first to keep her last name. During her abolitionist lectures, mobs drenched her tiny hundred-pound frame with cold water and hit her with apples.

Born two years later in Adams, Massachusetts, Susan B. Anthony had grown up in a simple Quaker community that taught her the value of conformity. But those lessons did not stick. She became a teacher and turned down the proposal of a rich widower with a sixty-cow dairy. At first she crusaded for the temperance movement, but after hearing Lucy Stone and other suffragist speakers, she turned from temperance to suffrage. With her piercing blue eyes and bear-trap mind, she became one of the strongest speakers, carefully outlining arguments that few could challenge. For her efforts, she was hanged in effigy and pelted with eggs, called a "hermaphrodite" and "Amazon."

Anthony and Stone became allies and even friends. When the women's movement became caught up in issues like "bloomers" and proper dress codes, Stone told Anthony that the right to vote did not revolve around such trifles and brought her back to their shared purpose. During the 1850s and 60s they both increasingly fought for the abolition of slavery, joining Harriet Beecher Stowe and others in the greatest cause of the 19th century.

Now that the war was over, women picked up pens, lobbied state and federal officials, and organized for their own civil rights. In 1868 Lucy Stone, Isabella Beecher Hooker, Julia Ward Howe, Frederick Douglass, and William Lloyd Garrison founded the New England Woman Suffrage Association. A year later Lucy Stone and Susan B. Anthony both attended the American Equal Rights Convention, where like-minded women and men met to discuss voting rights for everyone.

The convention did not go well. Frederick Douglass and others were concerned that the Fifteenth Amendment had not been ratified by all the states yet and wanted to put all efforts into that. Mentioning the hundreds of African Americans recently murdered during the 1868 election, he said, "I do not see how anyone can pretend that there is the same urgency in giving the ballot to woman as to the negro. With us, the matter is a question of life and death, at least in fifteen States of the Union."

Susan B. Anthony replied that "Mr. Douglass talks about the wrongs of the negro; but with all the outrages that he today suffers, he would not exchange his sex and take the place of Elizabeth Cady Stanton." Lucy Stone agreed that women's rights were important but was willing to take the victory of the Fifteenth Amendment for now, saying, "I will be thankful in my soul if anybody can get out of the terrible pit."

Women's rights supporters split into two camps. Susan B. Anthony and New Yorker Elizabeth Cady Stanton created the National Woman Suffrage Association, while Lucy Stone established the American Woman Suffrage Association. There would be no unity throughout the 1870s and beyond. Worse, the division allowed journalists to make fun of both, calling them "hens at war." They often thought of each other as "enemies" too; Stone called Anthony selfish and egotistical while Anthony sarcastically named Stone "Saint Lucy."

But there was little time for that. After debating Frederick Douglass in 1870 in Worcester, Massachusetts, Stone spent the rest of the decade lecturing around the country on "The Disappointment of American Women" and other topics. She tried to bring the federal and state auxiliaries of her organization into line. Sometimes she struggled against arthritis and despair. "I have no country and no hope of a country," she wrote.

She was helped in the cause by adoptive New Englander Julia Ward Howe, who had brought up her children in Boston. In 1861 she had watched soldiers march by singing "John Brown's Body," and decided the song needed better lyrics. She wrote them in half an hour, creating the anthem of the Grand Army of the Republic. Now Howe fought a different war, first helping Stone found the New England Woman Suffrage Association, then the AWSA. She edited the *Woman's Journal*, and during the 1870s began to write antiwar tracts, arguing that the Fourth of July should be changed to "Mother's Day."

Meanwhile, in 1871, Anthony gave 171 lectures over thirteen thousand miles. "I ask you to forget that you are women," she said. "And go forward in the way of right, fearlessly, as independent human beings." But later in the decade, she struggled against the hijacking of their agenda by "free love" advocate Victoria Woodhull and her crusade against Minister Henry Ward Beecher. The "trial of the century" against the popular but ethically questionable preacher at first seemed to help, then began to hurt, the cause of women's rights. Anthony finally brought Isabella Beecher Hooker and others back to that cause. She was less successful when it came to questions like granting immigrants the right to vote and courting openly racist politicians who vowed to fight for women's suffrage. How far were they willing to go to gain allies?

The right to vote was not the only cause that women took up after the Civil War; they were also finding their voices in matters of religion and the spirit. In Boston's West End, Eliza Ann Gardner had been taught by abolitionists, and her family home was a sanctuary on the Underground Railroad. Trained as a dressmaker, she became a Sunday school teacher in the African Methodist Episcopal Zion church, and in 1876 founded a society to raise money for missionaries to Africa. When confronted with resistance from the men of the church, she said, "I come from Old Massachusetts, where we have declared that all, not only men, but women, too, are created free and equal. . . . If you commence to talk about the superiority of men, if you persist in telling us that after the fall of man we were put under your feet and that we are intended to be subject to your will, we cannot help you in New England one bit." She went on to convince the AMEZ to allow women to be ordained and served herself as a chaplain.

Meanwhile, Maine's Ellen Gould White was building a new church. She had been converted to the Millerite movement at age twelve, was baptized in Casco Bay, and began experiencing powerful visions. She published accounts of her prophecies, promoted the building of schools, and advocated vegetarianism. Then in 1863 she became one of the founding members of Seventh-Day Adventism, which published its founding documents in 1872. Her writings soon became the most important in the early history of the church, shifting it toward a mainstream religion that would become one of the largest Christian denominations in the world. By the 20th century, White would become the most translated American author of nonfiction.

Her only competition as both an author and spiritual founder might have been Mary Baker, who grew up on a hill farm above the Merrimack River with five horses, eight oxen, and three cows. With a laughing mouth, deep-set blue eyes, and a love of the written word, she learned the strictures of theology from her father and was educated at the village school, unlike many girls of her day. After moving to Lynn, Massachusetts, she dabbled with spiritualism and mesmerism, psychics and magnetics, as so many did in the 19th century. Then one day in 1866, she fell on the ice of Swampscott Pond and appeared to be paralyzed. She asked for the Bible, and while reading the Gospels, she was healed. "That short experience," she wrote later, "included a glimpse of the great fact that I have since tried to make plain to others, namely, Life in and of spirit; this Life being the sole reality of existence." From that day on, she worked her beliefs into *Science and Health*, a runaway best seller, published in 1875. It marked the beginning of another new faith: Christian Science.

The women who founded or participated in these new religious congregations may or may not have been on board with Lucy Stone and Susan B. Anthony's cause, and vice versa. "We will keep our platform free from controverted theological and social types," Stone said. But there was one topic on which almost all agreed—the eradication of alcoholic beverages.

Temperance had been a popular cause since before the Civil War, particularly in New England. The Massachusetts Society for the Suppression of Intemperance had been formed in 1813, though it only accepted men, and failed miserably. Connecticut's Lyman Beecher was slightly more effective, publishing a popular book in 1826 that called drunkenness a "national sin." He helped form the American Temperance Society in Boston, and it quickly expanded, finding sympathizers from every walk of life. Even Bridgeport showman P. T. Barnum was converted to an alcohol-free lifestyle, running the play *The Drunkard* at his museum for thousands of performances. Maine banned alcohol in 1851, in order to stop the drunken brawls in lumber camps and accidents of shipyard workers. Twelve other states followed, to one degree or another.

But it was women who really brought energy to this cause, some hating alcohol for personal reasons and others seeing in it the cause of societal poverty and degradation. The leaders of other movements like Mary Baker Eddy and Susan B. Anthony supported and even preached temperance. "Nine tenths of those who are taken to prison are those who have learned to drink," wrote Ellen Gould White. For better or worse, suffrage, piety, and temperance would be linked in both the popular imagination and in reality for decades to come.

In the meantime, there were other wrongs to right and reforms to champion—child labor, birth control, the eight-hour work day, and dozens more. And though some of these issues overlapped or blended, others divided and fractured the women who cared about them. After all, for these New Englanders, as for so many others over the centuries, the world of ideas was not abstract, but as real as a photograph on the table. It was getting others to see the same picture that was so much trouble.

CHAPTER 27

Starlings and House Sparrows

1880s

In 1872 German immigrant and journalist Charles Nordhoff visited Hawaii, where among the palm trees he was shocked to find "white frame houses with green blinds, the picket-fences whitewashed until they shine, the stone walls, the small barns, the scanty pastures, the little white churches scattered about, the narrow 'front yards,' the frequent schoolhouses, usually with but little shade: all are New England, genuine and unadulterated." This was the work of a half-admirable, half-naïve people "who knew no better country than New England, nor any better ways than New England ways, and to whom it never occurred to think that what was good and sufficient in Massachusetts was not equally good and fit in any part of the world."

But while tiny New Englands cropped up around the globe, the prototype seemed to be drying up. By 1880 many grizzled, old whalers and hawk-faced, old wool-spinners exchanged greetings across rows of empty pews. The fisheries off the coast were beginning to collapse, and falling beef and dairy prices drove many farmers to bankruptcy. The two million sheep grazing the hills of Vermont were now competing with a billion in Montana. A landlord and tenant system changed the way people thought about property; farms were mortgaged rather than owned outright; and class distinctions became more and more defined. Cedar islands emptied, cottages crumbled, and tools rusted in the sun. Barrett Wendell of Harvard wrote a few years later, in 1893, "We are vanishing into provincial obscurity. America has swept from our grasp. The future is beyond us."

In the cities, it was an age of corruption and political machines, the structures of which would remain basically unchanged for the next century. Slums had appeared in Boston in the 1840s, but now every factory town had them. Few read Latin, the classics were abandoned at Harvard, and business took over the schools. San Francisco ruined the China trade, and New York drew more and more commerce away from Boston. "Numbers is the king of our era," said Harriet Beecher Stowe. The sorrowful sound of a train whistle in the distance was no longer the sound of the future; it was a signal that the future had passed by.

But maybe things were only changing. After all, change can feel like death to those who know nothing else. Innovations like elevators, typewriters, phonographs, bicycles, and brand-name dungarees were new and scary, but not necessarily the end of civilization. And conveniences like electric fans, irons, and streetlamps were already improving the lives of millions. Of course, to produce these appliances and accessories required factories, and New England kept building more and more of those, trying to stay at the forefront of the industrial age. Bridgeport, Connecticut, alone would boast five hundred by the turn of the century.

New England's only remaining natural resource was lumber from its north woods, with Burlington, Vermont, becoming the third largest lumber market in the United States. The pulp mills of Maine drove the state's economy now far more than fishing or shipbuilding, and Westbrook's Cumberland Mills was the largest paper manufacturer in the world. However, the size and number of these mills had polluted the nearby areas, and both workers and residents complained of lung and skin problems. It was not only paper—pollution from the huge factories on the Merrimack and Housatonic literally drove people from adjacent homes.

One solution to this side effect of industrialization had been proposed by Hartford's Frederick Law Olmsted, who invented the profession of "landscape architect." Throughout the late 19th century he designed parks and green belts to act as the "lungs" for coughing city dwellers, allowing them to get healthy exercise away from their tenements and row houses. The other solution was to spread out and away from the factories and densely populated city centers. Streetcar railways began taking residents out to formerly small communities like Jamaica Plain, South Providence, and Fair Haven. Horse powered, they would electrify by the end of the decade, doubling the speed and reducing the prices. It was the beginning of "suburbanization," which at first was a way for poorer residents to live more cheaply away from the center of town.

The people who flooded into these "streetcar suburbs" were largely immigrants. During the mid-19th century, immigration to the United States sparked editorials in every newspaper and arguments in every town meeting. Was this a good or a bad thing? Should certain countries be excluded? These questions had first arisen four decades earlier, when large numbers of people fleeing the potato famine made Boston the most Irish city in the United States. The native-born population had objected to such large numbers of immigrants, particularly Catholic ones, and had even burned down a convent in Charlestown.

By 1855 Theodore Parker called Boston the "American Dublin," and by 1860 two-thirds of household servants there were Irish women. Men worked in construction or as dockworkers, though others found success in business, like Dorchester's Christopher Blake, who built a furniture factory, and Thomas Ring, founder of the Union Institution of Savings. Irish-born Andrew Carney progressed from tailor to financial genius, helping found the First National Bank of Boston and John Hancock Insurance Company. During the Civil War, ten thousand Irish Americans from Massachusetts fought for the Union.

In 1877 Boston's mayor, Frederick Prince, didn't get reelected because he supposedly put too many Irish on the police force. However, by 1882 Boston was the first American city with a majority Irish population and an Irish-born congressman, Patrick Collins. In 1884, with the help of powerful Irish neighborhood leaders like the Fitzgeralds and the Kennedys, Hugh O'Brien became mayor, remaining in that role until the 20th century.

The Irish were clearly here to stay, but proposals to keep out new groups or limit their citizenship were floated throughout the 1870s by male politicians and female activists alike. Only one of these proposals was successful on a national scale—the 1882 Chinese Exclusion Act, signed by President Chester A. Arthur, born in Vermont and part of the New York political machine. He reformed civil service and led a generally blameless administration, drawing praise from even the cynical Mark Twain. However, the Chinese Exclusion Act was the first to completely ban an ethnic group from immigrating. It mostly affected the West Coast of the United States, but New Englanders like Yung Wing, who had graduated from Yale University, eventually had their citizenship revoked.

Other immigration remained largely unchecked, and Jews, Armenians, Lithuanians, Greeks, Poles, Scandinavians, and Syrians all came to work in the factories of Lowell, Lynn, Brockton, Dover, Rochester, Willimantic, and New Britain. Portuguese fishermen had been fishing New England waters since the 1600s, but during the late 19th century, towns like Taunton, Fall River, and New Bedford became their chief destination for emigration from Portugal, the Azores, and the Cape Verde Islands. Quebecois flooded into Vermont, New Hampshire, and Maine to work in lumber camps, pick apples, and tap maple trees. French could be heard again throughout northern New England, ringing from brickyards, cotton mills, and farmstead kitchens.

Large numbers of Italians began to arrive in New England for the first time, with a thousand families arriving in Boston during 1880. Stoneworkers from Carrara, Varese, and Lake Como now mined granite in Barre, Vermont, and "Little Italys" sprang up in Hartford, Providence, and Springfield. It was part of the largest voluntary emigration in history, and New England would gain its share. Eventually Rhode Island would become the most Italian state in America, closely followed by Connecticut. All these immigrants would soon add their own customs and ideas to the culture, and absorb the culture already present, paradoxically creating diversity and unity all at once.

Empty fishing villages and boarded-up farmhouses, factories full of women and neighborhoods full of immigrants—to some this must have seemed like the end of an era, maybe the end of what New Englanders had thought New England meant for the past century. Many writers called the 1880s the "dreadful decade" or the "brown decade" for its gloomy despair. But who exactly was despairing? Not the successful factory owners and railroad entrepreneurs. Not the eager immigrants starting a new life in a new land. And certainly not the New Englanders who had left that land to spread their culture to the far ends of the earth.

In Hartland, Vermont, one morning in 1888, Mrs. Williamson woke up, then "made a fire, mended pants, set the breakfast going, skimmed ten pans of milk, washed the pans, ate breakfast, went to the barn and milked two cows, brought the cream out of the cellar, churned fifteen pounds of butter, made four apple pies, two mince pies, and one custard pie, done up the sink." Then the clock chimed 9:00 a.m. Change and endurance were not mutually exclusive concepts.

CHAPTER 28

The Chief End of Man

1890s

DURING THE 1880s IN BEAUTIFUL, PARKLIKE HARTFORD, SAMUEL CLE-
mens lived the happiest years of his life. He played billiards, smoked
cigars, and lampooned New England cleverness in *Connecticut Yankee in
King Arthur's Court*. He also invested in schemes and technologies that
would bankrupt him in 1894. And he was not the only happy man to get
caught up in the spirit of the age and be ruined. Newport's Clarence King
first went west as a geologist because he loved the mountains, but went
back as a speculator. He made a fortune, then lost it, and died alone in a
tavern in Arizona. "What is the chief end of man?" Clemens had written
in 1871. "To get rich. In what way? Dishonestly if we can; honestly if we
must." As usual, the great author was joking, but by the 1890s that joke
must have worn out its welcome.

Clemens's alter ego, Mark Twain, and friend Charles Dudley Warner would provide a name for this "Gilded Age" in their book, satirizing
the thin sheen of wealth that overlay moral corruption. While railroad
workers went on strike and economic panics destroyed fortunes, graft and
bribery rotted democratic institutions. Swindlers and the swindled shook
hands, parted, and returned again to make another deal. Despite, or perhaps because of this, it was also an age of astonishing growth in commerce and industry. Collis P. Huntington of Harwinton, Connecticut,
and Cyrus Field of Stockbridge, Massachusetts, left to become "railroad
barons," while Hartford's J. P. Morgan became America's financial wiz-
ard, reimagining how huge companies were created. Monopolies created
titanic wealth, and though much of that wealth flowed into New York

City, the wealthy did not want to live there amidst the shantytowns and smoke. Their solution was to move out to Long Island and the Hudson Valley, but most of all to New England.

Clarence King's Newport was one of their main destinations. Since the 1840s, wealthy plantation owners had been escaping southern humidity on Narragansett Bay, and Yankee merchants had joined them. But by the 1890s the country's richest people, including the Vanderbilts and the Astors, built their dream homes here. Though they were not necessarily the biggest houses in America, they were certainly the most desirable, the most fashionable, the most copied. Of course, not everyone thought them so attractive. Author Henry James had grown up in a simpler Newport and, though a fan of luxury himself, called the mansions "grotesque." He thought that the quiet beauty of Ocean Drive had been trampled by "white elephants," unwanted by their absentee owners, symbols of wealth without taste.

For three seasons these Italianate, Gothic Revival, and French Renaissance mansions often lay fallow, but during the summers the lawns filled with men in boat shoes and white waders, and women in bustles and feathered hats. Marble corridors rang with music, laughter, and the tinkling of cocktail glasses, in what socialite Elizabeth Lehr called "that brilliant chain of balls and parties which made its season the gayest in two continents." Novelist and heiress Edith Wharton, who lived in several Newport "cottages" during the Gilded Age, remembered the immaculate hairdos, four-seated carriages, and elaborate rituals of "calling" on other members of the elite, which took up endless hours every day.

Newport was not the only destination for the wealthy—the Pulitzers and Rockefellers built their own summer cottages on Mount Desert Island, creating Millionaire's Row amongst Maine's broken shells and barberry bushes. The Berkshire Hills had been a summer retreat for decades, and now industrialists and their heirs began building magnificent homes there. Just across the border from New York, Greenwich had become a haven for wealthy socialites just after the Civil War, and now their houses spread along railway corridors to Darien, New Canaan, and Westport. The protected anchorages of Long Island Sound and the four thousand islands of Maine soon became the country's most desirable locations for boating. Empty fishing marinas now filled with the gold-trimmed yachts of the rich.

Of course, things were not always as nice as the gilding promised. Trapped in a loveless marriage, Elizabeth Lehr wrote checks for her "adventurer" husband, while the walls of her elegant Newport home "would echo to the bitter reproaches, the recriminations." Young Eugene O'Neill lived down the coast in New London with his celebrated actor father and addicted mother, living his long day's journey into night. In nearby Fall River the wealthy Borden family was torn apart by murder and scandal.

But this was merely the human conflict that twisted every social class, regardless of wealth. It was the conflict between those classes that began to trouble New England society more and more at the end of the 19th century. For two hundred years, this had been one of the most egalitarian places on the planet, but now things were changing. In Newport, the upper, middle, and lower classes bathed on separate beaches, and seasonal residents tried to keep visitors from the fabled Cliff Walk. They may have had a point—vandals destroyed their property and curious sightseers broke into houses for impromptu "tours." But these clashes about access would grow louder and louder over the next century, as more and more coastline became privately owned, enclaves of the superrich and upper middle classes alike.

Middle-class tourists had also begun to arrive in great numbers, sunning themselves on Martha's Vineyard, swimming in New Hampshire lakes, and setting up easels along Narragansett Bay. They came to discover their heritage as Americans, and to escape the summer heat of the Midwest and Great Plains. They came for the lighthouses, for the stone walls, for the clambakes. They gazed in wonder at the village greens and little red schoolhouses. They ate imported California oranges, drank Coca-Cola, and knew themselves to be the luckiest people in the history of the world.

The leisure time for the new middle classes needed more than yachting. Bridgeport's P. T. Barnum had brought gasp-inducing entertainment to every small town in America, but by the 1890s the circus competed with vaudeville and motion pictures for everyone's attention. Lake Compounce in Bristol, Connecticut, had pioneered the amusement park back in the 1840s, and now dozens sprang up around New England. During a summer day both men and women might participate in golf, tennis, or even cycling and then watch a band play a concert of popular tunes in the local park. More and more people enjoyed simply watching sports, too, with prizefighting gaining widespread acceptance, at least for male spectators. The first postseason games in baseball had been played in 1884 between the Providence Grays and the New York Metropolitans, and cheerleading and fight songs had just been added to the annual Harvard-Yale football game. In 1891, in Springfield, Massachusetts, James Naismith invented an indoor activity to pass the time between the baseball and football seasons, and soon basketball would take its place among America's games.

Domestic architecture had begun to matter to these new classes more than ever before, and not just in the Stick Style and Beaux Arts mansions of Newport. Queen Anne and Victorian houses with ornate porches and elaborate spindle work sprang up on every street. Inspired by some of the other villas in Newport that harkened back to earlier centuries, less impressive versions began to crop up—two-story rectangular blocks with high gables or one-story "Cape Cod" cottages that developed from eastern Massachusetts folk homes. These "colonial revivals" would soon spread a kind of old-fashioned New England charm to every corner of America.

While big cities like New York and big open spaces in the West continued to draw people as places for economic opportunity, some had reimagined New England as a sanctuary of old-fashioned charm. But others refused to give up on the future. In 1897 the first subway in America was built in Boston, using an electric motor invented by Frank Sprague of Milford, Connecticut. It was in response to the influx of immigrants, and constant jamming of trolleys, horse-drawn carriages, and wagons on the narrow 18th-century streets. Former mayor of Boston Dr. Samuel Green said that this "would probably disturb the bones of many an old Bostonian, but this now cannot be helped." It was both a literal and figurative statement.

If New England was going to be more than a weekend retreat in the next century, many believed the rural charm and romantic past would have to go. Future generations would have to find a different sort of nostalgia, a different kind of beauty, on the storied streets of Boston and the enchanted, rose-tinged cliffs of Aquidneck Island.

CHAPTER 29

The Wolf Is at the Door

1900s

BY THE TURN OF THE 20TH CENTURY, NEW ENGLAND HAD FULLY embraced industrialism. Fishing had collapsed and farming was reduced to specialty products like artisanal cheese, shade tobacco, and varietal apples. Water rights became an issue of contention between farmers and factory owners, and the factories won. Whale oil had lost almost all its cachet to petroleum products like kerosene, and even whalebone corsets had been replaced by more flexible fibers. The giant mammals had been overhunted and became harder to find, with only a few whaling vessels still sailing from the ports of Massachusetts. Connecticut's last whaling ship, the *Margaret*, returned to port in April 1909.

Not that the region was poverty-stricken—thousands of factories dotted an increasingly urban landscape, creating a wealth never before seen in the world. The problem was that only a few shared in that wealth, and many felt that the rich were getting rich on their labor. The average factory worker saw no benefits when the factory made money and worked long hours with little safety regulation and no job security. With so many potential workers coming in from Europe and the southern states, bosses could pay whatever they wished and still have employees.

People had been poor before, but in previous centuries they usually owned land they could farm and hunt. Communities had been closer then, too, and neighbors and family could help each other. But as the 1800s had chugged along faster and faster, spewing coal smoke and brick dust, the urban poor had multiplied and become poorer. Unemployed men sat morosely on the docks or at the fences of factories; unemployed women lounged outside taverns and textile shops. Those that found employment became trapped in a cycle of commerce in a way that their ancestors had rarely been. The pennies they earned went toward food their family no longer grew and clothing they no longer wove themselves. Any weaknesses—liquor, sugar, tobacco, trinkets—became luxuries that broke a family.

Established churches and aid societies tried to deal with the problem, but often fell short, particularly with immigrants, Catholics, and other marginalized groups. So in the late 19th century, the workers themselves started to organize into cooperative unions, and by the turn of the 20th these groups were becoming well established and nationally effective. Many immigrants from Quebec, Italy, and Poland moved into neighborhoods that had their own newspapers in their own languages, as well as mutual benefit associations, formed to make up for the loss of kinship circles in the old country. These often became networks that fed into unions, and sometimes into political organizations: anarchists, socialists, and Communists made their first appearances in New England during those Gilded Age years.

Another group that was often left out of economic and social equality was women. After Lucy Stone's death in 1893, the American Woman Suffrage Association and Susan B. Anthony's National American Woman Suffrage Association finally joined forces. But after the brief successes of the 1870s and early 1880s, little progress was made. State referenda lost over and over again. Susan B. Anthony went "across the river" in 1906 without seeing any of her many causes come to fruition.

Women in the workforce turned to unions to solve this problem. At a 1903 Boston meeting of the American Federation of Labor, women were left out of both the conversation and membership. So Mary Kenney O'Sullivan and Leonora O'Reilly decided to create the Women's Trade Union League to organize female workers. By the following year it had branches in the big cities, and over the next two decades fought for minimum wage and the eight-hour workday. It helped support strikes in the garment industry and boycotted clothing manufacturers.

Charlotte Perkins Gilman, the grandniece of Harriet Beecher Stowe, agreed that, at a local level, unions might solve these gender inequalities.

However, she went even further, connecting the suffrage movement and socialism, calling it "all the same." Born in Hartford, she was abandoned by her father and grew up poor and unloved, often spending long periods with the wealthier Beecher family or at the public library in Providence. She enrolled in classes at the Rhode Island School of Design, painting and writing. In 1898 she published *Women and Economics*, which argued that more opportunities for women in the workplace were necessary, both for their mental development and for society. It made her an international star, and she toured Europe and America lecturing on poverty, gender, and socialism. "To work, to work!" she wrote, trying to spur others to activism. "In Heaven's name, the wolf is at the door."

The new economy also left behind many African Americans, though not all. Son of a member of the Massachusetts Fifty-Fifth Infantry, William Monroe Trotter was born and raised in elegant Hyde Park, Massachusetts, and went to Harvard for undergraduate and master's work, the first African American to earn a Phi Beta Kappa. He joined the temperance movement, invested in real estate, and married accountant Geraldine Pindell. However, he experienced a political awakening when he encountered racial segregation in Boston's hotels and restaurants, and in 1903 organized protests around New England. Along with Geraldine, he founded the *Boston Guardian*, which argued that African Americans should not "accommodate" racism but rather fight against it actively.

They were joined in this effort by William Edward Burghardt Du Bois. Born in Great Barrington, Massachusetts, Du Bois lived in an integrated community and attended an integrated school, both of which recognized and encouraged his blistering intelligence. The First Congregational Church raised money to send him to college, and though he first went to Fisk University, he ended up at Harvard, where he studied under William James and became the first African American to earn a PhD there. In 1903 he published *The Souls of Black Folk*, which had an immediate impact on American society, saying that "the problem of the Twentieth Century is the problem of the color line." It heralded him as one of the preeminent thinkers in the country.

In agreement in their opposition to "go slow," thinkers like Booker T. Washington, Trotter and Du Bois helped found the National Association for the Advancement of Colored People. But by the end of the decade, the two men fell out, with Trotter promoting boycotts and activist protests, and Du Bois supporting socialist solutions to the "color problem." Indeed, all these groups and the individuals in these groups varied widely as far as their political beliefs, from anarcho-syndicalism to socialism to republicanism. They all wanted equality of opportunity, but often had different approaches to getting there.

Unions made the most progress during those years, helping pass the 1908 workman's compensation law in Massachusetts. But progress went slowly, and often suffered reversals. Throughout the decade, the "Hat City"—Danbury, Connecticut—remained a flashpoint for union and management fights. Hatters had unionized as early as 1880, trying to deal with the continual problem of "hatters' shakes" or "mad hatter disease," caused by mercury used in the felted-fur process. A strike in 1893 had locked out four thousand workers, and in 1902 a nationwide boycott of nonunion manufacturer Dietrich Loewe had led to a lawsuit against the American Federation of Labor, arguing that they were violating antitrust laws. Six years later the case reached the Supreme Court, and the union lost the suit. The workers also continued getting the mercury shakes, and though they protested and lobbied the government, it was not until 1937 that something was done about it.

Nevertheless, by the end of the decade, union memberships around New England had doubled, and small gains had been made, with unionized wages rising slightly, and the hours worked per week beginning to fall. In January 1912 the government of Massachusetts began enforcing one of the laws designed to protect laborers, which cut the work week from fifty-six to fifty-four hours. Not surprisingly, the mills cut the corresponding two hours of wages. The workers saw this not as a benefit to them but a detriment, and in Lawrence twenty thousand men and women from dozens of different nationalities immediately went on strike. Italian immigrants Joseph Ettor of the Industrial Workers of the World and Arturo Giovannitti of the Socialist Party of America took over union leadership, while the mayor of Lawrence called out companies of bayonet-wielding militia and mill owners turned fire hoses on the picketers in the dead of winter.

Some of these "bread and roses" strikers were sentenced to a year in prison for breaking windows. Another union worked against them, and the town tried to frame the leaders by planting dynamite, but these ruses were discovered. Then, Ettor and Giovannitti were thrown in jail, charged as accomplices to a murder. Out-of-work strikers began sending their children to families in other states, which garnered sympathy with the general populace and federal government. When the city tried to stop some of the mothers from putting their children on the trains, the poorly trained police began clubbing everyone involved. The national press covered this horrific event, reporting that one woman had miscarried after being clubbed.

Congressional hearings discovered that the conditions in the mills and adjoining apartment buildings were disgraceful. Half the children born to these mill workers died before age six, and the life expectancy of the workers was thirty-nine. The humiliated mill owners gave substantial raises to their employees, which satisfied everyone for the moment. By March 30 the children had returned to their parents, and soon afterwards, Ettor and Giovannitti were acquitted.

It seemed like a happy ending to a long-fought battle, but the textile workers of Lawrence lost almost all their gains in the next few years. Other progress like prohibiting industrial poisons, establishing weekends, and putting limits on the length of working days would also have to wait. The wolf may have been at the door, but not everyone was ready to fight it yet.

CHAPTER 30

Either Dreams or Swords

1910s

On Saturday, July 2, 1911, temperatures reached a hundred degrees in Boston. It was the hottest day for a decade, but not too unusual. Then for almost two weeks the temperature kept rising throughout New England: 105 degrees in Vernon, Vermont; 106 in Bangor, Maine; and even the tops of the White Mountains reached the 90s. People went to the beach for relief, but found dead, still air. City-dwellers escaped the ovens of their apartments by sleeping in the grass of Boston Common. When it reached 110 degrees in downtown Boston, some drowned in the rivers trying to flee the heat. Others sweated to death, collapsing in heaps; still others committed suicide. Farm animals keeled over, and tar on the streets ran like maple syrup. At the height of the heat wave, a thermometer in Cumberland, Rhode Island, read 130 degrees. Over a thousand people died in Massachusetts, and nearly another thousand in the rest of New England.

Three summers later, a different kind of heat would sweep across Europe. As nations chose sides, the United States continued an isolationist path. Massachusetts senator Henry Cabot Lodge was perhaps the strongest voice to upbraid President Wilson for not declaring war against Germany. But Irish Americans, who made up the majority of the population in Boston and other major cities in the region, were angry at the United Kingdom's treatment of Ireland, and did not want to help them in a war with Germany. The crushing of Dublin's Easter Rising in April 1916 did not help the matter. The Irish American mayor of Boston, John Fitzgerald, wisely stayed out of these arguments, singing "Sweet

Adeline" at public functions and throwing out the opening pitch at Fenway Park in 1912. Charming and popular, "Honey Fitz" had also served in Congress, and now ran for US senator against Lodge, but lost. His grandson would be more successful.

Everyone in New England could agree that even before the United States entered the war, producing war materials helped the regional economy. Between 1915 and 1918, fifty thousand new workers flooded into Bridgeport, Connecticut, a third of whom toiled at the gigantic Remington Arms Company factory. The Remington complex included the largest building in the world and produced ten thousand bayonets per day, a hundred thousand rifles per month, and seven million rounds of ammunition per week. And it was not the only factory in town—dozens of other companies turned to the war effort, from Bridgeport Brass to Simon Lake's submarine factory, which racked up fifteen hundred patents, including airlocks and steering gears. By 1918, Bridgeport produced more munitions than any other city in America, and the other cities of the region, from Springfield to Lowell, were not far behind.

As soon as war was declared in 1917, New England organized a National Guard division that included troops from all six states. Called the "Yankee Division," it was assembled at Camp Devens, built on the site of a 1656 military base that had been used in King Philip's War and later by the Fifty-Third Massachusetts during the Civil War. Not long afterwards, the twenty-seven thousand men boarded ships for France, the first full-strength force of US soldiers to arrive. The war-weary French taught these inexperienced soldiers techniques like rolling barrages, and on February 5, 1918, Battery A of the 101st Field Artillery made the first shots by a National Guard unit in the war. On March 21, the German forces attacked, and in April the Yankee Division came under fire for thirty-six hours straight, suffering 80 killed, 424 wounded, and 130 captured.

The Yankee Division fought in the trenches and in the underground quarries, leaving behind graffiti applauding the Red Sox. In August they attacked along the Marne, in September they helped take Vigneulles, and in October they fought near Verdun. They spent 210 days on the line, with 45 of those days in combat, second only to the Regular Army First Division. A total of 1,587 New Englanders in that division alone were killed in action and another 12,077 were wounded. One celebrated officer in the division was Sergeant Stubby, a Boston terrier mix from Yale University who joined the division to sniff out gas attacks and German spies. He was wounded by a grenade attack, and returned home a hero.

New Englanders served in other divisions, and in other ways. New Bedford's Frank Leamon Baylies had vision problems that prevented him from enlisting in the US Army Air Service, so he enlisted with the French air force. Despite imperfect eyesight, he shot down twelve German fighter planes during spring 1918, becoming America's "ace of aces," even though it was not in the American military. He survived a crash landing in no-man's-land, outrunning a German patrol, but on June 17 he was finally shot down by a squadron of four Fokker Triplanes. The Germans respected such an accomplished flier, though, and buried him in honor, while the French awarded him the Légion d'Honneur, the Médaille militaire, and the Croix de Guerre.

With men enlisting in the army and securing factory jobs, many women took over farms. Recruited from colleges, suffrage societies, and local garden clubs, "farmettes" learned to drive tractors and fought to receive fair wages and eight-hour days. Close to a thousand of these women worked in New England to feed the armies. Others, like Margaret Chase of Maine, worked as volunteers with the Red Cross, collecting medical supplies to send to Europe.

Many in New England feared attacks, particularly when on July 21, 1918, a German U-boat attacked Orleans, Massachusetts, sinking a tugboat and barges before American planes drove it off. But most of the battles on the home front were civil conflicts. German Americans had to register with the federal government and Germans living in the country were often put into camps, including twenty-nine musicians in the Boston Symphony Orchestra. The war led to immediate inflation, and mobs in Providence smashed Italian businesses, throwing pasta into the street in what became known as the "Macaroni Riots." Factories increased hours to achieve their production goals, and often broke other commitments to workers. One hundred Portuguese workers at the Remington factory went on strike and a riot followed. President Wilson threatened to draft them.

By 1915 there were more than fourteen hundred local unions in Massachusetts alone, with 250,000 members. But during the war, some unions, particularly the IWW, actively tried to hurt the war effort and were shut down. This was accelerated by the Espionage Act of 1917, which prohibited any support for enemies during wartime, or in fact any interference with military matters at all. It was ruled constitutional during *Schenck v. United States* by a unanimous Supreme Court, and though the law ostensibly had nothing to do with unions, it was sometimes used to deter their protests, strikes, and boycotts.

Two of the members of that court were New Englanders: Oliver Wendell Holmes and Louis Brandeis. Holmes was the son of the author and doctor of the same name and had fought for the Twentieth Massachusetts Regiment in the Civil War. Later, he made a name for himself as a jurist and was nominated to the Supreme Court by Teddy Roosevelt. Brandeis had been born in Kentucky to two Jewish immigrants but, after Harvard Law School and marriage, had moved to Massachusetts. He pioneered the right to privacy, fought against monopolies, and became the "people's lawyer" in a variety of public cases. In 1916 President Wilson nominated him to the Supreme Court, and despite rampant anti-Semitism, he was confirmed.

Brandeis and Holmes sometimes agreed, sometimes did not, and both often dissented from the majority opinion. One of those disagreements came in a second case about the Espionage Act, *Abrams v. United States*, in which one defendant was arrested for taking flyers that criticized President Wilson's policies and throwing them out a hat-factory window. The court upheld the act again, but both Brandeis and Holmes dissented, arguing that in this case, at least, the defendants' freedom of speech had been violated, and that they were being prosecuted for their beliefs. It was not, they argued, a "clear and present danger" to the United States' war effort, but rather a protest protected under the first amendment.

Surviving unions like the AFL were more practical, arguing that their membership actually represented rather than worked against the war effort, and sometimes used this argument to get higher wages and fewer hours. But the vast majority of strikes ended in failure, and by the end of 1918, unions had not gained much ground. The end of the war also meant the end of war production, and this caused an immediate recession in New England. Remington and other factories had to lay off workers, while Lowell's United States Cartridge Company would close completely in a few years.

One successful strike was staged by the Boston Telephone Operator's Union, who were incensed by the failure of the nationalized industry to increase wages as promised. Julia O'Connor from Woburn, Massachusetts, and nine thousand of her fellow female operators shut down telephone service throughout New England in April 1919. Though college students were hired as replacements, they were attacked by men who supported the strikers. A settlement was reached fairly quickly, and O'Connor went on to organize a national campaign.

But the dynamic changes that shook New England in those years were not in the workplace. Both political parties had "wet" and "dry" factions, and so they often fought amongst themselves about whether to ban alcoholic beverages. However, anti-immigrant sentiment against Italians was high, and the war increased feeling against German Americans, allowing government officials to ignore those constituencies, which were both "wets." Between 1909 and 1913, the "dries" had helped ratify the Sixteenth Amendment, which instituted the income tax, in order to get the federal government funded without taxing alcohol. Then in 1917, various dry factions banded together to propose the Eighteenth Amendment to the Constitution, which would prohibit the sale of alcoholic beverages nationwide. State after state ratified it, and on October 28, 1919, Congress passed the Volstead Act to enable enforcement.

The relationship between temperance and women's suffrage had hurt the latter for decades, faced with the liquor lobby and men who liked whiskey after dinner. But now the two issues walked hand in hand together toward victory. Rising numbers of middle-class and upper-class women from New England, many with careers and degrees, helped argue for universal suffrage. On March 22, 1920, Washington became the thirty-fifth state to ratify the Nineteenth Amendment, and on August 6 it became law, just in time for women to vote in the presidential election that autumn. Equal representation in politics and society would take a little longer.

CHAPTER 31

The Roar and the Silence

1920s

ON DECEMBER 20, 1920, VICE PRESIDENT–ELECT CALVIN COOLIDGE addressed a crowd at Plymouth, Massachusetts, on the three hundreth anniversary of the landing of the pilgrims. "On that abiding faith has been reared an empire magnificent beyond their dreams of Paradise," he told the gathering. "What an increase, material and spiritual, three hundred years has brought that little company is known to all the earth. No like body ever cast so great an influence on human history."

Born July 4, 1872, in the tiny village of Plymouth, Vermont, and descended from the Great Migration settlers of 1630, the red-haired Coolidge grew up in a frugal but not poor house, walked to the district school, and worked on the family farm. He attended Amherst, studied law, and got a job nearby as a lawyer. He was elected to the city council of Northampton, Massachusetts, served on several committees and clerkships, and married Grace Goodhue of Vermont, a teacher at the Clarke School for the Deaf. They remained happily married for the rest of their lives.

In 1907 he entered the Massachusetts House of Representatives, where as a Republican he tried to shrink the footprint of government and decrease legislation. However, he believed in the power of government to help people, and voted for and supported many of the bills considered "progressive" at the time, such as women's suffrage and pensions for teachers. He moved up through the ranks, becoming mayor of Northampton in 1910, president of the state Senate in 1914, and then lieutenant governor in 1916. He never seemed to seek higher office, and perhaps that is why it was offered so readily.

In 1918 he became governor of Massachusetts just at the end of the First World War. During his administration, the police force in Boston tried to join the American Federation of Labor, but the commissioner had denied it. A police strike followed, stores were ransacked, and Boston Common became a gambling den. Coolidge called out the state guard of Massachusetts to keep order, and urged the police to return to duty. "I call on every citizen to aid me in the maintenance of law and order," he said. "There is no right to strike against the public safety by anybody, anywhere, any time." This made him even more popular with the Massachusetts public, and also made him a national figure. Despite being from the opposing party, President Woodrow Wilson sent him a note of congratulations. Coolidge was reelected as governor and later that year nominated for vice president as a sort of compromise amongst the factions of the Republican Party.

By the time he took office, the prohibition of alcohol had taken effect. Hundreds of breweries and wineries around New England disappeared nearly overnight. Many in Massachusetts, Vermont, New Hampshire, and Maine had welcomed the new amendment, cheering the destruction of "demon liquor." After all, Portland mayor Neal Dow had been called the "Father of Prohibition" and even ran for president on that platform in the late 19th century. When the law took effect, a mock funeral was held in Boston, with evangelist Billy Sunday telling the crowd that "the reign of tears is over."

However, not everyone was pleased with this new constitutional amendment. The only two states in the Union that did not vote for the Eighteenth Amendment, before or after ratification, were Connecticut and Rhode Island. The Hartford *Courant* called it a "dangerous invasion of the rights of individual states." Hotels concealed booze behind false walls, while doctors and drugstores prescribed whiskey for "medicinal purposes." Italian immigrants continued to make wine in their backyards, the wealthy in Newport and Greenwich kept extensive wine cellars, and farmers quietly made bathtub gin. And the rebellion against Prohibition led to rebellion against other standards. Stamford's Lois Long became one of the age's famous "flappers," telling people in her pseudonymous column, "Tomorrow we may die, so let's get drunk and make love." On the beaches of Long Island Sound, defiant teens wore tight-fitting women's swimsuits or, in the case of men, began to go shockingly bare-chested. Couples could actually be seen kissing in public on the New Haven Green.

As Prohibition continued, many in northern New England shifted their opinions as well. Canadian towns along the border began to stock up, and you could hear songs like "Four and twenty Yankees, feeling very dry, went across the border to get a drink of rye. When the rye was opened, the Yanks began to sing, God bless America, but God save the King!" Smuggling through the forests of the north or the dark water of the southern coasts soon led to the rise of organized crime in the cities of New England. Police officers and politicians were bribed with all the untaxed money being made off liquor sales, while "baby-carriage bootleggers" smuggled it in plain sight. Democrats began to argue that Prohibition was causing more crime than it was stopping, and for the first time since the Civil War the party began to make gains in New England.

Vice President Coolidge was in his tiny Plymouth Notch farmhouse when he was awoken by his father, John, calling upstairs in a trembling voice. President Warren Harding had died, and Coolidge would have to step up and serve. After a prayer, he and his wife went downstairs to find reporters and a few friends in the parlor, lit in the darkness by a small kerosene lamp. At 2:47 a.m. on August 3, 1923, he took the oath of office from his father, who was a notary public and justice of the peace, and then he and Grace went upstairs and back to sleep. When asked about his son's qualifications for the presidency, his father remarked, "It always seemed to me that Calvin could get more sap out of a maple tree than any of the other boys around here."

His presidency came as the nation worked itself out of the recession that had followed World War I, and the economy was booming again. Mass-produced cars parked in old carriage houses, jazz blared from radios in soda shops, and films brought thousands into downtown movie palaces. Films with sound had begun to be produced, and by the end of the decade would become the world's most popular art form. The ability of unions to strike had weakened due to espionage and sedition acts during the war, and membership declined due to low unemployment.

In 1924 Coolidge signed an act granting automatic citizenship to Native Americans, and spoke in favor of African Americans, saying that their civil rights were "just as sacred as those of any other citizen." He repeatedly asked Congress to pass laws to prevent lynching, but they refused. However, he signed the Immigration Act of 1924, the most restrictive such law passed to date. It limited entry for immigrants from Asia, eastern Europe, and southern Europe. Italians had been coming to America at a rate of several hundred thousand per year, working in construction and granite carving, walking police beats and opening grocery stores. This law cut that number to a maximum of four thousand.

The issue was thrown into strong relief by a Massachusetts trial that aroused international attention. During an armed robbery in Braintree, Massachusetts, on April 15, 1920, a guard and a paymaster were murdered, and two Italian immigrants, a fishmonger named Nicola Sacco and a shoemaker named Bartolomeo Vanzetti, were arrested for the crime. Both sides saw this apprehension as an anti-immigrant roundup, and though some booed, others cheered. For many, including the trial judge, the fact that Sacco and Vanzetti were anarchists made them likely to be guilty. Witnesses placed them at the scene, but others swore they were elsewhere. Physical evidence was inconclusive and contradictory. At the murder trial in Dedham, the courtroom was fortified with steel doors and iron shutters in anticipation of an attack by other radicals or Italian "mobsters." The jury deliberated for three hours, ate dinner, and then returned their verdict—both guilty.

The judgment was appealed on the grounds of recanted testimony, conflicting evidence, and the stated prejudices of the jury foreman. They were denied. As the date of their execution got closer, protests rocked not only Boston, but the entire world, from Tokyo to Buenos Aires. The Massachusetts governor appointed a commission to investigate, but the verdict was upheld, and President Coolidge declined to grant an appeal to stay the execution. Sacco and Vanzetti were executed by electric chair on August 23, 1927; hundreds of thousands of people marched in solidarity with them during their Boston funeral procession. The trial had bitterly divided New England, and the nation.

Meanwhile, Coolidge was dealing with a more private tragedy. While playing tennis on the White House's South Lawn, his son got a simple blister, which somehow led to a case of blood poisoning, and his early death. "I do not know why such a price was exacted for occupying the White House," Coolidge said later, in a rare show of emotion. His father, John, soon followed. "When I reached home he was gone. It costs a great deal to be President," Coolidge wrote. He took comfort in the white collies that he and Grace kept, and got a reputation as "Silent Cal." True to his roots, he remained thrifty, cautious, and balanced in all areas throughout his life, and the presidency did not change that. "I think the American people want a solemn ass as a president," he said, "and I think I will go along with them."

For many, he had been a calm, steady presence in a tumultuous decade, but though he was asked, he did not run for a second full term, returning to his Vermont farm as silently as he came. It was a good decision. The following year on Tuesday, October 29, Wall Street's stock prices cratered. Overnight, factories closed, banks folded, and investors committed suicide. Unemployment skyrocketed, and even Coolidge's fellow self-sufficient farmers dealt with dropping milk and lumber prices, selling off their land in record numbers. The economic freedom and laissez-faire attitudes of the 1920s had come to a thunderous end.

CHAPTER 32

The Winds that Shake the World

1930s

DURING THE STOCK MARKET TEMPEST OF 1929, THE FINANCIAL DIS-trict of Boston's State Street collapsed immediately, but the rest of New England took longer to feel the effects of the Great Depression. Most were still arguing the effectiveness of Prohibition during the early years of the 1930s. But by 1935 the Amoskeag Textile Mills of Manchester, New Hampshire, were gone, with fifteen thousand people out of work. Fall River, Hartford, Taunton, Providence—all the cities had tens of thousands of people on "relief." That winter, red snow fell in New England, filled with topsoil blown from the dust bowl–haunted West.

President Roosevelt was elected with supporting majorities in Congress in 1932, and Prohibition ended soon afterwards, to the great relief of nearly everyone in New England. It may have been a worthy experiment but had failed miserably in its goals. Now, both old "wets" and young jazz agers celebrated with a drink, while the government quietly raked in tax on alcohol again. But that would not be enough to end the Great Depression. What would? A seventy-eight-year-old Warren, Massachusetts, farmer named Jared David Busby proposed a solution "that everyone should work, in the first place, and work hard." He advocated the planting of small gardens, salting and pickling, and keeping two cows and some hens. "You know," he said, "I think I'm a socialist."

Perhaps he was joking, but many thought the same about President Franklin D. Roosevelt's administration, which advocated very similar values. Thousands of unmarried, unemployed young men joined Roosevelt's

Civilian Conservation Corps, working in New England's forests to build trails and lodges. Angelo Alderuccio from Bristol, Connecticut, joined "because my mother was going to get some money, and it took me off the streets." In Vermont, the clever lobbying of state forester Perry Merrill brought in over forty thousand workers to build dams, cut ski trails, and plant a million trees. Across the border in the White Mountain National Forest, the CCC cut logging trails, built ranger stations, constructed fire towers, and planted berries for small game animals.

Projects begun during the booms of the teens and twenties were finished and improved. Mostly financed and developed by John D. Rockefeller Jr., the first national park east of the Mississippi had been created in Maine, and in 1929 it was renamed Acadia. Landscape architect Beatrix Farrand designed the plantings along the crushed-stone carriage roads and granite coping stones, nicknamed "Rockefeller's Teeth." Now these wealthy patrons were joined by CCC workers, who built campgrounds and cleared thousands of downed trees. State parks and beaches throughout New England also acquired stone pavilions and lookout towers, stepped paths and parking lots.

Inspired by the Green Mountain Club's state-spanning Long Trail, Benton MacKaye of Stamford, Connecticut, had proposed an "Appalachian Trail" in 1921. It had been growing ever since, with Connecticut Forest and Park Association members Arthur Perkins and farmer Ned Anderson mapping the Connecticut leg, and Myron Avery from Lubec, Maine, taking over the Appalachian Trail Conservancy over the next two decades, becoming the first to walk every section of the completed trail. This private club was helped immeasurably by the new government work projects, and the CCC built most of the Maine section and completed the final link on August 14, 1937.

It was not only recreational areas that were being reimagined. Over 750 vessels had been wrecked off Cape Cod in the four decades before 1914, when the canal across its neck opened. Now, in the 1930s, workers replaced rail and car bridges, and expanded the canal to five hundred feet, making it the world's widest. Throughout the decade, Massachusetts's Swift River was dammed to create a water supply for Boston. Church spires, farmhouses, and the tavern where Daniel Shays planned his ill-fated rebellion all sunk beneath the spreading Quabbin Reservoir, sacrifices for a thirsty city.

Government had to deal with other 20th-century infrastructure needs too. Connecticut's Wilbur Cross had started as a Yale English professor, but at age sixty-eight became governor in a landslide, and shepherded the state through the Great Depression, resolving disputes with unions and championing the construction of the Merritt Parkway. The Works Progress Administration (WPA) helped build the first half of the road, which opened on June 30, 1938, as the "Gateway to New England." With Art Deco bridges and landscaping, the Merritt provided a model for "scenic parkways" around the country. It was also the first of many highway projects that would bring millions of new automobiles into the region.

However, there would soon be a different kind of work to be done. On September 21, 1938, a fine day with a gentle breeze brought many to the newly improved beaches and forests. Then, at 3 p.m. trees bent double along the Connecticut coast. There had been no warning, and no evacuation. People still standing on the beaches and on city streets were abruptly hit with walls of water or flying bricks. A tidal wave fifty feet high smashed into western Rhode Island, and the forty families of Napatree Point lost their town entirely. The wave swept up Narragansett Bay to Providence, where it was high enough to smash the skylight of the Providence Library. Startled pedestrians were instantly drowned.

The unexpected hurricane ripped up cemeteries, disintegrated docks, and turned boats into matchwood. Block Island nearly disappeared under Long Island Sound. In Jamestown, children drowned in their school bus. Storm surge swamped Falmouth and New Bedford, and smashed docks and chewed away beaches in every small coastal town. In Old Saybrook, Connecticut, actress Katharine Hepburn and her family struggled through waist-deep water toward safety while their house floated away into the mouth of the river.

Orchard apples flew through the air like bullets. A ship in New London crashed into a warehouse and burned down the business district in the worst destruction since Benedict Arnold struck the town in 1781. The Cape Cod Canal filled with boards, bricks, and houses. In northern New England, strong winds set fires, knocked down the trestle of Mount

Washington's Cog Railway, and blew over a billion trees. Salt from the ocean encrusted the windows of houses in Montpelier, Vermont.

An ice-jam flood in 1936 had already wreaked havoc on Hartford, but as rain gushed into the valley, the Connecticut River rose thirty-five feet above its banks, swamping cities and towns along its length. Foundations were undermined and concrete sidewalks cracked into pieces. Railroad tracks, roads, and bridges all swept away in the wind and water. Collapsed barns had killed thousands of farm animals, and millions of birds perished. One-quarter of the beautiful elm trees lining New England parks disappeared.

The human toll was staggering; at least seven hundred people were dead and many thousands wounded. Of a hundred fishing boats between New London, Connecticut, and Point Judith, Rhode Island, only three survived. Along with the thirty thousand destroyed or damaged homes, an almost equal number of automobiles were ruined. Twenty thousand miles of new electrical and telephone lines were little more than tangles of wire. Only 4 percent of the affected businesses were insured, and many that had survived the Depression now collapsed.

CCC and WPA workers cleaned water-damaged houses and built shelters for those made homeless by the storm. They had a big job: In two years they cleared over ten thousand miles of roads and six hundred thousand acres of debris—roughly the size of the entire state of Rhode Island. In the north woods, a few landowners refused to accept the free help from "Roosevelt's men," and trees rotted on their lands. The rest accepted the help that the larger American community could give. Nevertheless, it took the many paper mills of Maine and New Hampshire nine years to process all the downed timber.

Two months later, Governor Wilbur Cross gave a "sound film" Thanksgiving Day proclamation that would later become famous. He said that even in the midst of disaster, we should give thanks "for all the creature comforts: the yield of the soil that has fed us and the richer yield from labor of every kind that has sustained our lives—and for all those things, as dear as breath to the body, that quicken man's faith in his manhood, that nourish and strengthen his spirit to do the great work still before him: for the brotherly word and act; for honor held above price; for steadfast courage and zeal in the long, long search after truth; for liberty and for justice freely granted by each to his fellow and so as freely enjoyed; and for the crowning glory and mercy of peace upon our land;—that we may humbly take heart of these blessings as we gather once again with solemn and festive rites to keep our Harvest Home."

It was the sort of dramatic proclamation one might expect from someone educated in New England. Others retained their Yankee practicality about the disaster. When Katharine Hepburn finally reached her father by phone and told him their house had floated into the sound, he said, "I don't suppose you had brains enough to throw a match into it before it went, did you? It's insured against fire, but not against blowing away."

The cleanup from the deadly "Yankee Clipper" hurricane would continue until the end of the decade. Meanwhile, Europe was at war again and New Englanders, who had been shaken to their core by economic depression and natural disaster, now turned to meet this new wind blowing from the east.

CHAPTER 33

Along the Knife Edge

1940s

AT 7:48 A.M. ON DECEMBER 7, 1941, THE SKY WAS BLUE AND CLEAR OVER Honolulu as the first wave of Japanese planes dropped their bombs on the US Pacific Fleet. On the USS *Oklahoma*, Edwin Hopkins of Keene, New Hampshire, died when torpedoes capsized the ship. Ensign Joseph Taussig of Newport, Rhode Island, was officer of the deck on the USS *Nevada*, and though wounded horribly, he did not leave his station until his fellow sailors carried him away to have his leg amputated. The *Nevada* tried to escape the assault but after heavy damage was beached. Ensign Delar van Sand of Gloucester, Massachusetts, recalled "blood flowing three inches thick and a foot wide, flowing in the scuppers, being washed overboard by the fire hoses to clear the blood from the deck so that men carrying ammunition would not slip and fall, causing explosions."

Raymond Haerry of Warwick, Rhode Island, was on the deck of the USS *Arizona* and tried to fire back at the dive-bombing planes, but the unprepared antiaircraft guns had no ammunition. When the ship exploded, he was thrown high into the air and into the flaming waters of the harbor. Later, as one of the few survivors, he had the unenviable job of pulling the bodies of his fellow sailors from the water while the battleship burned and sank. "Japan Strikes All Over Pacific" the *Boston Globe*'s headline ran the next day. "Let's get 'em, and get 'em quick," a Boston man told the newspaper. "We're really in it now!"

Japan, Germany, and Italy declared war on the United States. Luckily, some had prepared ahead—the Selective Service Act had already gone into effect, industries had shifted to war production, and draft notices had already gone out. States with relatively tiny populations, like Vermont and Maine, gave huge numbers of citizens to the armed forces, as New England continued its tradition of punching far above its weight when it came to American wars. On Block Island, residents were warned of possible invasion and offered evacuation, but the leader of the civilian defense on the island, George Sheffield, had a typical New England response: "There ain't a thing here any enemy would want to get a hold of, so far as I can see."

Although programs like the CCC and WPA had benefits other than short-term economic ones, in 1940 there had still been thirty-six thousand unemployed men in Boston. Maine, Vermont, and New Hampshire voted against Roosevelt's reelection. But what the New Deal had promised, war now delivered in spades. Men not in the armed forces went back to work, and there was so much work to be done that many came to New England from nearby states and regions. Puerto Ricans began arriving in great numbers during World War II, laboring as farmhands and factory workers. Since Italy was at war with the United States, noncitizen Italians were considered "enemy aliens" and had to check in with the government. Those who were citizens served proudly in the armed forces or got jobs in the defense industry, despite suspicious looks from their neighbors and coworkers.

In Maine, the Bath Iron Works built hundreds of ships for the war effort. The Springfield Armory made rifles, and East Hartford's Pratt and Whitney made plane engines. Raytheon built radar tubes in Lowell, Massachusetts, and Russian immigrant Igor Sikorsky built helicopters in Stratford, Connecticut. Plants in New England produced half of the nation's rubber. Although the region gained money and factories during the war, it did not progress as fast or far as other areas of the country. Instead, factories began to move toward specialized industry using specialized labor. The Massachusetts Institute of Technology got its first substantial federal funding.

As in the First World War, women on the home front took over absent men's jobs. Telephone operator Mary Doyle of Arlington, Vermont, modeled for neighbor Norman Rockwell's famous painting of "Rosie the Riveter," which was on the cover of the *Saturday Evening Post*.

The image inspired legions of women to join the workforce, to buy war bonds, and to see physical strength as a vital part of womanhood. Mildred McAfee took a leave of absence as the president of Wellesley College in order to command the Women Accepted for Volunteer Emergency Service, or WAVES, eventually leading over eighty thousand women in their service during the war.

Everybody listened to the radio for reports of the latest battle and scanned the newspapers for casualty lists. But the war was not the only thing taking the lives of New Englanders. On November 28, 1942, an electrical fire at Boston's Cocoanut Grove nightclub killed 492 people, including many servicemen, when they couldn't get out through the revolving doors. Two years later the Hartford Circus Fire killed 169 when flames lit the canvas big top, which was treated with paraffin and gasoline. The dangers of chemicals and electric power were just beginning to become an everyday reality, and new safety laws began to be passed.

Soon, though, casualties overseas would mount higher and higher. On June 6, 1944, American and British troops landed on the white sands of Normandy, soon stained red with blood. Cambridge's Charles Henderson supervised the landing of tanks, and then walked through hundreds of dead marines to reach the survivors of his unit. He and thousands of other New Englanders went on to liberate Paris. The Yankee Division did not experience the epic battles it had during World War I, but assisted the advance across the Saar, helped stop the German armies at the Battle of the Bulge, and liberated the Gusen concentration camp.

Pilot John Katsaros of Haverhill, Massachusetts, was shot down in France, captured by the Gestapo, and liberated by the French Resistance. He went back up, was shot down again, and repeated the process. George Peters of Cranston, Rhode Island, served in the Parachute Infantry, and when he landed near the Rhine River his single-handed attack on a machine gun saved his comrades. He was not so lucky, and would never return. Frank and Charles Solomon of Coopers Mills, Maine, both served in the air force in Europe. Charles went missing in autumn 1943 while serving in a bomber squadron over France. His brother Frank was also shot down on New Year's Day of 1944 while carrying out an air raid on

Berlin. The Solomons' third son entered the service that same year but was kept out of the front lines.

In the Pacific, more New Englanders risked their lives to fight fascism. Born in Brookline, Massachusetts, on May 29, 1917, Lieutenant John F. Kennedy had been chief of the "muckers" at Choate, played football with larger boys at Harvard, and sailed boats off Hyannis amongst the scoters and cormorants. After training as a navy PT officer in Narragansett Bay, he took command of an eighty-foot speedboat called PT 109. He survived the air attack at Guadalcanal on April 7, 1943, though an explosion fractured his neck. Then, during action near Kolombangara in the Solomon Islands, the PT 109 collided with a Japanese ship, sending an explosion into the air and covering the sea with fiery gasoline. After rescuing some of his crew, they jumped off the sinking boat into the Pacific and, after an astonishing swim, struggled up onto the beach of a small green island with naqi naqi trees and kidokidoga bushes. Kennedy survived, though a back injury from the collision would plague him for the rest of his life. His brother Joe was less lucky. On August 12, 1944, on a secret mission during Operation Aphrodite, his Boeing BQ-8 blew up over Suffolk, England.

When the Americans invaded the Philippines in January 1945, one of their objectives was to save the five hundred survivors of the Bataan Death March, left on the island two years earlier. The Imperial Japanese military had already started executing prisoners of war when it looked like they would be rescued, so the Americans needed to do it quickly. Colonel Henry Mucci from Bridgeport, Connecticut, had survived the attack on Pearl Harbor and trained the Special Forces Sixth Ranger Battalion. "You're going to bring out every last man," he told his team, "even if you have to carry them on your backs." One hundred twenty-eight Rangers and 250 Filipino guerrillas snuck past enemy lines to the POW camp. The guerrillas set up ambushes for the return journey, and the silent Rangers crept between three thousand sleeping Japanese soldiers to the fence of the camp, taking out the guards quickly and efficiently, and piling wounded and sick prisoners onto their backs. In thirty minutes, they had all 513 POWs out of the camp and on the way back to American lines, suffering only two Ranger casualties and twenty-one Filipino casualties, while killing five hundred Japanese troops. It was the largest and most successful rescue mission in the history of the United States.

That autumn, after witnessing the suicidal butchery on Okinawa and the buildup of thirty million troops on mainland Japan, the US high command decided to drop their new atomic bombs to end the conflict without further American deaths. Unaware that the emperor was already considering surrender, pilot Charles Sweeney of Lowell, Massachusetts, flew the plane carrying the "Fat Man" atomic bomb into heavy cloud cover over the East China Sea. Sweeney could not see the primary target, Kokura, and diverted to the secondary, Nagasaki, and the Mitsubishi arms production plants. Forty thousand people were killed immediately. "There's no question in my mind that President Truman made the right decision," Sweeney said forty years later. But, he declared, "As the man who commanded the last atomic mission, I pray that I retain that singular distinction."

As the war ended and the nuclear age began, some might have questioned the first statement, but none questioned the second. Millions of other New Englanders had banded together in encampments, hospitals, and factories to fight the largest and deadliest war in the history of civilization, and no one wanted to repeat that experience. They had walked upon the edge of a knife and made it to the other side. And if that had taught them anything, it was, as a recently promoted John F. Kennedy said sixteen years later, "Mankind must put an end to war before war puts an end to mankind."

CHAPTER 34

The Shifting of the Plates

1950s

CORPORAL JOSEPH VITTORI OF BEVERLY, MASSACHUSETTS, HAD enlisted in the marines just as World War II was ending in 1946, and four years later he was sent to Korea. In the Battle of the Punchbowl he engaged in brutal hand-to-hand combat before single-handedly preventing an enemy breakthrough with his automatic rifle, firing a thousand rounds in three hours until he was killed. Other soldiers, sailors, and civilians joined the effort, and to many it seemed like World War II never ended.

Information about the Korean War was censored in the newspapers and on radio as World War II had never been, part of the new Cold War between Communist states and capitalist ones. This larger conflict also led to a hunt for "reds" and their sympathizers. In 1947 the House Un-American Activities Committee held hearings on Hollywood's "red propaganda," and over the next few years, hundreds of artists were blacklisted and boycotted. In 1951 eighty-three-year-old W.E.B. Du Bois was dragged in front of a Justice Department panel as a Soviet agent, for distributing antinuclear pamphlets. Although acquitted, he was relieved of his passport for eight years and eventually driven into exile in Ghana.

In the Senate, Wisconsin's Joseph McCarthy railed against "enemies within" the government itself, charging individuals with disloyalty, sex crimes, socialist leanings, and homosexuality. The accused were encouraged to "name names" and thus reduce their own punishment. This sort of hearsay destruction of peoples' lives was quite familiar to New Englanders, and Roxbury, Connecticut's Arthur Miller would forever link this incident with the Salem witch trials in his play *The Crucible*.

One person who stood up to the intimidation and hysteria was Margaret Chase Smith. Born in Skowhegan, Maine, to a family of old Puritans and French Canadians, she worked at a local five-and-dime, played high school basketball, and wrote for the local newspaper. After high school, she cofounded the local Business and Professional Women's club and worked in a textile mill, before becoming politically active. Her husband served in the US House of Representatives, but after he became ill she took over the seat in a special election, the first woman elected to Congress from Maine. She won another three elections easily and sponsored the Women's Armed Services Integration Act, which enabled women to serve permanently in the armed forces. She voted her conscience and, though a Republican, sometimes broke ranks to vote for Roosevelt and Truman's legislation. She ran for senator in 1948, defeating the incumbent Republican and the Democratic challenger easily, becoming the first woman to represent Maine in the Senate, as well as the first woman to serve in both houses of Congress.

In 1945 she had voted against the peacetime use of the House Un-American Activities Committee, and now in 1950 she stood up on the Senate floor to condemn McCarthy's anti-Communist "witch hunt." She remembered thinking that "surely one of the Democrats would take the Senate floor." But none did, paralyzed with the fear of being the next one on the list of Communists. Standing alone, she denounced the "unproved charges" and the "hate and character assassination" that had poisoned her own party. All Americans, she said, had the "right to hold unpopular beliefs, the right to protest, the right of independent thought." Six other Republican senators joined the protest, but it would be four more years before McCarthy was officially censured.

For many New Englanders, though, the red scare was far away. Closer to home was the ground-shaking development of infrastructure in the 1950s. Macadam rolled out over the old Indian paths like black dough, and new Goodyear tires smoothly circled along them. Everyone had a car in the driveway now, and these metal beasts became nearly as personal as horses had been to earlier generations. The long stoplight stretches of

Route 1 followed the old Post Road, and along the way drugstores, grocery stores, and gas stations sprang up on every mile. Billboards, which even P. T. Barnum hated, proliferated along highways and byways, while electrical lines, telephone wires, and underground pipes now snaked from house to house, gridding and interconnecting both rural and suburban landscapes.

Traffic had already grown too heavy for interstate roads like the old Route 6 from Cape Cod west through Providence and Hartford. So four-lane highways and turnpikes were built, like the toll highway in Maine, which had opened in 1947 and expanded throughout the decade. The I-84 Yankee Expressway was built across Connecticut, and the Massachusetts Turnpike soon stretched from Boston to West Stockbridge. By the end of the decade I-91, I-95, and I-90 connected the New England states, designated part of the growing interstate highway system. People moved out into the suburbs in greater numbers, and others began to drive south for the winter.

Not everyone found increased mobility and spreading suburbs to be comforting, and some rebelled against unchecked progress in significant ways. New Englanders built parks and saved green spaces at a rate never seen before. Hikers began mapping and walking the old trails again, and cutting new ones through the forests, now growing thick again. Groups dedicated to protecting and preserving the small pieces of wilderness and natural habitat gained members, while hermits and hobos tried to live their Thoreauvian dreams in the spaces between the suburbs. But mostly people settled onto their small plots, as villages spread into farmlands and met cities growing the other way. The green spaces became all the more precious, emerald gemstones in the strip-mall expanses.

Although some in the suburbs of Boston and Fairfield County began living in flat-roofed modern homes with huge glass walls and rectangular profiles, most still chose neocolonials and Cape Cods, with clapboards or plastic siding. They filled them with mass-produced items of metal and plastic as consumer culture began to take over everyday life. Families replaced the chipped china with plastic plates and chrome tableware, sniffed the new chemical scents of pool chlorine and household cleaner, and heard the whirring sound of a lawnmower and the whock-whock-whock of sprinklers. The small, happy tasks and pleasant silence of housekeeping disappeared into the blare of television, the ring of the telephone, and the hum of the vacuum cleaner. Sounds like crunching gravel and the clip-clop of hooves retreated from daily imagination.

Culture changed more quickly too. With penicillin and other drugs, parents could expect all or most of their children to live to adulthood, and therefore each one became that much more treasured. Social security was also now a growing reality for millions of elderly Americans, who in the new industrial-urban culture of the 20th century couldn't exactly live on the family farm anymore. Corporate fathers drove from suburban houses to urban jobs, but many of those jobs began to move into the suburbs too. Women wore pants as often as skirts, and could even be seen on Nantucket beaches in two-piece bikinis.

Other changes were even more shocking. The elm trees that had survived the Yankee Clipper hurricane in 1938 were in trouble, attacked by micro-fungi spread by beetles that had been brought to America in the 1930s. The famous elms on New Haven Green were among the first to die, and soon the rest of New England's shaded streets and parks were barren. The chestnuts had been blighted earlier in the century, and by the 1950s they disappeared too.

On August 11, 1955, Hurricane Connie largely missed Connecticut, and everyone breathed a sigh of relief. Six inches of rain was nothing to ignore, but not deadly. Then, just eight days later, Hurricane Diane dumped another foot or two of rain on the state in thirty hours, along with more upriver in Massachusetts. The nearby states experienced flooding, but the already saturated ground in Connecticut could not absorb the water. Every small river and brook began to overflow its banks, with the Housatonic reaching nearly twenty-five feet and the Naugatuck rising so quickly that families were trapped before they could get out. A house in Waterbury washed away carrying the entire Bergin family to their deaths. In Putnam the flood reached the second story of apartment buildings, and when it ripped open Belding Hemingway Magnesium Plant, barrels of the volatile magnesium crashed into bridges, exploding and burning for two days.

Over the next week Sikorsky helicopters rescued those trapped on upper floors throughout the state, but eighty-seven people had been drowned or electrocuted in the disaster. The cost to the economy was devastating, with three thousand houses severely damaged or destroyed, over five hundred factories wrecked, and another fifteen hundred businesses damaged. Nine hundred farms lost their crops that year. Riverfronts were left in tangles of steel girders, piles of bricks, twenty-foot splinters of wood, with bridges bent and broken and dams shattered. Rust and mold followed, causing incalculable damage. "In Waterbury, railroad cars were on top of tenement houses," Governor Ribicoff noted. "Industry has suffered a terrible loss." In October another tropical storm contributed another foot of rain, and more flooding drove many to utter despair.

Already losing money after the war, some manufacturers in Connecticut reluctantly gave up the ghost. Luckily, some had seen already that the loss of textiles and heavy industry to the south and abroad was inevitable, and new technology companies like Pratt and Whitney and General Dynamics would survive the flood and thrive in the new age. The first nuclear submarine had already launched from Groton on January 21, 1954.

But it was Massachusetts that would see furthest into the future. Outside of Boston, Route 128 had been built to ease traffic, but had failed in its original purpose. However, the substandard land along the road was an opportunity for the real estate firm Cabot, Cabot, and Forbes, which began to create the first "industrial parks," with buildings, small ponds, and plenty of parking for new businesses. For many, it seemed a nice place to work, a reachable and pleasant alternative that had adjusted to the automobile age. And it was perfect for the new technology industries that had been boosted by World War II, which did not need river-powered mills or huge turbines. It was also close to the brain trust of MIT. Soon Route 128 would be "America's Technology Highway," with companies like Raytheon, GenRad, Digital Equipment Corporation, and General Electric. They would develop products like the commercial transistor and semiconductor, vital components of the electronics revolution to come.

A few looked even further. Born in Everett, Massachusetts, in 1890, Vannevar Bush worked with other electrical engineers at MIT to help create the first analog "computer" in the late 1920s. Then, in 1940, at Harvard, mathematician Howard Aiken built the thirty-five-ton Mark I digital computer, capable of complex calculations in just seconds. And after getting a PhD at Harvard, Chinese immigrant An Wang founded Wang Laboratories in Massachusetts, where in 1955 he pioneered magnetic-core memory.

The rest of America still thought of New England as the soda-shop village of Thornton Wilder's *Our Town*, or maybe the secretive, gossipy *Peyton Place* of Grace Metalious. Until now, some folks had in fact actually lived rural lives barely distinguishable from that of the early settlers. Even industry had motored along for more than a century, barely unchanged. But now, the very land beneath our feet was shifting.

CHAPTER 35

Ask Not

1960s

ON THURSDAY, JANUARY 20, 1961, POET ROBERT FROST STOOD UNDER a cloudless blue sky in the freezing wind and recited "The Gift Outright" at the inauguration of John F. Kennedy. "The land was ours before we were the land's," the voice of New England echoed off the marble. Breath steaming in the cold air, Kennedy took the oath of office and his words crackled into the winter air. "Ask not what your country can do for you," he said in what would become one of the most famous lines ever spoken by an American President. "Ask what you can do for your country."

In fifteen years, "Jack" had gone from war hero to US representative to senator, despite health issues that bothered him nearly every day. His back injury from the war still ached, he almost died of a fever in Japan, and he was diagnosed with Addison's disease. Like many New Englanders, he remained stoic and endured the daily pain. He debated with his brothers over dinner, read almost as much as John Quincy Adams, and listened to his wife, the brilliant Jacqueline Bouvier. In 1960 he had beaten both liberal and conservative candidates for the Democratic nomination, and gone up against Vice President Richard Nixon in one of the closest elections in American history. Many thought he won it in the first televised debate. Others thought he won it with his grueling tour of speeches and appearances, like the one on November 6 in Waterbury, Connecticut, where in front of a crowd of thousands he cinched the state's eight electoral votes at three o'clock in the morning.

Now he had to make good on his promises and justify the belief so many had come to have in him. But the transition did not go well. That spring, the disastrous invasion of Cuba at the Bay of Pigs, already planned in the previous administration, may not have been his fault, but it was now his responsibility. It was not a good beginning. He was a little more successful fixing the growing recession, when he used the budget as an "instrument of economic stabilization." He urged Congress to extend unemployment insurance, increase minimum wage, and find ways to increase construction. They passed a bill to do all that and more within six months.

Meanwhile Soviet leader Nikita Khrushchev met with Fidel Castro, worried about American missiles in Italy and Turkey and about another American invasion of Cuba. They secretly agreed to construct missile bases only a few minutes by rocket power from Miami. A U-2 spy plane took photographs of the facilities, and on October 16 Kennedy was informed of the crisis. He ordered a naval blockade of the island in lieu of a full-scale assault, which hard-liners pushed him to do. For the next two weeks, the two superpowers jockeyed for position, with Castro telling Khrushchev that he was ready to launch a preemptive nuclear strike. On live television, Kennedy addressed the American people, saying, "It shall be the policy of this nation to regard any nuclear missile launched from Cuba against any nation in the Western Hemisphere as an attack by the Soviet Union on the United States, requiring a full retaliatory response upon the Soviet Union." China announced that its 650 million people stood ready to fight alongside Russia.

Fingers hesitated over red buttons in the tensest standoff in human history. Children practiced hiding under desks while the armed forces remained on high alert. Military experts at the time estimated a third of the world's population would be killed, even without fully understanding the radiation poisoning and nuclear winter that would follow. Kennedy and Khrushchev negotiated with each other by telegram, and negotiated with hard-liners in their own governments. As the deadlock loosened, it became clear that neither man wanted war. A secret arrangement was reached, and the Soviets pulled their nuclear missiles out of Cuba, much to the annoyance of Castro. Eventually, they even removed the ones that US intelligence didn't know about.

Kennedy's nuanced and careful handling of those thirteen days would secure his legacy as one of the most capable presidents, though it would not be until much later that most Americans realized how close the world had come to a full-out nuclear war. Throughout his presidency, he dealt with these terrifying weapons, organizing a test ban and trying to urge disarmament. He was only partially successful in this, as in many things, like reforming health care and avoiding war in Southeast Asia. He was a little more successful negotiating in Europe, mending fences with Latin American countries, and solving the Berlin crisis.

His brother Robert was the attorney general, in one of the most fortuitous acts of nepotism in the country's history. Robert dissolved the McCarthy anti-Communist legacy, struggled with organized crime, and fought for civil rights. As president, John began speaking for civil rights, too, and increased the number of African Americans in civil service. At the integration of Ole Miss in 1963, students threw bricks and shouted racial epithets to prevent one African American student from taking classes. As Eisenhower had done in Little Rock, Arkansas, the Kennedy brothers sent in the National Guard to stop the riots.

Jack took breaks to walk on the beach at Hyannis with Jackie and the children. He sailed with ambassadors and cabinet members on the presidential yacht, *Honey Fitz*, named for his grandfather. But the pain that wracked his body kept him from enjoying life as much as he should have. In Newport, he spoke to other sailors at the America's Cup race: "We have salt in our blood, in our sweat, in our tears." When asked once what he regretted, he said, "I wish I had more good times."

On October 26, 1963, the president returned the favor to Robert Frost, speaking at Amherst College in a ceremony honoring the recently deceased poet. "I look forward to a great future for America," he said. It would be a country that "will be safe not only for democracy and diversity but also for personal distinction." Whatever that future might have looked like will never be known. A month later Kennedy went to Dallas, shots rang out on Elm Street, and he could never look forward again.

Days of mourning all over America followed. "What happened? What happened?" People wandered the streets of Boston in shock and grief, weeping openly. "The president's been shot." A few who hated Kennedy rejoiced secretly or openly, but some of his political opponents rose to the occasion to praise and mourn him. Margaret Chase Smith laid a single rose on his former Senate desk. The international outpouring of grief was unified, immediate, and profound. "Ah, they cried the rain down that night," one Irishman in Limerick said. Memorials to him sprang up from Liberia to Japan. Even Khrushchev mourned. When Jacqueline could finally speak, she told a reporter that "there'll be great presidents again . . . but there will never be another Camelot."

After the shock wore off, life went on in New England, as it had to. Vietnam escalated, and some were drafted and left for Southeast Asia. Others took former Harvard professor Timothy Leary's advice and turned on, tuned in, and dropped out. Some started experimenting with LSD and other drugs, looking for transcendence. The Civil Rights Act was signed by Kennedy's successor, Lyndon Johnson, but there was still much work to be done, even in New England. In April 1965 Martin Luther King Jr. marched from Roxbury to Boston Common to protest the discriminatory policies of Boston's public schools. As the casualty lists from Vietnam grew, antiwar protests ramped up, with many following King's adaptations of Thoreau's civil disobedience to passively and peacefully protest, and others taking a more violent approach. Riots broke out in Boston and in New Haven, but other areas of the country had it much worse. Counterculture movements joined with, and sometimes fought against, antiwar movements and civil rights activists.

Thoreau's philosophy of environmentalism finally came into its full power during those years too. It was a necessary adjustment. Long Island Sound's oyster industry was collapsing due to industrial waste and sewage, and a 1966 study of the Naugatuck River, once the center of brass and clock manufacturing in America, found not one fish alive along its thirty-nine-mile length. The oxygen level of Maine's Androscoggin River was zero; and though New Hampshire's fabled Merrimack still had fish, they tasted like sewage. The Watertown Arsenal's destruction of the

Charles River had been apparent for years, with *Harper Magazine*'s Bernard DeVoto describing it as "unlikely to be mistaken for water." Cleanup of New England's rivers would continue for the next fifty years.

Some tried to preserve the good that was left. President Kennedy had created the Cape Cod National Seashore in 1961—one place in all the long New England Coast, at least, not given over to private homes. By the end of the decade, Vermont decided to maintain its rural character by banning billboards and limiting rampant development. Some young people turned back to the land, forming collective farms and other communal projects that would have seemed very familiar to the Brook Farm idealists of the 1840s. Vermont in particular became a haven for peace-loving activists, who migrated there in search of greater freedom.

Others turned their eyes to the stars. In 1961 after the Soviets put the first human being into space, Alan Shepard of Derry, New Hampshire, slammed his hand down on a table at NASA in competitive frustration. A month later Shepard himself made it into space on the Freedom 7, despite the fact that, as he put it, "every part of this ship was built by the lowest bidder." After President Kennedy set the nation's eyes to the moon, the "space race" was on. A decade after he became the first American in space, and despite suffering from Ménière's disease, Shepard himself would become the fifth person to walk on the surface of earth's satellite. He was also the oldest, and will always remain the earliest born, though it is possible someone else will smuggle a golf club there and play another round amongst the craters.

Those who had not given up on traditional politics when Kennedy died put hope into this candidate, or another. In 1964 Margaret Chase Smith ran for president on the Republican ticket, the first woman whose name was placed in nomination at either of the two political parties' conventions. Two years later, Massachusetts's Edward Brooke became the first directly elected African American senator. And Smith's fellow senator from Maine, Edmund Muskie, became one of the most vocal official spokesmen for the environment in the 1960s. But it was John's brother Robert Kennedy who seemed to hold the most promise in the 1968 presidential election. On April 4, just a few hours after Martin Luther King was shot, Robert spoke from the heart, asking his fellow Americans to "tame the savageness of man and to make gentle the life of this world." Two months later, he was also killed by an assassin's bullet—another hostage to fortune, another fleeting wisp of glory, another question without an answer. What more could anyone ask.

CHAPTER 36

Over the River and through the Woods

1970s

IN SOME WAYS, NEW ENGLAND NEVER RECOVERED FROM THE GRIEF OF its lost Camelot. Throughout the 1970s, the remaining hopes began to crash down one by one. In the younger generation, faith in the political establishment was already gone long before the time the Watergate scandal disgraced the presidency. In 1969 when Secretary of State Henry Kissinger stood up to address Brown University's commencement, two-thirds of the students turned their backs.

Tens of thousands of New Englanders served in the Vietnam War, and over two thousand did not make it home. They included Donald Skidgel from Bangor, Maine, who was only twenty years old when his unit was ambushed from the tall grass near Song Be, and he ran through a hail of bullets to draw enemy fire. Others, like Richard Allen Stratton of Quincy, Massachusetts, were captured and tortured as prisoners of war. Those that came home safely sometimes returned to neighbors who blamed them for "losing" the war and, as more than a few experienced, to "people with hatred throwing rocks and spitting on you."

Antiwar rallies continued to grow through the end of the sixties into the seventies. Students went on strike, shutting down Yale, Harvard, and other New England schools. Some canceled classes entirely. The antiwar protestors were soon joined by many Vietnam veterans who through bitter experience had also come to hate the war. One of those veterans was John Kerry, who had played soccer for Yale and won awards for his debates and orations. During Operation Sea Lord, he earned praise for both his competency directing his unit and his bravery leading an assault party onto the shore of the Bay Hap River.

After Kerry's return, he joined the Vietnam Veterans against the War, participated in the Winter Soldier Investigation on atrocities, and was nearly court-martialed for antiwar activity. On April 22, 1971, he sat in front of a Senate committee to give testimony on his experiences, and the following day demonstrated in front of the US Capitol with a thousand other veterans, many of whom tossed their uniforms and medals over a makeshift barrier. "I'm not doing this for any violent reasons," he said, "but for peace and justice, and to try and make this country wake up once and for all."

As Vietnam wound down, many in the munitions industry found themselves out of work. In 1969 the Springfield Armory, linchpin of New England's war industry, shut down. Lynn and Beverly's huge shoe factories, once the world leader in shoemaking, shut down one by one due to global imports. "My dad used to tell me that at lunch time he'd go out to the central square and the people would come pouring out of the factories like ants," said Richard Rothbard of Barry Manufacturing, Lynn's sole surviving shoe company. Brass from Waterbury, clocks from Torrington, silver from Meriden all disappeared. The giant complex of Remington factories in Bridgeport emptied of workers and products one by one, long before the company left for Arkansas. From the end of the war to 1980, New England lost 1.5 million factory jobs, producing less and becoming a consumer-based culture.

Many of these lost industries left chemically destroyed brownfields, littering the landscapes of Massachusetts, Rhode Island, Connecticut, and New Hampshire. The oil crisis of 1973 added to this misery, leading to soaring prices, rationing, and many questions about the sustainability of this limited resource. Writers, politicians, and philosophers walked the old path around Walden Pond, trying to reckon with the bitter fruits of the industrial revolution.

Some turned to nuclear power as a solution. But for others, with new information about radiation and meltdowns, the power of the atom that seemed to hold so much promise in the 1950s now felt scary and hostile. In New Hampshire, activists formed the Clamshell Alliance in 1976 to protest the Seabrook Nuclear Power Plant, eventually occupying the construction site in May 1977. Police arrested 1,414 protestors, and the subsequent publicity hurt nuclear power in the region. Massachusetts governor Michael Dukakis delayed the opening of Seabrook, citing both environmental and safety concerns. Years of protests in New England cities and towns, as well as bankruptcies and red tape, would eventually encourage the shutdown of the Yankee Rowe and Maine Yankee power plants.

The highways pioneered by Robert Moses in New York City webbed New England now, and lines of cars slid along their rain-spattered macadam. But in smaller cities, the concrete barriers cut off downtowns from foot travel, dividing rather than uniting neighborhoods. And instead of bringing more people into the downtowns to eat and shop, the highways siphoned more and more people into the suburbs, to strip malls and comfortable homes. Places like Waterbury and New London, Worcester and Fall River, Pawtucket and Manchester, already struggling with the loss of industry, dried up like old leaves.

The bicentennial celebrations during the summer of 1976 were a welcome distraction, with Boston taking a leading role in the nationwide festivities. For a few months, patriotism surged, although sometimes it took new forms, like the "tea party" that threw packages labeled with the names of oil companies into Boston Harbor. The parades, picnics, fireworks, and fleet of tall ships made for one of the best Fourth of July celebrations of the century. Many people were also celebrating the renovation of Quincy Market and Faneuil Hall, which became models of downtown and seafront renewal for other projects around the nation.

The urban renewal of the rest of Boston was less successful. Nearly a third of the older parts of the city were knocked down for high-rises and government buildings. Unlike Quincy Market, this sort of urban renewal became an example of what not to do. And Boston was not the only mistake—New Haven cleared its "slums" but did not have enough money to rebuild. Hartford's huge Civic Center, one of the first buildings designed by computer, collapsed during a snow storm just three years after it was built. The Little Italy neighborhood of Portsmouth, New Hampshire, was swapped for a parking lot and hotel, and Senator Daniel Webster's home was leveled for a grocery store. Smaller towns like Laconia suffered even more damage from well-meaning urban developers, who in a 1975 project left it with a "renewed" pedestrian mall on the old main street, which retailers promptly abandoned.

Many of these projects directly affected minorities, who lived in neighborhoods knocked down for new highways or skyscrapers. The growing population of Puerto Ricans in New England experienced upheavals throughout the decade, with many poverty-stricken youths in violent confrontations with police. Civil rights for African Americans continued to move slowly, hampered by the controversial New Haven trials of the Black Panthers. The mid-1970s were marked by protests against segregation in Boston public schools, and as desegregation began and compulsory busing shifted racial politics, counter-protests and riots rocked the city. In 1978 the NAACP sued over Boston Housing Authority policies, which discriminated against African Americans when awarding home mortgages, even after adjusting economic and other factors.

That same year, winter storm Larry blew in, dumping three feet of snow on the region. Ella T. Grasso of Connecticut, the first female governor not replacing a husband in the job, shut down all roads and slept on her office sofa while directing operations. With the interstate highway system, though, it was easier for middle-class people to escape the frozen-shut garage doors, the drifts burying mailboxes, the cars slipping sideways into ditches. Who wanted to stick around to put chains on the salt-crusted tires, to scrape the frosted windshield clear in one tiny spot over the wheel, to chat with a tow-truck driver full of coffee and grim jokes? Many fled to Florida or Arizona, becoming snowbirds or just leaving forever, to return once in a while to visit family for a white Christmas or a flowering spring.

Those that stayed found joy at the Newport Folk Festival or an Aerosmith concert at the Boston Garden. They went to the local theater to see *Jaws* or *The Friends of Eddie Coyle*. Professional sports had become central to American culture, and the many championships Bill Russell and the Celtics brought home in the 1960s had assuaged a desperate Massachusetts. The Celtics continued to win throughout the 1970s and 80s, and with a few championships by the Boston Bruins, New Englanders had plenty of distractions to buoy their spirits on the coldest winter days.

Many continued to douse themselves in bicentennial nostalgia, longing for the days of the revolution, which they imagined as simpler and purer than the dissatisfying present. Some looked further back to the storied past of colonial times, and memberships in historical and preservation societies soared. Others reminisced about the 1950s, which now seemed a golden age before chaos, corruption, and death. When artist Norman Rockwell died in Stockbridge, Massachusetts, in 1978, his small-town-Americana paintings soared in value, and prints hung in every home. It was an understandable urge, and as the next few decades went by, many New Englanders would continue to search through the complicated galleries of history, hoping to find some bright, clear image to take into the future.

CHAPTER 37

No Wider than the Heart Is Wide

1980s

ON NOVEMBER 7, 1979, TED KENNEDY ANNOUNCED THAT HE WAS RUN-
ning against the incumbent President Carter. Carter's approval rating
was at 28 percent, and both Democratic Party officials and labor unions
encouraged Kennedy in this coup. All three older brothers had died serving their country, and maybe he was trying to live up to their promise.
But although many in Massachusetts had forgiven him for the night at
Chappaquiddick when Mary Jo Kopechne drowned, the rest of the country was less sympathetic. He lost the nomination, though his speech at the
Democratic Convention brought a thunderous applause: "For all those
whose cares have been our concern, the work goes on, the cause endures,
the hope still lives, and the dream shall never die."

On the Republican side, George Herbert Walker Bush had posi-
tioned himself as the sensible alternative, with decades of experience in
both military and government. Born in Milton, Massachusetts, in 1924,
Bush grew up in Greenwich, Connecticut, and spent summers at the Kennebunkport, Maine, retreat his great-grandfather had built. After attending private schools like Greenwich Country Day and Phillips Academy,
he enlisted in the US Navy during World War II, becoming the youngest
naval aviator at that time, participating in the Battle of the Philippine Sea.
After his plane was hit by flak during a bombing raid, he parachuted into
the ocean before being rescued by a submarine. After the war, he went to
Yale University, married his wife Barbara, and after his son George was
born, moved to Houston, Texas.

Bush won seven primaries, including Massachusetts, but lost the nomination to Ronald Reagan, who reluctantly picked him as running mate. After they swept the election, it was left to another Massachusetts politician, the Speaker of the US House of Representatives Tip O'Neill, to provide balance. O'Neill had been both friends and enemies with James Michael Curley, the famous Irish politico who for five decades ran Boston in one way or another. Now, O'Neill both fought and compromised with Reagan every step of the way as Roosevelt's New Deal was dismantled. However, as the economy recovered from the "malaise" of the late 1970s, optimism returned to America, and to New England.

Tax cuts for the wealthy and booming military-industrial spending seemed to many to herald a new Gilded Age. As if to prove it, young businessmen ate pizza with caviar or drank gold flakes in cocktails. Developers added gables, wings, and huge garages to neocolonial houses, so that one middle-class family might occupy something the size of a 17th-century chateau. The very wealthy in Southport and Hyannis built mansions larger than the largest houses of the 19th century, far grander than the now-quaint mansions of Newport. Leisure and recreation became the order of the day. Ski runs and hiking trails snaked across the northern mountains, while racquetball and squash courts filled city gyms. Television antennas became hard-wired cables, and available channels soared into the double digits. Microwaves, first patented by Raytheon in Massachusetts decades earlier, now took their place in every home along with cordless telephones, video games, and VCRs.

In Providence a 1904 structure called the "widest bridge in the world" was removed, and the river was opened to the sky, transforming the downtown in an attempt to "become kind of like the baby brother of Boston," according to the mayor. But at the same time some cities were trying to renew their downtowns, shopping moved to huge indoor malls in the suburbs. In 1986 the Danbury Fair in Connecticut, a center of gathering since 1821, was transformed into one of these huge new complexes, complete with food courts, department stores, and convenient parking. People could spend a rainy day walking between Thom McCann and G. Fox, and even ride on the old carousel, now conveniently placed inside.

Per capita income rose while population growth lagged in New England. The three dozen small cities became greater than their size, as museums and restaurants, libraries and theaters, turned the people toward culture, as societies often do when industry leaves. Tiny Dunkin' Donuts and Pete's Subway expanded into international chains. *Cheers* turned Boston's Bull and Finch Tavern into a tourist mecca, and Maine's coast became "vacationland" as tourism grew to its largest industry. Everyone wore the latest L. L. Bean clothing in both summer and winter, frolicking on beaches and in big woods, enjoying islands and highlands.

Meanwhile, another change simmered behind the scenes. In 1969, in Maine, while trying to help the Passamaquoddy Indians, a lawyer named Tom Tureen discovered a law had been passed by George Washington that gave Native Americans federal protection, particularly preventing land deals. Of course, nearly all of Maine had been acquired in these sorts of land deals. Eventually the state reached a compromise by giving the Passamaquoddy and other Maine tribes money to purchase real estate.

Federal tribal status followed for many New England tribes who had been left out of the national conversation about Native American rights. The Houlton and Aroostock Bands of Micmac, the Wampanoag Tribe of Gay Head, and the Narragansett Tribe would all earn federal recognition. The Mashpee Wampanoag Tribe would have to wait until 2007. But it was in Connecticut that this new movement would have the most immediate impact on the surrounding culture and economy.

A small Pequot reservation had been founded back in 1666, but by the 20th century the population had dwindled. When the federal government started to reclaim the land, the grandson of the last inhabitant, Skip Hayward, sued to recover it. In 1983 President Reagan signed the Connecticut Indian Land Claims Act, and the Pequots were secure. But in the entrepreneurial spirit of the 1980s, the Pequots were thinking bigger. The Penobscot Tribe in Maine had operated high-stakes bingo as early as 1973, one of the first in the nation. Now the Pequots did the same. On July 5, 1986, a bingo hall opened in Ledyard, Connecticut, and in one year made $26 million. Two years later, Congress passed the Indian Gaming Regulatory Act, and with a willing state government, the Pequots began to construct the largest and most profitable hotel-casino in the United States.

Meanwhile, the space shuttle program had captured the imagination of a generation brought up on *Star Wars*. A social studies teacher from Concord, New Hampshire, named Christa McAuliffe applied for the Teacher in Space Project, and beat out eleven thousand other candidates to join the space shuttle *Challenger* for a mission. What set her apart was her "infectious enthusiasm" and "broad-based" and "balanced" character. She trained for a year and answered questions from legions of reporters. "How does it feel?" one asked, and she replied, "I'm still kind of floating. I don't know when I'll come back to earth." At 11:38 a.m. on January 28, 1986, the rocket boosters ignited, and a few minutes later, the shuttle disintegrated in the sky over Cape Canaveral and horror-struck school-children across America were whisked away from classroom television screens.

Vice President Bush met with the families, and pledged to a shattered NASA that the space program would go forward. When he ran for president two years later, his opponent was another Massachusetts-born politician, Governor Michael Dukakis. Dukakis was born in Brookline, but had stayed in his home state after attending Harvard. He had served as governor during the high-tech glory days of Route 128, and had improved Boston's mass transit. Though initially in the lead, Dukakis fared poorly in the debates, and Bush attacked him as a "Massachusetts elitist," which coming from the son of a wealthy New England senator was a bit ironic. However, Bush won this cross-Massachusetts presidential election easily, saying at his inauguration: "We are not the sum of our possessions. . . . We cannot hope only to leave our children a bigger car, a bigger bank account. We must hope to give them a sense of what it means to be a loyal friend, a loving parent, a citizen who leaves his home, his neighborhood and town better than he found it."

One of Dukakis's lieutenant governors, John Kerry, would run against Bush's son sixteen years later. By then, the "Massachusetts miracle" was seeming less of a miracle. Minicomputer research kept the state going throughout the 1980s, and aerospace and defense continued to be important for New England. But by the end of the decade, California's Silicon

Valley drained more and more business away, and Massachusetts companies failed to break into the personal-computer market. Many of the office parks along Route 128 put up "for sale" signs.

Bush's presidency would also end in a fiscal quagmire—with another recession, new taxes, and high unemployment rates. He would soon be accused of the same thing he accused Dukakis of: being one of the out-of-touch New England "elite." But for a few brief years he presided over a booming economy, the end of the Cold War, and a huge coalition of nations in the successful military operation of Operation Desert Shield. He returned again and again to his roots in Kennebunkport before, during, and after he served in the White House. "It's where my family comes home, and it's our anchor to windward," he said in 1989. "It's a point of view. You can feel it, in the land and in the water here." He was unquestionably right about that.

CHAPTER 38

The Things You Gave Your Life To

1990s

As the St. Patrick's Day festivities wound down in Boston at midnight on Sunday, March 18, 1990, two police officers asked for entry to the Isabella Stewart Gardner Museum. Except they were not police officers, and after handcuffing the security guards to a pipe in the basement, they made off with thirteen works by artists like Rembrandt, Degas, and Vermeer valued at $500 million. It was the largest theft of private property ever recorded and led to decades of unsuccessful investigations of suspects from Hartford to Paris.

Later that same year, between October 28 and November 2, a clash between a nor'easter and Hurricane Grace created a Halloween gale that damaged President Bush's vacation home in Kennebunkport and countless others along the coast. Then it got worse, with waves off Nova Scotia reaching over one hundred feet high and boats swamping in marinas and out to sea. Amongst the death and damages, the swordfish vessel *Andrea Gail* of Gloucester and its six crewmen went down in the graveyard of the Atlantic.

Crime and catastrophe would weave their way through the decade. In 1992 unemployment and poverty reached temporary highs, as New England shifted more and more from manufacturing to services, finance, real estate, and insurance. Everyone had a personal computer now, but not from Massachusetts's former computer hub of Route 128 as Silicon Valley began to suck more and more intellectual capital and technological production. Cities around the region lost commerce and tax bases, and corruption followed. Graft, misappropriation, and peculation tempted politicians and businessmen in every state.

In Providence, the Heritage Loan and Investment company collapsed, taking with it forty-five credit unions and banks. The president, Joseph Mollicone Jr., had embezzled millions of dollars, and three hundred thousand Rhode Islanders lost access to their money. Demonstrations, hearings, and an eighteen-month nationwide manhunt for Mollicone followed. Local representatives, mayors of several major cities, and even the governor of Connecticut would go to jail over the next decade, and many others went unpunished. The last time corruption had peaked like this was a century earlier in another Gilded Age, and again the nation seemed to pass a weary New England by.

The most reliable profession for hundreds of years had been fishing, but as large companies took over, small fishermen found themselves out of work. Worse, the use of huge, long-distance trawlers and oceangoing "fish factories" by many nations had collapsed the once-immortal fishing grounds of the Grand Banks, with giant sixty-two-mile lines and acres of nets clearing out the depths. The cod that had survived centuries of fishing disappeared under the pressure and by the end of the 1990s were a mere 1 percent what they had been a few decades earlier. Families who for generations had set sail from New England ports now found themselves looking for new work. The "Sacred Cod" carving in the Massachusetts State House now seemed a tribute to the past instead a celebration of the present.

The valuable lobster grounds and oyster beds of Long Island Sound began to fail too. After improving during the 1980s, the water temperatures spiked, and in 1997 parasitic MSX destroyed over 80 percent of Connecticut's oysters. The Housatonic River suffered from mercury poisoning by the old Danbury hat factories and PCB pollution from the General Electric plant in Pittsfield, which the EPA pronounced a hazardous Superfund site in 1997. Eating fish or birds from the area was declared a health risk. Heavy metals and sewage from that river and others added to the damage in Long Island Sound.

Not everyone was having a bad decade. As lobstering failed in southern New England, it began to boom in Maine. The biotech industry in

Massachusetts replaced computing, anchored by Nobel Prize–winning Phil Sharp's Biogen. Women began to make more gains, led by politicians like Vermont's Madeleine May Kunin and scientists like Dr. Tenley Albright of Massachusetts. And thanks in part to intense lobbying by Speaker of the House Tip O'Neill, Boston had received billions of federal dollars to deal with Boston's legendary traffic jams.

As early as the 1970s, an ambitious "Big Dig" was envisioned to put a huge section of obtrusive expressway underground, and in 1991 construction began with crews tunneling under the city. It was one of the most complicated projects in the world—at one point the highway was dug under the railway tracks of South Station, requiring artificial induction of permafrost and specially designed jacks. Unsurprisingly, the project overran its costs, and construction continued well into the next decade in the most expensive single public works project in American history.

The Pequot Nation opened Foxwoods Resort and Casino in 1992, raking in billions of dollars from eager gamblers, shoppers, and tourists. They used part of the money to build the Mashantucket Pequot Museum & Research Center, which at over three hundred thousand square feet quickly became the leading Native American museum in the country. However, they soon had competition. The Mohegan Tribe gained federal recognition on March 20, 1994, and Ralph Sturges, the tribal chief, said, "We are no longer the little old tribe that lives upon the hill. We are now the nation that lives upon the hill."

Governor Lowell Weicker soon cleared them to build their own casino, saying, "I don't think there is one of us as American citizens that isn't proud to go ahead and rectify the mistakes of history." On a spot on the Thames River, formerly used to build nuclear reactors for submarines, the tribe opened the Mohegan Sun Casino in 1996. Only a few miles away, at Foxwoods Resort, Skip Hayward remained philosophical about the competition. "The Pequots and the Mohegans have a long history together," he said. "It's wonderful again to come together as one people." The two casinos also created an even more enticing destination, and became a small but significant victory after centuries of defeat.

Another traditionally marginalized group was also making unexpected gains. Same-sex couples had been suing for rights since the 1970s, and in 1993 a Hawaii court ruled briefly in favor of civil unions before being overturned by a popular referendum. Two lawyers from Vermont were watching carefully. Beth Robinson and Susan Murray created the Freedom to Marry task force, whose object was to "seek the legal protections and obligations of civil marriage." They joined with the Boston-based Gay and Lesbian Advocates and Defenders in 1997, and started litigation against the state of Vermont. They lost, but appealed to the state supreme court, which in 1993 had ruled in favor of gay adoption rights. The court scoffed at the government's "procreation" argument, and affirmed the rights of same-sex couples to form civil unions. Democratic, Republican, and Independent legislators in Montpelier were generally supportive, and despite a split opinion in the polls, the bill creating civil unions passed in the state House and Senate before being signed by Governor Howard Dean.

It was the end of the century, and the end of the millennium. Everyone panicked briefly about what "Y2K" would do to their new "email" accounts and their computerized bank statements. Others popped champagne corks and watched midnight bonfires in downtown Providence or waited for the first sunrise in America at Quoddy Head Light. It was a chance to reflect on the past, but also an opportunity to start anew. Some brave spirits looked toward the next thousand years as a chance for New England to dig its way out of debt and disaster.

CHAPTER 39

The Curse, Reversed

2000s

AT 7:59 A.M. ON SEPTEMBER 11, 2001, A BOEING 767 LIFTED OFF FROM the tarmac at Logan Airport. Fifteen minutes later, another did the same. Five terrorists were on each plane, and less than a half hour later, both planes had been hijacked and flown toward the Twin Towers of the World Trade Center. Lynn Angell and her husband, David, producer of *Cheers* and *Wings*, were on board the first plane, which hit the North Tower at 8:46. At 8:52, Peter Hanson of Easton, Connecticut, called his father to tell him they had been hijacked, and then again at 9:00, saying "I think we are going down" and reporting that the terrorists intended to steer into a building. "Don't worry, Dad. If it happens, it will be very fast." The plane hit the South Tower at 9:03.

The next hour and a half of horror was witnessed live all over the world, as two other planes crashed into the Pentagon and onto a field in western Pennsylvania. Then the towers collapsed. Among the 2,996 people who lost their lives that day, more than four hundred were from New England, many on the planes from Logan and many in the Trade Center doing their jobs at companies like Cantor Fitzgerald. In the immediate confusion, skyscrapers in downtown Boston were evacuated, fighter jets scrambled across otherwise empty skies, and US Navy ships moved into Long Island Sound. Judy Cobden of Warwick, Rhode Island, was working in the New York Stock Exchange during the attacks, but survived. "I watched so many people die," she said later. "I could have died. I really thought I was going to."

Since the Persian Gulf War ten years earlier, New Englanders had continued to serve as soldiers around the world. During United Nations operations in Mogadishu on October 3, 1993, two Black Hawk helicopters were shot down, and Gary Ivan Gordon from Lincoln, Maine, and his team heroically dropped to the ground to protect the wounded soldiers until they were killed by Somali militia. A film about the incident came out just a few months after September 11, as thousands of soldiers from the region were deployed to the Middle East, and thousands more joined the armed forces to fight the War on Terror.

Britt Slabinski, who hailed from Northampton, Massachusetts, had been an Eagle Scout before joining the navy, and after 9/11 was deployed to Afghanistan. In 2002, at the Battle of Roberts Ridge, he went beyond the call of duty and charged toward enemy fire to help a stranded teammate. Ryan Pitts from Lowell, Massachusetts, watched nine of his comrades die as the Taliban besieged their outpost. "They were my brothers," he said. "My best friends." And the fighting went on and on through the end of the decade. Many more died, like Eric Shaw from Exeter, Maine, who sacrificed his life rescuing twelve Afghani soldiers from a Taliban ambush in 2010.

To those on the home front, it seemed an age of fear and uncertainty. Rumors of biological weapons gripped cities, and ethnic prejudices tore through communities. Many became addicted to news channels and websites, waiting for the next disaster. Politics briefly united, then divided the region, and the nation. After the mission shifted from Afghanistan to an invasion of Iraq, protests grew in number and volume, especially as the seemingly easy victory turned into a quagmire for the soldiers serving there. Every election turned into a referendum on patriotism, and nearly every family conversation was peppered with words like "freedom" and "war."

Despite the larger political and global conflicts, life went on. Technology leaped into everyone's hands, and though a tenacious few lived in the pleasant shady lanes of their ancestors, others began to live in virtual realms. People walked the streets with cell-phone wires snaking to their ears, talking to relatives in Florida and Baghdad. They discussed whether the Big Dig had made traffic better or worse and whether to buy an electric car or an SUV. Autumn stayed autumn, children were born, people fell in love and got married.

But one constant characteristic of New Englanders is their argumentativeness, and even marriage became a contentious issue in this age of political outrage and partisanship. Emboldened by the civil-union victory in Vermont, a group of seven same-sex couples sued Massachusetts. A judge ruled against them, but the legislature stopped an amendment designed to define marriage as heterosexual only, and an appeal was expedited. The state supreme court overruled the judge in a narrow decision, stating "whether and whom to marry, how to express sexual intimacy, and whether and how to establish a family—these are among the most important of every individual's liberty and due process rights." Some of the celebrations in Provincetown that night lasted a decade.

At midnight, in Cambridge, Marcia Hams and Susan Shepherd stood alone under an awning to receive their marriage license, wondering if someone would kill them. For twenty-four hours they waited, as hundreds of couples lined up behind them. On May 17, 2004, after swearing an oath in front of a clerk, they walked into a cheering crowd as the first same-sex married couple in America. Hams nearly fainted. "I'm shaking so much," she said. When they had their official wedding at their church later, Shepherd noted that, "We couldn't stop people from coming."

At first, polls in the state remained split, and following the will of a slim majority, Governor Mitt Romney tried to limit and even ban the practice. But opinions were shifting in this new century, and over the rest of the decade that majority disappeared, at least in New England. Connecticut governor Jodi Rell signed civil unions into law in 2005, and three years later its judiciary ruled to extend equal protection for same-sex marriage. New Hampshire followed the same path, granting civil unions in 2006 and marriage in 2009. When civilization did not collapse, as some had predicted, many New Englanders took their usual tolerant attitude of "live and let live."

In 2004 Senator John Kerry of Massachusetts won the Democratic primaries and went up against President George W. Bush, losing to the New Haven-born politician who three decades earlier had attended Yale with him and even joined the same fraternity. Kerry's actions in and after

Vietnam came under scrutiny in a close election, but he nearly beat the popular incumbent, even at the height of the Iraq War. Four years earlier, Connecticut's Joe Lieberman had been the losing vice presidential candidate, and eight years later, Mitt Romney would be the Republican nominee. All four presidents, from the elder Bush to Barack Obama, attended New England universities, adding to the region's total of one-third of all commanders in chief. If, as so many pundits asserted, New Englanders no longer steered the destiny of America, there certainly seemed to be a lot of them standing around near the tiller.

With the world in chaos and politics dividing every conversation, many turned to something simple to believe in. In the dark days after 9/11, many New Englanders rallied around the Patriots, which started the season considered one of the worst teams in football, but after win after win throughout that bitter autumn faced the Rams on February 3, 2002, in Super Bowl XXXVI. With 1:30 left in the fourth quarter, the game was tied, and a young quarterback named Tom Brady drove down the field, spiking the ball with seven seconds left. A field goal gave the team their first Super Bowl victory.

Two years later, in 2004, the Red Sox made it to the World Series. For nearly a century the so-called "curse" of trading Babe Ruth to the Yankees had allegedly put the hex on Fenway Park's team, and many Bostonians had been born and died without ever seeing their team win a World Series. A number of trade betrayals and late-inning screwups had poured salt on the wound, leading Denis Leary of Worcester, Massachusetts, to compare being a Sox fan to "masochism." So many believed in the jinx that when someone graffitied a "Reverse Curve" sign on the Longfellow Bridge to read "Reverse the Curse," city officials left it up.

When, in 2004, the Sox lost three games in a row to their division rivals, the Yankees, many expected yet another loss, yet another crushing defeat for Boston. But in Game 4, trailing by one in the bottom of the ninth inning, pinch-runner Dave Roberts stole second, and a single by Bill Mueller tied the game. In extra innings, David Ortiz hit a two-run walk-off homer for the win. Then the Sox won another, and another, and became the only team to ever come back from three games down in a series. They maintained that momentum throughout the World Series, crushing the Cardinals. "I don't believe in curses," said MVP Manny Ramirez.

Some could not understand the glory of it, or why it mattered so much in an age of terror and war, saying, "It was just a game." Perhaps. But to millions of New Englanders it was more. "I hope that after we are long gone our children's children will speak with wonder about these years," said historian and Red Sox fan Doris Kearns Goodwin. "They did it for the old folks in Presque Isle, Maine, and White River Junction, Vermont," wrote Dan Shaughnessy of the *Boston Globe*. "They did it for the baby boomers in North Conway, New Hampshire, and Groton, Massachusetts. They did it for the kids in Central Falls, Rhode Island, and Putnam, Connecticut." Shortly afterwards, that road sign on Longfellow Bridge above Storrow Drive was changed to "Curse Reversed."

The Patriots won again in 2003 and 2004, the Red Sox won for a second time in 2007, and many New Englanders began to think of their home as a place for champions. For others it was a home for brave men and women who served and led the country. For still others, this was where new ideas germinated and spread, pushing out across a larger America. All these perspectives had one thing in common—a sense of pride in place, a pride that had seemingly returned, as it so often did during the darkest hours, in the midst of disaster. By the end of a decade of conflict, a few even began to believe that a new age might herald new possibilities, a new spirit, and a new love. Maybe all the curses that the 20th century had cast on New England could somehow be reversed.

CHAPTER 40

The Day's Work

2010s

"THOSE WHO CANNOT REMEMBER THE PAST ARE CONDEMNED TO REPEAT it," wrote philosopher and Harvard professor George Santayana. Easy to say but difficult to do when the past is always slipping away. We might tap maple trees at the living history museum of Sturbridge Village, read *Moby Dick* on the *Charles W. Morgan* whaling ship at Mystic Seaport, or eat Indian pudding at Boston's Union Oyster House, the country's oldest restaurant. But the sand dunes of Cape Cod creep eastward a few inches every year, and robots roam the halls of MIT.

Many things improved for New England in the second decade of the new millennium. Oysters rebounded in Long Island Sound, and lobsters continued to thrive off Maine. The universities and liberal arts colleges remained the best in America, aided by dozens of Nobel laureates in the nearby hills. Over a thousand biotech companies gathered around the hub of Kendall Square in Cambridge, supported by a 2008 Life Sciences Act that gave $1 billion to their development. Hospitals around the region became cutting-edge research and teaching institutions, while art galleries, restaurants, theaters, and wineries all appeared with astonishing rapidity. The Patriots and the Red Sox and UConn women's basketball continued to win championships. And every four years, New Englanders lined up to run for president of the United States.

New challenges arose: new diseases, new weather patterns, new human failures. Ash trees started dying off, hurricanes increased in power, and opioid addiction struck every community. Debt and high taxes continued. Ticks made a comeback. At the Big Dig, corrosive saltwater leaks, a ceiling collapse, and deadly guardrails all caused damage and deaths, and the replacement of light fixtures cost millions more dollars. On December 14, 2012, twenty school children and six teachers were killed in Sandy Hook, Connecticut, by a former student, the second deadliest school shooting in American history to that day. A few months later, on April 15, 2013, two bombs built from pressure cookers exploded near the Boston Marathon finish line, killing three and injuring hundreds. After-wards, some came together, while some sowed more division. Some found purpose; some found only sorrow.

Other events in those years had hazier consequences, as events usu-ally do. Beavers returned to dam the streams and coyote-wolf hybrids hunted them. Marijuana was declared legal in Massachusetts and Maine, and more gambling casinos appeared throughout the region. The Internet became more and more useful, but also more and more indispensable. Handheld devices connected us to the entire world, and separated us from everyday life. Social media designed to bring us together, somehow also pulled us apart.

The future always meant changes, but humans themselves changed little. In the face of increasing globalization and technological depen-dency, home, community, and family began to matter more to some. The same people who embraced new cultural and scientific realities also gath-ered at local farmers' markets, breweries, bookstores—places where every-body knows your name. They looked for the constancy in cranberries and stone walls, in mountain laurel and coffee milk. They sailed their boats off Martha's Vineyard, climbed Mount Washington, and took their children apple picking. The shared experience of being in a place inspired some to look forward, some to look back. But more often they did a little of both.

As the four hundredth anniversary of the Pilgrims' landing approached, tourists gathered around to take selfies with the broken piece of Plymouth Rock in its tiny cage. Perhaps this unsatisfying, circumstan-tial fragment, this remnant of a half-remembered legend, held some key to the whole business. Or maybe it was the people themselves who held the answer, with all their flaws and weaknesses. Somewhere deep in the forests of the north woods or in a high school classroom or in a nearly deserted office park, a few creative souls might be imagining a transformation that could guide us through the next four centuries.

They will be in good company. There have been others who lived on these same hills and shores—pioneers, inventors, and prophets—who knew how to build, how to love, and how to die. To face the future, New Englanders will need the stubbornness of a woman going back to the gallows, the serenity of a bookish asthmatic eating breakfast before battle, and the strength of a man hated by his own country who held the flag while those around him fell. They will need the political abilities of Uncas, the conviction of Lucy Stone, the hope of John F. Kennedy. They will need to have minds of winter, of rubber, of magnetic complexity. They must imagine a world rooted in the past, but marvelously, astonishingly, strangely new.

If history teaches anything, it is that there is never a final victory or defeat. There is only the day's work, anchored in lived realities like raking autumn leaves and arguing your point over a dessert of fresh-baked blueberry pie. We live in that ever-changing now, in the flickering beginning of something new. And in the antique sea chest in the corner, we might find a few dependable tools for that journey.

Selected Bibliography

Adams, Charles Francis. *Three Episodes of Massachusetts History*. New York: Russell & Russell, 1965.

Adams, Henry. *The Education of Henry Adams*. New York: Modern Library, 1997.

———. *The United States in 1800*. Ithaca, NY: Great Seal Books, 1958.

Adams, James Truslow. *The Founding of New England*. Boston: Atlantic Monthly Press, 1921.

Alcott, Louisa May. *Hospital Sketches*. Carlisle, MA: Applewood Books, 1993.

Anderson, Virginia DeJohn. *New England's Generation*. Cambridge: Cambridge University Press, 1991.

Bailyn, Bernard. *The Barbarous Years: The Peopling of British North America: The Conflict of Civilizations, 1600–1675*. New York: Vintage Books, 2012.

Baker, Jean. *Sisters: The Lives of America's Suffragists*. New York: Hill & Wang, 2005.

Banks, Ronald. *Maine Becomes a State*. Middletown, CT: Wesleyan University Press, 1970.

Beals, Carleton. *Our Yankee Heritage*. New York: David McKay, 1955.

Benedict, Jeff. *Without Reservation*. New York: HarperCollins, 2000.

Black, Robert. *The Younger John Winthrop*. New York: Columbia University Press, 1966.

Blake, John Ballard. "The Inoculation Controversy in Boston: 1721–1722." *New England Quarterly* 25, no. 4 (1952).

Boynton, Cynthia Wolfe. *Connecticut Witch Trials: The First Panic in the New World*. Charleston, SC: History Press, 2014.

Brooks, Van Wyck. *The Flowering of New England*. Boston: E. P. Dutton, 1936.

———. *New England: Indian Summer*. Boston: E. P. Dutton, 1940.

Brewer, Francis. *The Puritan Experiment*. New York: St. Martin's Press, 1976.

Buel, Joy Day, and Richard Buel Jr. *The Way of Duty*. New York: W. W. Norton, 1984.

Burke, Alan. "Remembering Pearl Harbor: Local Veterans Remember a Day That Changed Their Lives." *Gloucester Daily Times*, December 7, 2016. http://www.gloucestertimes.com.

Cairns, William. *Selections from Early American Writers*. New York: Macmillan, 1910.

Carbone, Gerald. *Nathanael Greene*. New York: St. Martin's Press, 2008.

Carr, J. Revell. *Seeds of Discontent: The Deep Roots of the American Revolution 1650–1750.* New York: Walker, 2008.

Carse, James. *Jonathan Edwards and the Visibility of God.* New York: Charles Scribner's Sons, 1967.

Clark, Charles E. *The Eastern Frontier: The Settlement of Northern New England 1610–1763.* New York: Alfred A. Knopf, 1970.

———. *Maine.* New York: W. W. Norton, 1977.

Clark, George Larkin. *A History of Connecticut: Its People and Institutions.* New York: G. P. Putnam's Sons, 1914.

Coolidge, Calvin. *Autobiography.* New York: Cosmopolitan Book, 1929.

Craker, Wendel D. "Spectral Evidence, Non-Spectral Acts of Witchcraft, and Confession at Salem in 1692." *Historical Journal* 40, no. 2 (1997): 331–58. www.jstor.org.

Donovan, Robert. *PT 109: John F. Kennedy in World War II.* New York: McGraw Hill, 1961.

Earle, Alice Morse. *Home Life in Colonial Days.* Stockbridge, MA: Berkshire Traveler Press, 1898.

———. *Stage Coach and Tavern Days.* Mineola, NY: Dover, 1969.

Emilio, Luis. *A Brave Black Regiment.* 3rd ed. Salem, NH: Ayer, 1990.

Fawcett, Melissa Jayne. *The Lasting of the Mohegans: Pt. I, The Story of the Wolf People.* Uncasville, CT: Mohegan Tribe, 1995.

Feintuch, Burt, and David H. Watters, eds. *The Encyclopedia of New England.* New Haven, CT: Yale University Press, 2005.

Gardon, Charlotte. *Mistress Bradstreet.* New York: Little, Brown, 2005.

Gilman, Charlotte Perkins. *Women and Economics.* New York: Source Book Press, 1970.

Green, Constance. *Eli Whitney and the Birth of American Technology.* Boston: Little, Brown, 1956.

Gutman, Herbert, and Donald H. Bell. *The New England Working Class and the New Labor History.* Urbana, IL: University of Illinois Press, 1987.

Hall, David, ed. *Witch Hunting in 17th Century New England.* 2nd ed. Boston: Northeastern University Press, 1999.

Haller, William. *The Puritan Frontier.* New York: AMS Press, 1968.

Hansen, Chadwick. *Witchcraft at Salem.* New York: George Braziller, 1998.

Harris, John. "Politics and Politicians: Of All of Callahan's Highways, Route 128 Seems to Be 'It.'" *Boston Globe,* July 22, 1951. http://www.mass moments.org.

Hatch, Nathan, and Harry O. Stout, eds. *Jonathan Edwards and the American Experience.* New York: Oxford University Press, 1988.

Historic Storms of New England. Salem, MA: Salem Press, 1891.

Holder, Robert. *I Touch the Future: The Story of Christa McAuliffe*. New York: Random House, 1986.

Hollie, Pamela. "Shoe Industry's Struggle." *New York Times*, May 28, 1985. http://www.nytimes.com.

Hurd, D. Hamilton. *History of New London County, Connecticut*. Philadelphia: J. W. Lewis, 1982.

James, Henry. *The American Scene*. New York: Charles Scribner's Sons, 1946.

James, Sydney. *Colonial Rhode Island*. New York: Charles Scribner's Sons, 1973.

Jones, Matt Bushnell. *Vermont in the Making*. Hamden, CT: Archon Books, 1968.

Judd, Richard M. *The New Deal in Vermont: Its Impact and Aftermath*. New York: Garland, 1979.

Junger, Sebastian. *The Perfect Storm*. New York: W. W. Norton, 1997.

Kimnach, Wilson, Caleb J. D. Maskell, and Kenneth P. Minkema, eds. *Jonathan Edwards's "Sinners in the Hands of an Angry God": A Casebook*. New Haven, CT: Yale University Press, 2010.

Lader, Lawrence. *The Bold Brahmins: New England's War against Slavery: 1831–1863*. New York: E. P. Dutton, 1961.

LeBlanc, Jeanne A. "The Lost." *Hartford Courant*, August 2, 2005. http://www.courant.com.

LeClerc, Cherise. "New Hampshire Man Killed at Pearl Harbor Finally Buried Next to His Parents." *WMUR.com*, October 15, 2016. http://www.wmur.com.

Lehr, Elizabeth Drexel. *King Lehr and the Gilded Age*. Philadelphia: J. B. Lippincott, 1935.

Lepore, Jill. *The Name of War: King Philip's War and the Origins of American Identity*. New York: Vintage Books, 1999.

Marsden, George M. *Jonathan Edwards: A Life*. New Haven, CT: Yale University Press, 2003.

Martin, Wendy, ed. *Colonial American Travel Narratives*. New York: Penguin Books, 1994.

Matthews, Lois Kimball. *The Expansion of New England*. New York: Russell & Russell, 1962.

McCullough, David. *John Adams*. New York: Simon & Schuster, 2001.

Menta, John. *The Quinnipiac: Cultural Conflict in Southern New England*. New Haven, CT: Yale University Press, 2003.

Merrill, Perry H. *Roosevelt's Forest Army: A History of the Civilian Conservation Corps, 1933–1942*. Montpelier, VT: Perry H. Merrill, 1981.

Meyer, William B. "The Worst Weather Disaster in New England History." *Yankee Magazine* (January 1997). *New England Living Today*, March 8, 2018. http://newengland.com.

Miller, Perry, and Thomas Johnson. *The Puritans: A Sourcebook of Their Writings.* New York: Harper Torchbook, 1978.

Moers, Ellen. *Harriet Beecher Stowe and American Literature.* Hartford, CT: Stowe-Day Foundation, 1978.

Morgan, Edmund S. *The Puritan Dilemma: The Story of John Winthrop.* Boston: Little, Brown, 1958.

Morrisey, Charles. *Vermont.* New York: W. W. Norton, 1981.

Mumford, Lewis. *The Brown Decades.* San Diego, CA: Harcourt, Brace, 1931.

Murphree, David, ed. *Native America: A State by State Historical Encyclopedia.* Westport, CT: Greenwood, 2012.

Murray, Iain H. *Jonathan Edwards: A New Biography.* Edinburgh: Banner of Truth, 1987.

O'Neill, Tip, and William Novak. *Man of the House.* New York: Random House, 1987.

Osborn, Norris Galpin. *History of Connecticut.* Vol. 2. New York: States History, 1925.

Palfrey, John Gorham. *History of New England.* Vols. 1–5. New York: AMS Press, 1966.

Paresh, Dave. "First Same-Sex Couple to Get Marriage License Marks 10th Anniversary." *Los Angeles Times,* May 17, 2014. http://www.latimes.com.

Perry, Jack. "R.I. Man, One of Last Survivors of USS Arizona, Dies." *Providence Journal,* October 7, 2016. http://www.providencejournal.com.

Pierceson, Jason. *Same-Sex Marriage in the United States.* Lanham, MD: Rowman & Littlefield, 2013.

Quarles, Benjamin. *The Negro in the Civil War.* New York: Russell & Russell, 1968.

Roach, Marilynne K. *The Salem Witch Trials: A Day-by-Day Chronicle of a Community under Siege.* Lanham, MD: Taylor Trade, 2004.

Roth, David Morris. *Connecticut's War Governor: Jonathan Trumbull.* Hartford, CT: American Revolution Bicentennial Commission of Connecticut, 1974.

Salisbury, Neal. *Manitou and Providence.* New York: Oxford University Press, 1982.

Schlesinger, Arthur. *The Colonial Merchant and the American Revolution.* New York: Atheneum, 1968.

——. *A Thousand Days: John F. Kennedy in the White House.* Boston: Houghton Mifflin, 1965.

Selesky, Harold. *War and Society in Colonial Connecticut.* New Haven: Yale University Press, 1990.

Shay, Michael E. *The Yankee Division in the First World War: In the Highest Tradition.* Texas A&M University Press, 2008.

Silverman, Kenneth. *The Life and Times of Cotton Mather*. New York: Columbia University Press, 1985.

Simpson, Alan. *Puritanism in Old and New England*. Chicago, IL: University of Chicago Press, 1955.

Stearns, Monroe. *The Story of New England*. New York: Random House, 1967.

Stuart, Isaac Williams. *Life of Jonathan Trumbull, Senior, Governor of Connecticut*. Boston: Crocker and Brewster, 1859.

Szatmary, David. *Shay's Rebellion*. Amherst, MA: University of Massachusetts Press, 1980.

Trumbull, J. Hammond, ed. *The Memorial History of Hartford County Connecticut, 1633–1884*. Vol. 1. Boston: Edward L. Osgood, 1886.

Turner, Frederick Jackson. *The Frontier in American History*. New York: Henry Holt, 1921.

Unger, Harlow. *John Quincy Adams*. Cambridge, MA: Da Capo Press, 2012.

Van Doren, Carl. *Secret History of the American Revolution*. New York: Viking Press, 1941.

Weeden, William B. *Economic and Social History of New England, 1620–1789*. Vol. 2. Boston: Riverside Press, 1891.

Whiting, Edward Elwell. *Changing New England*. New York: Century, 1929.

——. *President Coolidge: A Contemporary Estimate*. Boston: Atlantic Monthly Press, 1923.

Yardley, William. "Connecticut Approves Civil Unions for Gays." *New York Times*, April 21, 2005. https://www.nytimes.com.

Zeichner, Oscar. *Connecticut's Years of Controversy*. Williamsburg, VA: Institute of Early American History & Culture, 1949.

Zinn, Howard. *The People's History of the United States*. New York: Harper Perennial, 1980.

INDEX

About the Author

Eric D. Lehman is an associate professor of English at the University of Bridgeport and the author of eighteen books, including *Yankee's New England Adventures*, *Quotable New Englander*, *Homegrown Terror: Benedict Arnold and the Burning of New London*, *Insiders' Guide to Connecticut*, *A Connecticut Christmas*, and *Becoming Tom Thumb*, which won the Henry-Russell Hitchcock Award from the Victorian Society in America and was chosen as one of the American Library Association's outstanding university press books of the year. His novella *Shadows of Paris* was judged the novella of the year by the Next Generation Indie Book Awards, was awarded a silver medal in romance from Foreword Reviews, and was a finalist for the Connecticut Book Award.